Bobby Maduro and the
Cuban Sugar Kings

ALSO BY LOU HERNÁNDEZ
AND FROM MCFARLAND

*Manager of Giants: The Tactics, Temper
and True Record of John McGraw* (2018)

*The 1933 New York Giants: Bill Terry's
Unexpected World Champions* (2017)

*Chronology of Latin Americans
in Baseball, 1871–2015* (2016)

*Baseball's Great Hispanic Pitchers:
Seventeen Aces from the Major, Negro
and Latin American Leagues* (2015)

*Memories of Winter Ball: Interviews
with Players in the Latin American
Winter Leagues of the 1950s* (2013)

*The Rise of the Latin American
Baseball Leagues, 1947–1961: Cuba,
the Dominican Republic, Mexico, Nicaragua,
Panama, Puerto Rico and Venezuela* (2011)

Bobby Maduro and the Cuban Sugar Kings

Lou Hernández

McFarland & Company, Inc., Publishers
Jefferson, North Carolina

ISBN (print) 978-1-4766-7526-8
ISBN (ebook) 978-1-4766-3482-1

LIBRARY OF CONGRESS CATALOGUING DATA ARE AVAILABLE

BRITISH LIBRARY CATALOGUING DATA ARE AVAILABLE

© 2019 Lou Hernández. All rights reserved

No part of this book may be reproduced or transmitted in any form or by any means, electronic or mechanical, including photocopying or recording, or by any information storage and retrieval system, without permission in writing from the publisher.

Front cover: Bobby Maduro, 1957; the 1959 Sugar Kings baseball team, champions of the International League and Junior World Series champions

Printed in the United States of America

*McFarland & Company, Inc., Publishers
Box 611, Jefferson, North Carolina 28640
www.mcfarlandpub.com*

For all those who lost everything,
and had to start anew
in a most welcoming country

Acknowledgments

First and foremost, I am beholden to the Maduro family for their receptiveness and support for this project. To Rory Costello, whose SABR online biography of the title subject served as an excellent blueprint. I found myself referring to it often. Thanks to Ralph Maya and César López for their photo contributions. And to Miami History Museum Archives Associate Ashley Trujillo, for her generosity and warm assistance. Lastly, I am grateful for the handful of surviving players from the era who took the time to speak to me. Their unique reminiscences delivered enhanced perspectives in the way only former ballplayers can.

All present-day monetary conversion equivalents came from dollartimes.com.

Table of Contents

Acknowledgments	vi
Preface	1
Introduction	4
Prologue: Establishing Tropical Roots	6
One—Stadium Builder	9
Two—Team Owner	19
Three—Birth of the Sugar Kings	35
Four—"Los Cubanitos"	65
Five—Championship Glory Amid Political Discord	88
Six—End of the Sugar Kings	129
Seven—Starting Over as "a Millionaire in Friends"	150
Eight—Cuban Sugar Kings Foundation	174
Epilogue: Special Latin American Committee and International Hall of Fame Wing	184
Chapter Notes	187
Bibliography	197
Index	201

Preface

In August 2017, as part of my research for this book, I traveled to the capital of the longest-lasting dictatorship in the history of the Western Hemisphere. The trip was facilitated, in part, by the normalization of relations by the United States with Cuba initiated in December 2014. Although a Cuban-born American citizen, I still had to pay over $200 for a one-visit visa to enter and exit the country. (The visa cost for a U.S. tourist to enter Cuba is $50 by air, $75 by sea.) Cuba is the only nation on earth that requires its nationals, or former nationals (through separate visa or passport requirements), to pay to enter its country, a violation of Article 13 of the Universal Declaration of Human Rights, which stipulates that all citizens of the world have the right to freely leave and return to their native countries.

The purpose of the trip was to see first-hand where my subject had lived and, in some remote way, get a sense of how he lived. The latter attempt required quite some imagination. Apart from an abundance of tourist spots, foreign embassies or related institutions, military residential zones, and pre–Revolution UNESCO World Heritage sites, Havana is a city in ruinous decay, mirroring the rest of the country. (I had previously visited eastern Cuba on more than one occasion under already-allowed "family reunification" visits.) The failure of Fidel Castro's rebellion is starkly evident not only in the crumbling facades of Havana's buildings but in the struggling faces of its average citizens outside of the tourist areas. The "elitism" derived from private enterprise that Castro targeted and excoriated to build internal support for his six-decades-old insurrection is alive and well under Cuba's current system of military capitalism, through its armed forces–backed conglomerates. Combined with the state's entrenched totalitarian machinery, virtually every sector and segment of the Cuban people's lives is controlled.

In 2017, Mercer, the world's largest human resources consulting firm, once more ranked Havana as the worst city in which to live in Latin America. "Access to healthcare, quality of education, housing and environmental factors" are the main measuring sticks used by the corporate giant for their determinations, according to their website report. Even with the advantage of a subtropical climate, Havana ranked 191 (worst in the hemisphere) out of 231 major cities of the world. San Juan, Puerto Rico, incidentally, placed as the best Latin American metropolis in which to reside. Cuba's decades-long boasts of superior education and healthcare systems are exposed again as nothing but threadbare propaganda tools.

Twenty percent of Cuba's population has fled the island in the more than half-century since Castro's revolution. Bobby Maduro was one of those two million-plus individuals compelled to abruptly leave behind an established career or cultural way of life. Although he lost all of his wealth in the process, he was luckier than many Cuban émigrés in that he escaped with his immediate family unit intact. Maduro's biggest dream in Cuba was to establish the first international franchise in the major leagues. He was one step away with the Havana-based, Triple-A Cuban Sugar Kings. Those dreams were forever dashed by the socio-political maelstrom that convulsed Cuba in the mid–20th century. Though it had its warts, as did the United States, Cuba was one of the most progressive nations in Latin America prior to the political chaos that befell it and turned it into a third-world country. (A Cuban doctor, Carlos J. Finlay, discovered the cure for yellow fever at the turn of the last century. The nation recorded the first transatlantic flight from any country in Latin America, Havana to Madrid, in 1946. It was the first country in Latin America to have television.) The utter shame of it is that with its proximity to the United States, Cuba would have, economically speaking, become another Taiwan, as contemporary Miami journalist Maria Elvira Salazar is so fond of saying.

Following his death, the editorial page of the November 27, 2016, *Miami Herald* stated, "[Fidel Castro] also ruined an economy that had been the third-largest in Latin America when he took power." But such a place of wealth and resources could not have been driven by external factors alone. "[After the end of the second World War] Cuba had the highest literacy rate in Latin America and the second-highest standard of living," wrote Latin American specialist and *Secret Missions to Cuba* author Robert M. Levine.

Castro's revolution snuffed out many wonderful things in Cuba, including its Golden Age of baseball, replacing it with what can only be characterized as Cuba's Tragic Age of baseball. Ballplayers—like all gifted components of Cuban society—were exploited, and extraordinary individuals were not permitted to realize the full potential of their talent. How many Cuban players were denied a chance at playing in the major leagues before the tidal wave of defections of more recent times? How many Hall of Famers? Cuba's footprint in the major leagues could have equaled the Dominican Republic's—*before* the Dominican Republic. Instead, for decades, Cuban ballplayers had to settle for "amateur" dominance against overmatched international competition—the baseball equivalent of the Soviet hockey team during the Cold War.

Bobby Maduro, whose love of baseball flowed through his veins, dedicated his adult life to the sport. This book entails his lofty accomplishments and unfulfilled aspirations, and how his legacy is not forgotten today in the youth recreation leagues of Miami.

And that, perhaps, may be his most shining memorial.

Introduction

Perhaps no one in baseball history has worn as many important hats within the game as Roberto "Bobby" Maduro. He was a stadium builder, owner of multiple clubs, general manager, scout, agent, youth baseball organizer, founder of a league, and MLB's only named ambassador.

In a life of selfless dedication to the sport he loved, Maduro tirelessly applied himself in all of his various capacities, with promotion and expansion as resonating themes.

Maduro was born in Cuba on June 27, 1916. Raised in a well-bred, wealthy family, he received his higher-grade schooling abroad in North Carolina, perfecting language skills that helped him navigate the cultural divide between the United States and Cuba. In later years, because of his earlier accomplishments and reputation, Maduro was able to integrate himself into different levels of U.S. corporate baseball.

Maduro became co-owner of the Cuban Winter League's Cienfuegos Elephants in 1949, and then the majority owner of the Florida International League's Havana Cubans a few years afterward. In 1954 Maduro, who believed "in the value of baseball as the most effective possible instrument for creating and maintaining Good Will and understanding between the U.S. and Latin America," shifted his Class B franchise to the International League as the re-christened Cuban Sugar Kings. A popular team both at home and away, the 1959 Sugar Kings won the AAA Junior World Series against the American Association's Minneapolis Millers in a thrilling seven-game series.

The baseball visionary's dream of establishing the first international franchise in the major leagues in Havana seemed close at hand. But like hundreds of thousands of other Cubans, Maduro fled into exile following the Marxist turn of Cuba's 1959 Revolution. With all his personal wealth and corporate assets confiscated, including the 15-year-old, cutting-edge stadium he co-built, Maduro was forced to start all over again, with a large family to support, in a new country.

In 1960, unable to guarantee the safety of its players, the International League had ordered Maduro's Sugar Kings team out of Havana, gutting the proprietary revenue stream associated with the club. Relocated to Jersey City, New Jersey, the renamed team did not draw well and moved again a year and a half later, to Jacksonville, Florida.

Incidentally, organized baseball did not abandon Cuba in the International League or shut down the Cuban Winter League as has often been falsely portrayed. The Cuban Winter League (as were all winter leagues in Latin America) was an autonomous institution with its own local directors and owners, and had completed its 77th season in February 1961 (with native players only). The following month, the demagogue Castro abolished professional sports in Cuba under National Decree Number 936.[1] In September of the same year, under "constitutional" Resolution 454, all Cubans who left the country, in particular for the United States, were branded traitors and would have their property confiscated if they did not return within 29 days.[2]

In December 1965, having sold his interests in his Jacksonville Suns, Maduro was appointed to a unique position in baseball Commissioner William Eckert's "cabinet." Maduro accepted the job of the first (and only) "Coordinator of Inter-American Relations"—a cultural liaison post between organized baseball and Latin American baseball's winter and summer leagues, including amateur development. Eckert's successor, Bowie Kuhn, came to appreciate the Cuban impresario as well.

More than a decade later, the 63-year-old father of seven undertook his most ambitious project, forming the Inter-American League. Seeing it as not only a vehicle to showcase Latin American talent but also as a conduit for Hispanic players hoping to reach the major leagues, Maduro's league incorporated with six teams, composed of five Caribbean-basin clubs and one U.S. entry from Maduro's adopted hometown of Miami. Because of unforeseen factors and occurrences, the AAA minor league did not survive its planned 130-game schedule, folding more than halfway through its maiden season of 1979.

In 1985, a year before his death, the man Hall of Fame manager Tommy Lasorda called the "Father of Latin Baseball" was elected into the Cuban Hall of Fame by the Federation of Cuban Professional Players in exile. The Dominican Republic–based *Salon de La Fama del Beisbol Latino* selected Maduro for its inaugural induction class in 2010—the only executive in the 11-person honorary field.

Prologue
Establishing Tropical Roots

In stark contrast to the second half of the 20th century, immigration abundantly flowed *into* Cuba in the century's first 50-odd years. Following the British-influenced abolition of the African slave trade in the early 1800s,[1] working-class migrants arrived from Europe (mostly Spain), and other parts of the globe, as skilled and unskilled laborers to the largest island of the Greater Antilles. Expansion in agricultural farming and a booming sugar industry contributed to the economic growth and prosperity that supported the growing native and immigrant population. In 1899, Cuba's population was 1.5 million. By 1960, it had topped seven million.

An example of the multiculturalism in Cuba was a thriving Chinese community that peaked at around 140,000 in the 1950s. A smaller, but no less important, ethnic composition was the island's Jewish population, which topped 25,000 in the 1930s. A member of that smaller ethnic group was Salomón Mozes Levy Maduro, a Curaçao-born businessman who migrated to Cuba in 1914 with his wife Abigail.

Levy Maduro was born on September 8, 1890, in Willemstad, one of six offspring born to Mozes Salomon Levy Maduro and Adela Naar. "The Maduro family was of Sephardic Jewish origin," writes historian Rory Costello. "Levy Maduro was a grandson of S. E. L. Maduro, who founded Curaçao's oldest company in 1837. Bobby Maduro's paternal grandmother also came from a prominent Sephardic family in Curaçao, the Naars. So did his mother Abigail Abinun de Lima."[2] Born July 29, 1890, Abinun de Lima's cultural background included ties to France, where she spent a great deal of her youth (to the extent of considering French as her native tongue) and where she continued to visit, travel documents show, after her relocation to Cuba.

Following an extensive genealogical check, Costello affirms that "along with many other Sephardim, the Maduros went first from Portugal to France and then, starting in the 1600s, the Netherlands. In Amsterdam, they joined the Levy family by marriage and the surname became Levy Maduro. In 1672 descendants went to the Dutch Antilles and from there to various other spots in Central America and the Caribbean."[3]

Precipitating the young couple's move to Cuba was the death of Mozes Salomon in 1911 and a sagging economic front at home. "During the three decades or so prior to oil refinery operations, the Curaçaoan economy stagnated and emigration rates were considerable," explains university lecturer Alan F. Benjamin. "Early in the twentieth century, this included migration to Cuba to participate in the sugar boom, first by Sephardi and then by Afro-Curaçaoans."[4]

Adapting to new tropical surroundings may have been easier for the Levy Maduros than most typical expatriates due to already acquired communication aptitude. "Both Spanish and English were (and are) widely spoken in Curaçao, along with Dutch, the official language of the island,"[5] advises Costello. Already imbued with a Caribbean sense of lifestyle, the multi-lingual skills possessed by the couple further eased the cultural assimilation.

Two years after settling in Havana, the Levy Maduros felt assimilated enough to welcome their first child. Roberto Maduro de Lima came into the world on June 27, 1916, a month and two days before his mother's 26th birthday. Two years later, the couple's second and last child was born, a girl christened Adrienne. "They were born Robert Levy Maduro [de Lima] and Adrienne Levy Maduro [de Lima],"[6] states Mercedes de Marchena, married for over four decades to Frank de Marchena, one of Adrienne's two children. (The other is a daughter named Adriana Teresita, born March 13, 1947.)

Sometime during the first-born's developmental period, the Levy name was forgotten, or discarded, "Robert" became "Roberto," and Adrienne became "Adriana." Similar to the U.S. custom of anglicizing Hispanic ballplayers' first names prevalent for many decades of the last century, it seems a Hispanicization of the younger Maduro children's names occurred. "Bobby's parents were non-practicing Jews,"[7] adds Mercedes, which may explain the eventual dropping of the Levy surname. Neither of his children used it.

"My father was born a Jew and he converted to Catholicism, and my grandfather eventually converted," affirms Bobby Maduro's youngest son, Alberto, or Al. "My father converted—when? It was before he married my mother. She was Catholic. It's unbelievable that no one in our family knows the exact reason but there was a lot of speculation.... You couldn't get into social clubs in Cuba if you were Jewish or black."[8]

The elder Maduro incorporated himself into Cuba's lucrative sugar industry, with an original home base in the flourishing sugar mill town of Central Cunagua, a little more than 300 miles from Havana. The Louisiana Planter and Sugar Manufacturer Company had an office in the capital. It published in 1919 the following account of a trip it made into the country's interior, which highlighted the industrial advancement in Cuba that men like the elder Maduro continued to bring about:

> On our trip into Camaguey Province we also visited Central Cunagua, the world's finest sugar estate, and although it is an inconvenient place to reach, one forgets all the inconveniences after arriving at the central. The batey houses are by far the finest, as a whole, in Cuba; the finest we might say in the world, and the same is true of the central itself. One must really see the place to appreciate [it], and considering it was developed in the short space of two years in what was practically wilderness, the results are little short of marvelous.[9]

Salomón Maduro branched out into the world of commercial finance in the mid–1920s. In Havana, he worked for different insurance companies, eventually rising to the presidency of one of them within a dozen years.

It was in this residual affluence that Roberto Maduro and his younger sister were raised.

ONE

Stadium Builder

In a home where at least four languages (French, Spanish, Dutch and English) were spoken by its masters, it can be easily conjectured that young Roberto and Adriana Maduro were instilled with a significant amount of educational focus.

Maduro's cultured upbringing expanded in his mid-teens when he was sent to the United States to broaden his education. In the early 1930s, he attended Asheville School, a private university preparatory institution in western North Carolina. It was during this youthful time abroad that he was probably tagged with his familiar nickname of "Bobby."

He then sought out higher learning at Cornell University, matriculating in the fall of 1934. Maduro joined the freshman baseball team but had trouble sticking, for reasons not involving talent. "I flunked chemistry," he later admitted, "and that took care of my collegiate career."[1] After completing his sophomore year, the 20-year-old engineering major left college following the death of his uncle, Elias Levy Maduro, in July of 1936. It was a move predicated on helping fill the void left by Elias in his father's businesses.

Three and a half years later, a more pleasing life-changing event occurred for Maduro. He wed Isolina Olmo Fernández Garrido on January 28, 1940. "She was a beautiful woman, inside and out, and from a very good family,"[2] relates Lourdes Reguera, whose namesake daughter Lourdes attended St. Patrick Catholic School in Miami Beach with Isabel Maduro, one of Bobby and Isolina's children. (Isolina was affectionately known as Fúfila, a term whose origins and meaning have escaped her descendants over the years.)

The union produced three children in a little over four years. Third child Adela, arriving on March 8, 1944, joined first-born Roberto Jr., and second son Felipe.

Within a year of Adela's birth, her father took his first major stride toward baseball prominence by initiating the building of the great municipal stadium. Partnering with another entrepreneur, Miguelito Suárez, Maduro approached Julio Blanco Herrera, owner of the park that was the primary home of the Cuban Winter League. "The plan at first was to lease Stadium Tropical and expand the grounds," explained sportswriter Fausto Miranda, "but the parties could not come to an arrangement. Maduro and Suárez then turned their attention to raising a new complex."[3]

The pair secured a 99-year lease on a tract of land in the Cerro district of Havana. Suárez's father, a real estate broker, may have been helpful in this initial phase of the enterprise. "Miguelito wasn't a baseball man," says Maduro's son Jorge, in retrospect. "I think, I'm not certain, he may have gotten into it [stadium building] as a real estate investment. And I don't think my dad ever bought him out."[4]

Maduro and Suárez had likely met years earlier—or had their friendship reinforced—at the swanky Vedado Tennis Club, where they were both members. Athletically inclined young men, Roberto played first base for the Marqueses, the club's favored amateur baseball team, while Miguelito

A mustachioed Bobby and Isolina on their wedding day, January 1940. The union would produce eight children and last until Isolina's death in 1974 (courtesy Maduro Family).

excelled in rowing and swimming competitions against other distinguished amateur institutions, including the University of Havana, the Biltmore Yacht & Country Club, Habana Yacht Club and Central Hershey. (A year earlier, a handful of Vedado Tennis Club members had united together to purchase the Almendares franchise of the Cuban Winter League.) Both impresarios were young men as they stepped off on their ambitious undertaking, with Suárez[5] two years younger than the 29-year-old Maduro in 1945. The two biggest stockholders of the endeavor incorporated under the simplistic-sounding *Compañía Operadora de Stadiums*, which managed all the operations of the facility.

"The stadium would be built on a patch of land about two miles east of the city's famous Cristóbal Colón Cemetery, named for Cristopher Columbus, who landed in Cuba in 1492," wrote baseball author César Brioso. "Havana's new baseball cathedral would be in the heart of the city and would easily surpass the [number of] fans Tropical Park was designed to hold. So as the final season of the Cuban League at La Tropical unfolded, construction crews broke ground, poured concrete, and erected steel girders for the league's future home."[6]

Eventually accommodating more than twice as many people as the 15,000-seat Stadium Cerveza Tropical, *Gran Stadium del Cerro de la Habana* officially opened October 26, 1946, as the new home of the Cuban Winter League. The league inked a 40-year lease with the stadium owners. The initial radio transmission license went for $20,000 to CMBZ-Radio Sala, which, in turn re-sold partial broadcasting rights to three smaller Havana stations for $7,000 each. Coca-Cola and Seven-Up gained soft drink distribution privileges, while Bacardí was given exclusive domain over alcohol sales. (This last contract may have hit a snag, as later reports suggest that beer was not sold in the stands during the first season.) The Almendares Scorpions defeated the Cienfuegos Oilers, 9–1. Former Chicago Cubs hurler Jorge Comelles earned the inaugural win. Knocked out in the sixth inning, Venezuela's big-league pioneer pitcher, Alejandro Carrasquel, suffered the defeat. Cuban star Roberto Ortiz slugged the stadium's first home run. Thirty-one thousand fans cheered the festivities, even as several thousand seats were not yet available to the public. Although a day game, the stadium was equipped with a modern, arc lamp electric system that rivaled any found in the major leagues.

Three months after opening, the fully completed stadium drew a call from none other than the publisher of baseball's most widely read periodical. "Gran Stadium represents a great deal of dreaming," *Sporting News* publisher J. G. Taylor Spink informed his loyal readers. "Two wealthy

Cubans—Miguelito Suárez and Bob Maduro—pushed the project through to completion in the face of all hazards. Construction difficulties, labor troubles and mounting costs hiked their expenditure to $1,800,000 when they had figured to spend one million."[7]

Cuban baseball at this time happened to be caught up in the "South of the Border War" between organized baseball and Mexico over contractual ownership of players. Earlier in the year, flamboyant Mexican tycoon Jorge Pasquel had lured a group of major league players into his newly branded Mexican League by offering significantly higher salary commitments than their major league clubs. Organized baseball faced not only a loss of talent but, more importantly, its biggest challenge to the indenturing "reserve clause" of its players' contracts. Emboldened athletes such as Sal Maglie and Luis Olmo (who finished third in the NL in RBI in 1945) skipped out on their respective clubs to play in the league. They were later accompanied across the Rio Grande by St. Louis Cardinals notables Max Lanier, Fred Martin and Lou Klein, among others. Most of the foreign recruits signed multi-year contracts, something rarely offered by their previous front office bosses.

Baseball Commissioner A. B. "Happy" Chandler decreed all players who skipped out on their major league clubs suspended for five years, ineligible to play under the organized baseball banner. The ruling carried broader sanctioning powers with the forthcoming amendment to Major League Rule 18 (b) that read, in part, "No player shall participate in any exhibition game with or against any team which, during the current season or within one year, has had any ineligible players."[8]

That fall in Cuba, the line had clearly been drawn by Chandler. But for years, Cubans had participated and starred in Mexican baseball as players and managers. Snubbing Chandler's edict, the 1946–1947 Cuban Winter League refused to turn its back on some of its most famous personalities and welcomed players from the United States as ever before—even if some of those players were named Lanier, Martin and Klein. Accentuating the Mexican association as being too deep and involved to sever in one fell swoop, Cuba's best-known baseball men, Adolfo Luque and Miguel Angel "Mike" González, accepted excommunication in 1947. Luque managed in Mexico in 1946 with Puebla and skippered Almendares during the 1946–1947 winter campaign. González, third base coach of the defending world champion St Louis Cardinals, was banned prior to the 1947 major league season. For Luque, who had left his organized baseball job as pitching coach of the New York Giants in 1945, the sanction was easier to swallow. But González owned and managed the Habana

Lions, and he could not have been expected to comply with Chandler's order and completely relinquish interests in his home winter league team.

From the obvious contentious atmosphere sprang up a second winter circuit in 1946–1947 called the National Federation League. Domiciled in Julio Blanco Herrera's Tropical Park, the league employed U.S. minor league players, Cuban and North American, including blacks of both ethnicities who were sensitive to the promise of integration on the near horizon in the major leagues. Up against a new, state-of-the-art stadium on the other side of town and the greater talent pool of the established Cuban circuit, the OB-backed league struggled to maintain four teams and complete an abbreviated schedule. It officially ceased to exist on New Year's Eve, 1946.

Meanwhile, Gran Stadium played host to the most celebrated Cuban Winter League season in history, with the championship decided on the next-to-last day of the season, between "eternal rivals" Almendares and Habana. The pennant-deciding victory on February 25, 1947, was hurled by Scorpions pitcher Max Lanier.

Attending many sellouts throughout the four-month-long campaign, Maduro and Suárez could not have asked for a better opening act for their ambitious business venture.

For an encore, Gran Stadium welcomed the major leagues just days after Lanier's 9–2, championship victory. The Brooklyn Dodgers, who had arrived in Havana and were training at the big stadium during the day in the waning days of the winter league season, played their first exhibition game on February 26—a five-inning, intra-squad game. Two days later, the Boston Braves flew in for a three-game weekend set, February 28 to March 2, versus the Brooklyn team. After splitting the first two contests, the Sunday finale was rained out. The low, rounded-up attendance figures of 5,000 and 1,000 fans for the respective games indicated that the Cuban fans were spent from the emotionally draining conclusion of their season.

The Dodgers brought along their Triple A affiliate from Montreal, whose roster included Jackie Robinson.[9] The parent club left Havana during the first week of March to travel to Caracas, Venezuela, to engage the New York Yankees in a three-game series. The Yankees had been in San Juan, Puerto Rico, for preliminary spring training workouts and exhibition games against local squads from that island's professional winter league. Montreal and Robinson bided their time clashing against a Cuban All-Star squad and the Florida International League's Havana Cubans. While Yankees general manager Larry MacPhail followed through on the admirable idea of promoting the game with his famous team in the burgeoning baseball hotbed of the Caribbean basin, his Brooklyn counterpart, Branch Rickey, sought a higher purpose in choosing the less racially sensitive venues of Havana and Panama City for his team that spring. The locales were chosen as part of Rickey's plan to help facilitate Robinson's historic transition as the first African American player in the major leagues.

The ground-breaking path of Robinson was smoothed along the way by a Cuban doctor. Wendell Smith, who had been shadowing Robinson since he left the States, was informed of a potential foot problem Robinson had incurred that could have delayed, or possibly, altered the course of history, if not treated. "Jackie Robinson's training camp drills will be interrupted for a week, and maybe longer, it was announced here Sunday by Dr. Julio Sanguily, because of an irritating callous on the toe of his left foot," wrote the *Pittsburgh Courier* sports editor. "Dr. Sanguily, one of the outstanding physicians in Cuba, was to have operated on the foot Monday afternoon [March 3] at 4 o'clock. He said the operation was a minor one but that the Montreal second sacker would have to take it easy for a while."[10]

During Robinson's recuperation, the Dodgers and Yankees returned to Havana from Venezuela for more exhibition action. On Sunday afternoon, March 9, the Yankees defeated Brooklyn, 4–1, in front of 7,000 fans at Gran Stadium. That evening the in-demand park showcased two three-round sparring matches featuring heavyweight boxing champion Joe Louis. The 32-year-old Louis easily defeated both opponents in the friendly bouts, flooring one in the second round. The *Associated Press* reported the 25,000 persons present as "the largest crowd in Havana boxing history." *United Press* listed the turnstile count at 20,000. Adding to the discrepancy, Wendell Smith put the crowd at half the *UP*'s total, due to competition from the annual Carnival celebrations occurring in Cuba. Robinson was photographed with the champ prior to the festivities, which culminated a lucrative two-month-long, 10,000-mile tour throughout Latin America by the popular pugilist.

After visiting Puerto Rico, Venezuela and Cuba, the Yankees returned to Florida to finish training, while Robinson headed with his Montreal teammates to Panama, where they took on the Dodgers in several games. Robinson's performances against Brooklyn in Panama and Havana were key factors in his promotion to the big club a few weeks later.

Following excursions to Venezuela, Panama and their extended stays in Havana, Brooklyn and Montreal left the Cuban capital following their final exhibition game on April 5. Robinson was briefly knocked unconscious on a collision at first base (the position he would man that season) and had to be removed from the game. The Dodgers and Royals did not attract a large following in their daily spring meetings at Gran Stadium. Not even the prior handful of major league match-ups could have been stated as having "drawn well." Perhaps still hung over, or drained, from their exciting championship season's finish, local baseball enthusiasts simply never warmed up to the famous foreign teams, in spite of the gleaming new stadium and practice games that also involved the Havana Cubans.

Four days after the Dodgers and Royals vacated the premises, those same Havana Cubans—the country's one-year-old entry into organized baseball—opened their second Florida International League campaign and first at Gran Stadium. Cubans left-hander Rafael Rivas shut out the Lakeland Pilots, 3–0. It was the first of 105 wins for the Class C club, managed by Oscar Rodríguez, on their way to the pennant and playoff championship. The winning Cubans were well supported throughout the season, drawing 226,813 fans in their 77 home dates, including several playoff games, a no doubt pleasing total to the owners of the team and home park.

During J. G. Taylor Spink's January 1947 visit, he cited three successes for the duo of Suárez and Maduro as they pertained to the stadium: success in the winter league, success in landing the Dodgers to train in Havana, and success in luring the Florida International League. At this juncture, Spink did not know it but another accolade Maduro would be jointly credited with was the success in guiding the Cuban Winter League toward a harmonious relationship with organized baseball.

Given their altruistically shared history of the sport, the training trips of major league teams, and their ties with the Florida International League, it seemed indefensible for Cuba and the United States to be baseball enemies. That realization eventually hit home to Cuban team owners and the country's National Sports Commission executives. "By April of 1947, Cuban League officials had been meeting in secret, trying to secure organized baseball's blessings for the league," disclosed César Brioso. "Miguel Angel González, Almendares part owner Dr. Julio Sanguily, and Bobby Maduro, owner of Gran Stadium, were dispatched to meet with Chandler and George M. Trautman, president of the National Association of Professional Baseball Leagues, the governing body of the minor leagues."[11] The disclosure reveals Maduro's early involvement with Cuban baseball development.

Only six weeks after Chandler had suspended Mike Gonzalez, hostilities between the mutual baseball lovers ended and, at the same time, put asunder Jorge Pasquel's audacious foray against the United States' sovereign sport. In late-April 1947, a deal was forged whereby Triple A minor leaguers from the States would be permitted to play in Cuba, boosting the winter circuit's caliber of competition to expected new heights. In return, Cuba had to disassociate itself from all branded "ineligible" players who had defied previous rulings and jumped their U.S. contracts, or those who had simply competed against these ostracized players. Chandler and Sanguily, nicknamed "July" ["Hoo-lee"], were the principle participants in the final accord. Ratified on July 11 by the voting members of the National Association of Professional Baseball Leagues, Cuba entered the auspices of organized baseball as a designated "unclassified affiliate."

But the previous success of the league brought about discontent among some participants, who felt they were not getting a fair salary shake from team owners. Led by a newly formed players union headed by wartime major leaguer Tommy de la Cruz and backed by Cuban entrepreneurs who witnessed the huge turnstile turnouts of Gran Stadium's inaugural season, a new league with four teams formed to compete against the newly-favored circuit. The clubs were Alacranes, Leones, Cuba, and Santiago, which withdrew after 21 games. Their playing home was Tropical Park.

Adolfo Luque, who had once again managed in Mexico over the summer, remained ex-communicated, along with former big leaguers George Hausemann, Danny Gardella, Sal Maglie, Luis Olmo and the St. Louis trio of Lanier, Klein and Martin. But they all were embraced by the new league. Notable North American and Cuban black athletes incorporated into the start-up circuit as well, with Ray Dandridge, Terris McDuffie, Ramón Bragaña, Héctor Rodríguez and Santos Amaro among them.

Although the rival loop began with great fanfare and crowds, it rather quickly developed that Gran Stadium was the place for baseball fans to be. More and more, as the season progressed, the majority of fans' disposable income veered toward the new concrete and steel structure. As crowds at Tropical Park waned, the NAPBL held their annual meeting in Miami, Florida, beginning on December 1.

From the convention came significant news with respect to Latin American baseball. The winter leagues of Venezuela, Puerto Rico and Panama agreed to join Cuba as unclassified affiliates of the National Association, starting the following season. The new leagues would be fused with U.S. minor league talent. Conditionally, as with Cuba, the members promised not to engage or employ anyone associated with Mexican baseball—further thwarting Pasquel's ambitions and ultimately isolating him from Caribbean basin baseball.

A photo in the December 10, 1947, *Sporting News* depicts NA President George M. Trautman standing next to an assembly of ten men, most representing the baseball interest of the previously named countries. In the picture, taken at convention headquarters in the McAllister Hotel, were Venezuelans Otto Antillano and Roberto Machado; Stamford Graham, Panamanian League president; and a delegation of five Cubans: Rafael Inclán, Cuban Winter League president, co-Almendares owners Mario Mendoza and Dr. July Sanguily, and stadium partners Miguelito Suárez and Bobby Maduro. Paul Miller, CWL treasurer, and Robert L. Finch, Public Relations Director of the NA, were also part of the group shot. (Puerto Rican Winter League president Jorge Luis Córdova Díaz was late in arriving and missed the momentous photo op.)

A byproduct announcement to the Miami accord splendidly advanced the framework agreement for a Latin American "ultimate competition" to be played by the championship clubs of the OB unclassified affiliate nations. "Prospects of a Pan-American World's Series," trumpeted one Magic City press release, "among the champions of Panama, Venezuela, Puerto Rico and Cuba—details of which remain to be worked out—brightened as a result of conferences between representatives of those countries and officials of the National Association here."[12] The annual tournament eventually became known as the Caribbean Series and was inaugurated in Havana only 14 months after the NAPBL gathering.

La Serie del Caribe began as a double round-robin tournament on February 20, 1949, at Gran Stadium with a doubleheader. Although the historic twin bill card did not produce a sellout, there was plenty of partisan excitement to make up for the scattering of empty seats. Pomp and ceremonies included multi-national flag-raising and national anthem-playing for the four representative teams. The participants of Spur Cola, Mayagüez, Cervecería Caracas and Almendares, spread out in the outfield before marching back to the infield and lining up along the foul lines. A fifth flag also flapped in the breeze that evening after the secretary-treasurer of Major League Baseball, Walter Mulbury, representing Commissioner Chandler's office, hoisted the *Confederación del Caribe's* flag to punctuate the occasion. (*La Confederación de Baseball Profesional del Caribe* was realized with an accord created between officials from Cuba, Panama and Puerto Rico on April 12, 1948, in Havana; there was an initiative for a fourth country, Venezuela, to join, which the country shortly afterward accepted. The newly-formed Caribbean Baseball Federation, or Caribbean Confederation, as it was also known, finalized the Caribbean Series groundwork initiated at the December NAPBL meeting in Miami.)

The sartorial appearance of the squads at the first Caribbean Series was contemplated by erudite author Roberto González Echevarría: "Before the first pitch was thrown ... most visible was the fact that, as opposed to Almendares and all other teams in the Cuban League, the teams from the other three countries either had commercial announcements on their jerseys or actually had the name of a commercial product."[13]

"Wilmer Fields, the starter for Mayagüez [Puerto Rican champions], had the privilege of initiating the Games by throwing the first pitch in Series history," recounted a latter-day historian. "His batterymate was Humberto Martí. At the plate was [Panamanian champion] Spur Cola's Stanley Arthurs. Umpiring behind the dish was Amado Maestri."[14]

To the disgust of Indios fans, Fields did not have it on the mound. Knocking him out of the box in the sixth inning and scoring ten runs in the frame, the Colonites went on to a 13–9 keepsake victory. Canal Zone native Patricio "Pat" Scantlebury hurled the eight-inning complete game, which was shortened by a frame so as not to infringe upon the scheduled starting time of the second contest between Cervecería and Almendares.

In the anticipated match-up that followed, the Scorpions romped to a 16–1 triumph behind pitcher and fan favorite Conrado "Connie" Marrero. Outfielder Dalmiro Finol accounted for the only run for the Venezuelan national champs, clubbing the Series' first home run for posterity.

Managed by Fermín Guerra, Almendares proceeded to dominate the competition over the next five nights and captured the initial championship hardware with a perfect 6–0 record.

With the well-earned laurels of the maiden tournament apportioned to Almendares, the man who had quickly made a name for himself in the diamond sport in Cuba begs a reflective look. In a period of 28 months, Bobby Maduro had opened to overwhelmingly positive reception a new baseball stadium, helped negotiate a strategic peace accord, which not only ended serious strife between Cuban and organized baseball but which partnered the two, and was involved in the eventual formation of a Latin American cooperative of nations that would broaden and shape the scope of baseball in the region for decades to come.

And he was just getting started.

Two

Team Owner

Two months prior to the Caribbean Series commencement, the pro-amateur Havana Country Club Invitation took place. Professional golfer Sam Snead won the best-ball tournament with a score of 193, 23 strokes under par. "In the unique tournament," read a wire report, "the pros teamed with two amateurs and could take either for a partner. Snead's mate was Bobby Maduro, son of a Havana business man."[1]

Jorge Maduro, Bobby and Isolina's fourth child, remembers with a smile his father self-deprecatingly talking about that victory later in life. "My father asked Snead after the competition, 'What do you think about my game?'" says Jorge. "Snead replied, 'Everything you do is wrong, but we won, so don't change anything.'"[2]

Either the elder Maduro, who was six feet tall with broad shoulders, or the golf pro Snead came down too harshly with the implied criticism. Several years afterward, *Buffalo Evening News* writer Cy Kritzer exposed some interesting facts about that pro-am that places Maduro and his abilities on the links in an altogether different light:

> The 17th hole at the Havana Country Club is near the clubhouse and visiting sportswriters are reminded that "this is Bob Maduro's hole."
> Playing as Sam Snead's partner in a pro-amateur tournament here a few seasons ago, Maduro made the shot that finished the tournament. Snead was on the green in two and looked a cinch for a par 4 but missed two putts. The gallery had paid little attention to his partner. Sam was playing such precision golf that Maduro picked up on most holes. But now Maduro was on the spot. He had a downhill lie just off the green.
> The crowd opened up a lane for his shot, and without lining up the ball for the hole he chipped it into the cup.[3]

Bobby Maduro may not yet have been known to the foreign press at the time of his pairing with Snead, but in Cuba, he was plainly becoming more and more preeminent in the national sport. In late spring of 1949,

Maduro linked with a longtime league notable, Emilio de Armas, and a large sporting goods impresario, Luis Parga, to buy the Cienfuegos franchise. One of the four Havana-based teams that comprised the Cuban Winter League, Cienfuegos—a colonial city in south-central Cuba—was the only one with a name affiliation outside the capital. De Armas[4] had been a part-owner of other teams in the league, dating back more than two decades, and had been serving the circuit as business advisor and promoter.

The Sporting News notified its readers of the sale in mid–June 1949. But Jorge S. Figueredo contends that the "sale" was not a sale. "With respect to Cienfuegos," proffered the Cuban baseball historian, "it was announced on May 13 that Messrs. Bobby Maduro, Luis F. Parga and Emilio de Armas rented the team for five years, paying 10,000 pesos annually for the right to use the green franchise."[5] (Several of today's online currency exchange sites verify the Cuban peso trading at a 1:1 rate with the U.S. dollar during this time—reflective of bright economic conditions on the island.)

The controlling trio changed the club's image, complete with a new nickname. Formerly known as the *Petroleros* (Oilers), Cienfuegos became the "Elephants." "Cienfuegos had the most elegant uniform in the league," recalled fan Roberto González Echevarría, "black and green lettering and piping, with black socks and cap. Though television was not yet in color, these uniforms appeared enticingly in magazines and advertisements."[6]

Also undergoing a radical redesign that season was Marianao, the league's fourth franchise (in popularity) and named after one of Havana's better-known city districts. The previously-called *Frailes Grises* (Gray Monks) aggressively morphed into "Tigers," to the consensus delight of their fan base. The Tigers' new orange and black uniform scheme may have suggested the New York Giants, but González Echevarría states that Marianao borrowed its striking color combination from the Atlético de Cuba, an amateur team. The Cienfuegos and Marianao team nicknames and colors complemented nicely the existing animal kingdom sobriquets of Almendares (blue uniform trim with white old-English lettering) and Habana (red uniform trim with Gothic-font script).

The next pressing order of business confronting the new landlords was to improve their last-place club from a year ago. The three quickly showed their willingness to do so. In a testament to that commitment, published shortly following the takeover, they announced a crisscrossing scouting trip of some 6,000 miles through the United States. Winter league clubs had permission to contact players directly, or their teams, with contracts to be filed through the National Association.

As the 1949–1950 winter league season arrived, the new operating chiefs were forced to wait an extra day, as the Tigers and Scorpions squared off on opening night. The next evening, October 8, Bobby Maduro experienced his first game as team overseer. Cienfuegos disappointed their fans and new front office, dropping a 4–3 decision to the Habana Lions, with Tommy Fine the losing pitcher. A Texas League recruit, Fine carved an honorable place in the circuit during the season. Bouncing back from the defeat, the left-hander accounted for 16 of second-place Cienfuegos' 36 victories. Pitching mostly in relief, he appeared in 35 of the club's 72 games, and at one point won nine straight contests, an all-time league record. The win total and appearances also topped all other hurlers in the league.

As the season reached its mid-point in early December, Maduro took to the road again to attend the NAPBL meeting in Baltimore. Signaling his increased international visibility, Maduro appeared as one of three men representing Cuba in a caucus of Caribbean Confederation delegates in the Charm City.

Over the first few days of January, Maduro and July Sanguily were de facto hosts for Chicago White Sox general manager Frank Lane in Havana. Maduro appeared tailor-made for the role into which he was evolving and apparently embracing. His command of English was an undeniably important factor in his progression.

In a year of extreme competitive balance, Almendares repeated as champions of the league with an unimpressive 38–34 mark. Cienfuegos finished two games behind, with Marianao and Habana tied for third with identical 35–37 records.

Almendares produced a disappointing showing in the second Caribbean Series, held in San Juan, Puerto Rico. Fermín Guerra's team split their six contests to finish in third place, behind the home country Caguas Criollos club and the Series' champions from Panama, the Carta Vieja Yankees. The teams posted identical 4–2 records after the final day, prompting a winner-take-all square-off, won by the Yankees, 9–3.

That summer, *Miami Herald* sports editor Jimmy Burns reported that Maduro had toured the minor leagues in the U.S. with a developed interest in placing a club in the Florida International League. The same writer, three years earlier, had circulated an unconfirmed rumor that Maduro desired to relocate the FIL's Lakeland Pilots to Matanzas, Cuba,[7] with their home games presumably at Gran Stadium. Fueling the current speculation, Clark Griffith, part-owner of the Havana Cubans, commented that he saw no reason why a second FIL team in Cuba could not thrive, agreeing with an earlier remark attributed to Miami Sun Sox manager Pepper Martin. These appear to be the earliest indicators of Maduro viewing greater international expansion for the game in Cuba beyond winter baseball.

Expansion on a personal level materialized for Maduro and his wife as the family welcomed their fifth child, Beatríz, born August 24, 1950. The birth helped balance somewhat the existing offspring gender gap, after son Jorge's arrival three years earlier.

In the months following the blessed event, even as Maduro kept an enterprising eye on the future, his role within the winter league seemed to be broadening. Coinciding with the opening of the 1950–1951 CWL season, it became known that minor league umpire Phil Skillin had turned down an offered posting in Cuba over the winter due to other considerations. "In order to accept the major league Grapefruit Circuit job, Skillin had to pass up earlier offers from the Cuban Winter League and Panama Professional League," explained one news story. "Roberto Maduro had offered to pay Phil's expenses to Havana and return as well as his salary for the four-month campaign."[8] Upgrading the officiating may not have been a high priority for many, but it did not escape the apparent quality-driven management approach of Bobby Maduro.

Improving his team was not as easy to define. Cienfuegos stumbled out to an 8–22 start in the winter campaign. A great deal of the woes could be traced to an inability to beat the Habana Lions. The Elephants dropped their first 15 head-to-head match-ups against Mike Gonzalez's club.

During the opening month of the season, Cuba became the first Latin American country to acquire television.[9] The winter league in turn began televising contests for the first time via Unión Radio Canal 4, with Rafael "Felo" Ramírez and René Molina as the announcers. Maduro installed a television in Gran Stadium's "Stadium Club," patterned after the one in Yankee Stadium. The social clubs were precursors to the large-scale suites found today in every amenities-driven ballpark. "I met Bobby Maduro in Havana during the construction of Gran Stadium," the 93-year-old Ramírez told me. "I remember the Stadium was built rather rapidly. I debuted [behind the mike] in 1945, the year before Gran Stadium opened. I called the Sugar Kings in the summer and the winter league. He was extraordinarily kind with me. He always treated the players well."[10]

Cienfuegos' terrible opening forced a change of managers. Excised was current skipper Salvador "Chico" Hernández, replaced by Billy Herman. The second North American to manage in Cuba since the league joined OB (Lefty Gómez in 1947–1948 was the first), the new selection fell squarely upon the man who more and more appeared to be taking the mantle of a mover and shaker. "When his team plummeted to the cellar," wired a visiting writer from Cuba, "Maduro took prompt action. Contacting Billy Herman at the winter meetings in St. Petersburg, Fla., he signed the former second baseman to pilot Cienfuegos."[11]

The former standout infielder with the Chicago Cubs had trained with the Brooklyn Dodgers in Cuba in the spring of 1946. He was released later in the year and then managed the Pittsburgh Pirates for virtually the entire season in 1947, resigning with one game left. Most recently, the 41-year-old had been player-manager of the Pacific Coast League's Oakland Oaks. Herman had the option of staying with the rest of the Cienfuegos players at a Maduro-owned apartment building in the city. Wages for U.S. players in the winter league were set at $1,000 maximum per month, plus living expenses (including wives, if married) and any incurred medical costs due to injury. A player's contract was guaranteed in this respect—but not if he was cut for underperformance or other team reasons. Herman's pay was not disclosed, but it was expectedly higher than any of his players.

As Herman was given the task of turning the Elephants around, *Sporting News* editor-in-chief J. G. Taylor Spink donated a trophy to the league, to be awarded to the championship club at the end of each campaign. It was no run-of-the-mill cup. With a one-foot-high, multi-tiered base, the trophy measured approximately 3½ feet in height.

In January, Maduro and one of his players made the news in a manner reflecting an owner with kindhearted personality traits. Rafael "Ray" Noble had been catching for Cienfuegos for the past five seasons, three as a starter. The 31-year-old backstop had recently been obtained from the PCL by the New York Giants. The big league club grew troubled over a purported wrist injury Noble was playing with. Maduro assuaged the Giants' concerns by flying Noble to New York for X-rays, which revealed nothing out of the ordinary, discrediting the prior narrative.

The first recipients of the *Sporting News* trophy were the Habana Lions, who won a one-game pennant playoff, 4–2, over the Almendares Scorpions. Adrián Zabala hurled the February 19 complete-game effort, after his 40–32 club had finished the season in a tie with their azurean rivals. The left-handed Zabala had been acquired earlier in the season from Cienfuegos.

Cienfuegos bettered themselves under Herman, gaining 20 victories in 44 remaining contests. The team directly influenced the exciting pennant

In the fall of 1950, *The Sporting News* publisher J. G. Taylor Spink donated a trophy to be awarded to the champion of the Cuban Winter League. Standing behind the impressive hardware are, from left to right: Mario Nin, general counsel of the league; Gustavo del Cueto, business manager of the league; Mike González, Habana Lions owner and manager; Rafael Inclán, league president; Paul Miller, league treasurer; Maduro, directly behind the trophy and in one of his last photographs without glasses; Alfredo Pequeño, owner of Marianao; Emilio de Armas, co-proprietor of Cienfuegos; Luis Azorbe, Almendares club official; Luis Parga, co-proprietor of Cienfuegos with de Armas and Maduro; Andrés Fernándes Morell, general manager of Gran Stadium (courtesy Ralph Maya).

finish by upsetting Habana on the next-to-last day of the season, and then losing to Almendares the following day, while the Lions also lost, setting up the one-game championship playoff. The only bright spot on the Elephants team was batting champ and stolen base leader Silvio García, who was named co-MVP of the league with Zabala. With obviously too much emphasis placed on his final victory in the MVP balloting, Zabala finished with an overall record of just 5–4. He won two more games in the Caribbean Series, accounting for half of his squad's victories in the tournament, making its first appearance in Caracas. But they were not enough to overcome the five triumphs in six games by a strong Puerto Rican League champion from Santurce.

In the off-season, Maduro returned to his old high school stomping grounds to participate in the Asheville Country Club Golf Tournament. The *Asheville-Citizens Times* posted a picture of him with other young amateur players. A husky-looking Maduro with baggy white golf shorts and dark T-shirt was described in the August 6, 1951, photo caption as "president of the Havana, Cuba baseball club in the Class B Florida International League."

Maduro's involvement with the Havana Cubans in a high administrative capacity appears to have begun prior to the season, coming at the tail end of the great success had by the franchise in the league. Heading into 1951, the Havana Cubans boasted five straight pennant-winning clubs (1946–1950), led on the field by manager Oscar Rodríguez, as the circuit had been elevated in status from its original Class C listing.

Later that summer, the major leagues would undergo changes at their top executive level, with the naming of a new Commissioner of Baseball, following the owners' ousting of Happy Chandler. When Ford Frick was named the sport's supreme leader two and a half weeks prior to the commencement of the 1951–1952 winter league season, baseball's top periodical sought out comment on the appointment all the way in Cuba. Maduro was one of three men (Mike González and Rafael Inclán, league president, were the others) whose quotes were printed in *The Sporting News*. Maduro, like the other two, approved of the selection, going as far as saying that Frick would make an "excellent commissioner."

This was not Maduro's only press clipping in the "Bible of Baseball" that year. Its editorial page had recently recognized the Cuban businessman's approach and savvy, harkening back to the since-resolved matter of permitting native-born big leaguers to play in the winter leagues, while at the same time calling for deepening ties with Latin America's most ardent followers of the game:

> Men like Roberto Maduro of Havana, one of the owners of Gran Stadium, have the welfare of baseball at heart as much as any club owner in Organized Ball.... Maduro has not only established friendly relations with club owners in the major leagues, but he has continued to maintain those relations by insisting that full protection be given to the U.S. club owners' interests.
>
> It would be a splendid thing for the game if the major leagues took steps to cooperate more fully with baseball in the Caribbean.[12]

Cienfuegos lumbered off to another slow start, winning only six of its first 20 contests, notwithstanding an opening game shutout hurled by Joe Black. The 27-year-old Dodgers pitching prospect four-hit the Marianao Tigers, managed by Adolfo Luque, 4–0, on October 6. Black accounted for four of the team's initial six wins and saved another.

But winning seven out of eight games in mid–November, the Elephants, who were again managed by Billy Herman, extricated themselves from the cellar. A 1–0 dazzler hurled by Black over the Tigers freed the team from the dungeon on November 25. The team made a second push higher in the standings five weeks later. Claiming ten victories in 11 tries, Herman's club found itself in a pennant struggle with first-place Habana in January.

For the campaign, Cienfuegos had been reinforced by three St. Paul Saints pitchers. The threesome, which included Black, Pat McGlothin and Johnny Rutherford, accounted for 32 of the Elephants' 39 victories. The biggest contributor was Black, who pulled in a league-high 15 victories in 27 games as a starter and reliever. The former Negro Leagues pitcher tossed shutouts in back-to-back starts on January 25 and 31. Both times the victims were the Marianao Tigers, whom he one-hit, 3–0, then followed up with a 2–0 three-hitter on January 31. In the former game, Black missed out on receiving the $1,000 standing prize Havana-based *Bohemia* magazine offered to any pitcher in the league who threw a no-hitter. A bloop single by Marianao shortstop Damon Phillips dashed the bonus hopes. Black's triumph on the last day of the month was his 12th and put Cienfuegos within one-half game of top-seated Habana.

"During January, the Cienfuegos Elephants had earned the moniker 'New York Giants' from the Cuban press," divulged a 21st century winter league archivist, "because of their near-miraculous resurrection from their early-season morbidity to challenge and then gain first place, similar to the Giants' exciting pennant rush of the most recent major league baseball season."[13] Indeed, culminating with their 15th win in 17 games on February 10, Cienfuegos had taken over the top spot from Habana by one-half game. But unlike the major league Giants, the Elephants crumpled at the end, dropping their final three contests of the season. The Lions did not waste the opportunity, leaping past the Elephants to win the flag by two games with a 41–30 record. A Sunday doubleheader season finale involving all four teams was washed out.

Black, with his win total, 78 strikeouts and a 2.42 ERA, won the Triple Crown of pitching. The right-hander somehow finished third (50) in MVP voting tabulations behind Habana's Bert Haas (187) and teammate Ray Noble (51). The winter league undeniably helped Black hone his trade prior to his upcoming "Rookie of the Year" season with the Brooklyn Dodgers. His 15–4 record with the Dodgers (all but one of the wins as a reliever) and 15 saves propelled Brooklyn to the National League pennant. The Cuban writers named Billy Herman "Manager of the Year."

A few days after winning the pennant, Habana flew off to Panama City, where it posted five victories, along with one tie, to capture the fourth Caribbean Series.

Branch Rickey had recently left the Brooklyn Dodgers to take over the front office of the Pittsburgh Pirates. In his new job, the groundbreaking general manager maintained his previous belief in the benefits of training in the "Pearl of the Antilles"—especially when it was on someone else's dime. Excluding a handful of springs, including war years, the Pirates had trained in California for the better part of the last quarter-century. That travel arrangement would again be briefly interrupted. "Branch Rickey announced yesterday that the 1953 Pirates would train in Havana, Cuba, at the invitation of the Cuban government," the *Pittsburgh Press* reported during the first week of the 1952 major league season. "Rickey met with Dr. Lorenzo Nodarse, Cuban director of sports, and Roberto Maduro, president of the Havana Stadium, in New Orleans recently and both expressed a desire that Rickey bring the Bucs to Havana in 1953."[14]

With that promotional feather in his cap, Maduro took his family to Europe. Upon his July 5 return to Havana, he offered some insights for fans on the upcoming season as it pertained to his team. He said he believed his team would be stronger than last year's, which had been nosed out for the flag, despite having to find replacements for Joe Black and Johnny Rutherford, Dodgers players who would not be returning to winter ball.

Six weeks prior to the start of 1952–1953 winter league campaign, Maduro took another, shorter holiday excursion with some family members. Sportswriter Edgar Munzel found the genial owner during one leg of his journey and profiled him for the *Chicago Sun-Times*, later reprinted by a national publication. "Maduro ... who speaks English fluently," wrote Munzel, "has been vacationing in this country with his beautiful wife and two of his five children, sons Roberto and Felipe. They spent part of the time following the White Sox, who now have four Cubans on their rosters."[15]

In what turned into a working vacation for the interviewee, Maduro lobbied, on behalf of his league, for more than just rookie big leaguers to be able to play in Cuba, as it currently stood. Major league owners were reluctant to allow this. But Maduro briefed them on how he had invited Frank Lane to Havana the previous winter. The White Sox GM had not been a proponent of winter play, but now had changed his mind. (Lane had ordered Orestes "Minnie" Miñoso to quit playing for Marianao halfway through the 1951–1952 season, but now had removed all related restrictions on the dynamic player.)

Maduro reiterated his continued aim to cooperate with major league baseball for the end purpose of elevating the game in both countries. "Baseball is a tremendous thing in Cuba," Maduro said for the benefit of the North American reader. "We have five radio stations that broadcast the games. Almost everyone that can't see the game, listens to it on the radio. We have a four-team league with a 122 playing dates. Last year we drew 1,500,000 and the year before 1,600,000."[16]

Billy Herman missed the CWL's opening night, October 7, as he was wrapping up his duties as coach on the World Series–involved Brooklyn Dodgers. He was spared witnessing a 3–0 defeat at the hands of Habana, hurled by Julio Moreno. Herman arrived in Cuba in time for his team's second game, but may have wished he had been absent from that one, too. Marianao's José Miguel "Mike" Fornieles dominated the Elephants, 9–1. Famed Mexican outfielder Felipe Montemayor homered for the only Cienfuegos run.

The two initial losses were indicative of a season-long trend of defeats that would quickly mire the pachyderm crew in last place. As the played out season would attest, Maduro had underestimated the loss of pitchers Black and Rutherford. Although Pat McGlothin returned, he barely contributed, and the Elephants wound up using more pitchers than any team in the league in futile stopgap measures for an all-around weak pitching staff—with the exception of 13-game winner Al Gettel. Incredibly, no other Elephants pitcher won more than three games.

As Herman tried in vain to keep his club on firm footing, "Gabe Paul of Cincinnati, the second major league general manager in two years to visit Havana, took in the sights and sounds of the Cuban Winter League for five days in November."[17] Paul came away from his trip as impressed as Frank Lane, indicating a willingness for Redlegs farmhands to be loaned to the league in the future.

Paul, as a matter of fact, returned to Havana in February, along with Redlegs manager Rogers Hornsby, to attend the Caribbean Series, the second played in Havana. Branch Rickey, Fred Haney and George Sisler from the Pittsburgh Pirates also attended. For the second year in a row, the Habana Lions (43–29) were Cuba's Caribbean championship representative, having won the pennant by six games over Almendares and Marianao. Cienfuegos, with a record of 29–45, brought up the rear, burdened by a 16-game deficit.

The Santurce Crabbers became the first team to win two Caribbean Series when they swept through the competition with a perfect 6–0 record, upsetting the favored home country team (3–3).

In February 1953, the first order of business for Maduro following the CWL season was to make last-minute preparations for the Pittsburgh Pirates' arrival. He began making arrangements as soon as he returned from Canada on January 26. He had traveled to the country with his youngest son, Jorge, in the first days of the new year. As previously noted, these "bonding trips" with his children would become a recurring theme for the strong family man. (In an upcoming year, *The Sporting News* would mention that Maduro, his wife and daughter Adela attended five games in three days in three countries in a 48-hour span. The first two were in Havana, the next one in New York, followed by a Sunday doubleheader in Toronto.)

Back in Havana, Maduro endured the disappointing finish of his Cienfuegos squad. But he quickly immersed himself in the task of welcoming and hosting the steel city team. Rickey and his party, including his wife, her sister Mabel Moulton, Mr. and Mrs. George Sisler, Pirates traveling secretary Bob Rice, Rickey's secretary Ken Blackburn, and several Pittsburgh newspapermen and photographers arrived in Havana on the evening of February 20—the opening night of the Caribbean Series. (Pirates manager Fred Haney had beaten the contingent to the city by a day.) Pirates players were given permission to delay reporting until March 1, if they wished.

"No favor is too small for Bob Maduro & Co.," wired one of the Pittsburgh newspapermen early in the visit. "He and his friends have worked night and day to make the stay of the Pirates pleasant. Maduro is an energetic young native who is a successful businessman and sportsman."[18] The contingent was quartered in two-bedroom apartments adjacent to the seaside Club Náutico de Marianao, where the players took their meals, in west Havana.

As the full squad of players gathered on time, there was one noticeable member missing, which threatened to throw an economic wrench into the entire tour. "Roberto Maduro, who arranged for Pittsburgh to train in Havana's Gran Stadium," clarified a *United Press* cable, "said today that Ralph Kiner's absence 'could ruin us financially here' as the National League home run king became Branch Rickey's first holdout in 23 years. Kiner's presence is required to fulfill the terms of a contract guaranteeing the cost of spring training which was negotiated with the Cuban government. The contract can be declared void if Kiner fails to appear."[19]

Kiner had been asked to accept a 20 percent cut from his $90,000 salary from 1952. Although the slugger had led the league in home runs for the seventh year in a row, his average had plummeted more than 60 points. The tight-fisted Rickey was leveraging this against him. The fact that spring training was going to be gratis for the Pirates, that Cuban sports authorities were covering all transportation, lodgings and food expenses for 50 players and 30 more Pirates' representatives, did not sway Rickey's position in the matter. (Cuba was to keep all gate receipts in the deal, except for two dates involving a second big league club.)

The Pirates, coming off one of the most atrocious seasons in history (42–112), played an exhibition schedule against Cuban All-Star squads and the Havana Cubans. Also scheduled were a pair of games against the Philadelphia Athletics, on March 9 and 10, which attracted low weekday turnouts. The Athletics came to Cuba with an advance guarantee. The combined attendance for the two major league baseball games was under 6,500, leaving the home country ledgers in the red. The games that followed drew even more poorly.

Kiner eventually signed for $75,000, plus $5,000 if he was traded during the season. On March 19, the Pirates' biggest drawing card flew from his Palm Springs, California, home to Miami, where he posed for photos at Miami Stadium before heading to Havana. Kiner arrived later in the evening and went straight to Gran Stadium. Arriving in the fifth inning of the game between the Bucs and Cuban All-Stars, he sat in Rickey's assigned box. There were only 350 other people in the stands.

Even with Kiner in town the rest of the way, things did not improve from an attendance perspective. They became worse. A week after Kiner's arrival, drastic cost-cutting measures were instituted by the underwriters of the Pirates' junket. "The Sports Commission and Gran Stadium co-owner Bob Maduro said the Bucs are not even worth the electric bills they run up," reported the *Pittsburgh Post-Gazette*. "The government, footing the bill for the team's training camp, rescheduled the remaining games, making them all daylight affairs—with no admission charged. Intra-squad games will be the fare until the Bucs depart April 4."[20]

"Last year the Pirates spent $70,000 for spring training [in San Bernardino, Calif.]," summed up one traveling writer, "but this year it was free. Thanks to our good neighbors in Cuba."[21]

Before the Pirates left Havana, a report from the capital may have caused much distress within the power circles of Cuban baseball. Warning of the departure of the island's best-known promoter, it read:

> Roberto Maduro, Mr. Executive Baseball in Cuba, has relinquished stock in the Cienfuegos team of the Cuban Winter League and resigned as president of the club. His partners, Luis Parga and Emilio de Armas, will carry through another campaign. Maduro, Parga and de Armas leased the club four years ago and have another year left on their contract. They were unable to get a renewal on the agreement and Maduro has decided to drop out of the game temporarily.[22]

Perhaps the disastrous affair with the Pirates and the repeated underperformances of Cienfuegos had disillusioned Maduro. But the 36-year-old shortly put aside any fear the public may have had that he had soured on what had become his life's passion. On May 4, 1953, Maduro broadened his interests in the Havana Cubans to the point of purchasing from Washington Senators owner Clark Griffith the majority stake in the team. The price tag was given at $40,000, and Maduro was unanimously approved by the Florida International League's board of directors in a convened meeting at Miami Stadium two days later.

The Cubans franchise had fallen on tough times since capturing the pennant the first five seasons of the league's existence. In recent years, home attendance had dramatically declined in line with the team's per-

Maduro and Joe Cambria, known for his long-time connection with the Washington Senators and for signing Cuban players to the major leagues. In 1953, Maduro purchased controlling interest of the Havana Cubans from Senators owner Clark Griffith and partial shareholder Cambria (courtesy César López).

formance, and Washington ownership had taken to selling off well-liked players, such as Napoleón "Nap" Reyes, Roberto Ortiz and Carlos Pascual. The team had fallen into such disarray that its managing director, Joe Cambria, had failed to secure a renewal lease with Gran Stadium for playing its home games in 1953. Forced to start their home schedule in the Key West, Florida, park of a former league member before an adequate lease in Havana had been secured, the club opened the season winning only nine of its first 28 games. "Far from the feared Havana beisbol performers of yesterday," recorded one F-I writer halfway through the season, "the '53 Cuban caballeros are the favorite sparring partners of Pepper Martin's Fort Lauderdale Lions. Even under new owner Bob Maduro's spirited direction the Cubans haven't been able to desert the cellar."[23]

"I want to do everything possible to get baseball back on a popular basis here," said a committed Maduro, who also stated that he would retain current Cubans manager Armando Marsans.[24] Maduro clearly had his work cut out for him trying to revitalize the once-successful franchise that had sent four pitchers to the major leagues since its inception.

In the wake of the purchase, the sports entrepreneur became briefly caught up in social controversy when a U.S. national publication called him out over an issue of alleged racial intolerance. *Jet* magazine accused Maduro of wanting to reduce the number of black players on the Cubans by quoting him as saying, "Frankly, there are too many Negroes [six] on the team."[25] Other news outlets picked up the story as well. The comment by Maduro may have been speculative in nature over the deep drop in home attendance (not taking into account the team's poor play), and more of an indictment on a less enlightened time rather than a reflection of personal character.

"I've known the Maduro family since I was very young," said Tony Pérez, remembering the baseball magnate in 2016. "To this day, we see and greet each other with the warmth and affection of family. You always remember the person or persons who helped pave the way for you and Bobby Maduro helped pave the way for me into big league baseball and eventually the Hall of Fame in Cooperstown."[26] Maduro's special treatment of another black player, Ray Noble, when it was suspected he may have been playing hurt, can also be recalled as a truer racial measure of the man.

The birth of Maduro's third daughter, christened Rosario, on June 3, must have helped temper much of the terse, negative publicity he experienced.

In August, Maduro and Emilio de Armas traveled to New York to meet with Commissioner Ford Frick and other representative members of the Caribbean Confederation. Maduro and de Armas were identified as being co-owners of the Cienfuegos baseball club in the *AP*'s report of the conclave. Maduro was said to be advocating for the continuance of the existing agreement allowing veteran Latin American big leaguers to play in their native winter leagues.

Maduro was back in the Big Apple the following month, but with a different traveling partner. Les Biederman, one of the Pirates' beat writers who had spent six weeks in Havana, mentioned Maduro in a few lines in one of his columns. The Pirates were in town to face the Giants, and the Biederman comment was a clear gauge of Maduro's personableness: "When I got back to the hotel, Bob Maduro, my Cuban friend, was on the line to say hello. He had brought his 11-year-old son Felipe to New York from Havana for a visit. The boy suffers from leukemia but was stricken with a virus infection and his father surprisingly reported the virus strangely removed some of the effects of the leukemia."[27]

Maduro's people charms also engendered respect. He requested and was granted the postponement of a FIL meeting the first week of October because it conflicted with the opening of the 1953–1954 Cuban Winter League season.

His desire to be in Havana at this time, along with the earlier account of his meeting with Commissioner Frick, strongly indicates that Maduro may have decided or been convinced to fulfill the final year of his contract with Cienfuegos, after all. In May, Al Campanis, a Brooklyn Dodgers scout, had been signed to manage the club, replacing Billy Herman. While possible, it is hard to see Emilio de Armas or Luis Parga pulling off the signing. Two months later, Maduro specifically stated to the Cuban press that the Cienfuegos club would be available to Ted Williams, if the superstar desired to use the winter league to return to playing shape following his imminent release from the United States Marine Corps. After being away for 15 months, Williams joined the Red Sox directly upon his release and hit .407 in 37 games for Boston in August and September, shredding Maduro's hypothetical proposal.

Final reinforcement to Maduro's attachment to the club was a trade pulled off early in the winter campaign. "In October 1953, Maduro orchestrated a transactional coup when he traded for 19-year-old Camilo Pascual," stated one baseball history. "In probably the most one-sided deal in the league's long history, Pascual was surrendered by Marianao to Cienfuegos for 25-year-old Rafael Fernández, who had not played in the league in four years and would never again."[28] A rookie in the winter league with no record to speak of, Pascual had been a ten-game winner for the Havana Cubans over the summer, where he could not have avoided Maduro's notice. The trade amounted to quite a parting gift from Maduro to Cienfuegos, as Pascual would blossom into one of the best pitchers in CWL history and greatly assist the Elephants in achieving two Caribbean Series titles.

The Cubans ended up in fourth place in the now-six-team Florida International League. Posting a 63–69 record, the club was ousted in the first round of single elimination playoffs by the pennant-winning Fort Lauderdale Lions, three games to one.

As a postscript, the FIL would begin play in 1954 with six clubs, with a new franchise in Tallahassee taking over for the Cubans and one in Miami Beach replacing the defunct Fort Lauderdale Lions. Two other teams folded early in the season, and the league disbanded in late July without completing their schedule. "The FIL was created for Habana," analyzed author John Phillips, "and without the city the league had no reason for being. Further, the FIL hadn't done well since the Cubans quit steamrollering everybody in 1951. There's a tradition that each major league needs a strong presence in New York. Maybe the FIL needed those old over-achieving Cubans."[29]

Three

Birth of the Sugar Kings

In November 1953, Maduro unveiled a "big picture outlook" few could have seen coming. As he was fulfilling the final year of his partnered obligations with Cienfuegos, he unveiled plans for achieving greater reach and recognition for Cuban baseball. Maduro's Havana Cubans franchise applied for entry into the International League. "There are a lot of details to be ironed out," cautioned the Triple A league's president, Frank Shaughnessy. "We could not admit Havana unless another team somewhere in between came into the picture."[1]

Maduro's push was calculatingly prepared, coming within a week of the league's post-season meeting in Montreal and with the knowledge that a group led by industrialist Harry Siebold would buy the Piedmont League's Richmond Rebels and also apply for admission, resolving the scheduling problem associated with an unbalanced number of teams. The path for Richmond had been cleared by the move of the Baltimore Orioles to join the American League. This November 14 *United Press* communiqué anticipated the big story: "A sweeping reorganization that would make the International Baseball League a far-flung operation from Canada to Cuba, involving three nations, was envisioned today as delegates gathered for Sunday's annual meeting."[2]

The following day, Havana and Richmond were approved as new associates of an expanded circuit of eight teams. From the league's Quebec headquarters, Shaughnessy left little question as to the driving force behind Havana's acceptance. "Maduro made us a proposition that you just don't turn down," the league's chief stated as part of his favorable announcement. "It's a great sport city and we can give the fans there just about the same class of baseball that they see in the Cuban Winter League and several classes better than they see in the Florida International."[3] (Despite being an "unclassified affiliate," the Cuban Winter League was widely thought to be on par with the AAA leagues at the time.) The jet age had also helped Cuba's cause. "Travel is no obstacle in the way of accepting Havana," Shaughnessy concluded. "After all you can get on a plane here and be in Havana in six hours. You can't go to Toronto that fast by train."[4]

The bulletin was met with great fanfare in Havana. Maduro made the long-distance call himself back home. The news flash reached Gran Stadium in the middle of a rain delay during a weekend doubleheader. Fans alternated cheering, whistling and applauding their approval. Havana newspapers—which numbered in double figures—of November 16 carried front page headlines of the announcement.

Minus the wild enthusiasm, many U.S. baseball executives embraced the international progress.

> Baseball men who know Roberto Maduro, the man who made it possible to bring Havana—and with it Richmond—into the International League, have a deep feeling that the cigar-smoking capitalist will turn out to be the greatest thing to happen to the national game since Milwaukee.
> They say Maduro brings fresh blood, a fresh sporting spirit, and a fresh, new baseball crazy country into the high minors at a time when all three were badly needed to hearten American magnates. Had Maduro not persisted in his determination to give Cuba class three-A ball, there is no question that the International would have lapsed into a bobtailed six-club league.[5]

(The reference to Milwaukee was to the rousing relocation success experienced by the former Boston Braves in that city the past season.)

From an economic perspective, Maduro willingly dug into his own pockets to procure the covenant. To secure the release of the Havana Cubans franchise, Maduro paid the Florida International League between $15,000 and $25,000, based on varied newspaper stories. His "proposition" to the IL also offered reimbursement of travel expenses to Havana for the associate clubs in the first year. "In order to swing the deal in the face of some skepticism," advised the *AP*'s Gayle Talbot, "the youthful insurance and sugar tycoon has guaranteed to fly each of the other league teams roundtrip between Richmond and Havana."[6]

For his part, Maduro said, "All Cuba is tremendously excited over this. It is the best thing that has ever happened to our people and, I believe, this is a fine thing for baseball. It is the first time that three countries have been in one league. That makes it really international. This is my country's first step toward eventually becoming part of major league baseball," he added, hinting for the first time at his greater vision for the national game of Cuba.[7]

In early January, a radio contest decided the question of the team's new sobriquet. "The Havana Cubans took a new name and a new nickname today," disclosed a newsprint blurb, "as they prepared to enter the Triple-A International Baseball League. Bob Maduro, wealthy young president of the club, said his team will use its old 'Cubans' nickname as its official name in the International and has adopted 'Sugar Kings' as a new nickname."[8]

Meanwhile, Maduro continued to be the "man of the hour" within the combines of the IL. Rochester Red Wings front office executive Bing Devine arranged for the local press to meet Maduro at the posh Rochester Club in upstate New York. A local sportswriter offered the following glimpse into Maduro's much-in-demand activities and his ever-innovative thinking:

> But even Devine did not anticipate an SRO response for an off-season function. Maduro was interviewed in the morning; interviewed during the luncheon; interviewed after the luncheon; he was photographed in the morning; photographed during the luncheon and after the luncheon.
> He did tape recordings for radio shows; and he did "live" radio shows. Then he did a television show. Then he was allowed to return to New York last night, where he is staying until the Baseball Writers dinner February 1.
> The man is thinking ahead, too. He talks about realignment of the leagues in the future, and you couldn't peg the man as a dreamer when he said: "Nobody can tell. Perhaps in a few years we might have a REAL world's championship series."[9]

Part of another printed profile provided more personal details about Maduro, the work he had cut out for himself to try and revitalize a fading product, and inside information on the Sugar Kings. "Maduro owns a 3,000 acre sugar plantation and is associated with his father in Cuba's largest insurance agency," reported Frank Eck. "Havana, fourth place club in Class B in '53 averaged only 800 admissions a game, but Maduro's entrance into organized baseball perked things up immeasurably. His Cienfuegos team in the Cuba's Winter League has been averaging 9,000 persons per game. [He] has controlling interest in the [Sugar Kings] team and stadium and three of his partners are Jose Bosch, head of a rum firm; Walter Fernándes, who has an automobile agency; and Fernando Vidal, a cattle owner. Fernándes is his vice president."[10] The *AP* sports editor also put to rest any notion that the Sugar Kings were anything but a private enterprise when he quoted Maduro as saying, "There have been reports that the Cuban government put up $200,000, but that is not true. The government hasn't put up a cent."[11]

As the 1953–1954 Cuban Winter League wrapped up their season and with the International League's opening not far away, there appeared to be no role Maduro was too busy to entertain for the good of the sport and its players. In February, he acted as intermediary for a Chicago front office man in his quest to re-sign star player Minnie Miñoso. "Frank Lane, White Sox general manager," updated a Chi-town scribe, "in a long-distance call with his Havana agent, Roberto Maduro, was informed that he had talked shop with the Cuban flash and accomplished nothing. Miñoso took a look at the revised contract mailed to Maduro and exclaimed, 'No sign. Want more money.'"[12]

Miñoso eventually signed several weeks after the CWL season ended, but with time to spare for spring training. Splitting their 72 games played, the Cienfuegos Elephants, though finishing in second place, were rarely in contention throughout the campaign. Almendares reclaimed the national title with an eight-game cushion and record of 44–28. The team, managed by Bobby Bragan, fell a game short of a second Caribbean championship, losing to Puerto Rico's Caguas Criollos, the tournament played on the winning country's home turf.

During the final weeks of winter, the Yomiuri Giants, not long after receiving part of a coaching tour headlined by newlywed Joe DiMaggio and Lefty O'Doul, in Tokyo, flew west to play exhibitions in Central and South America and the Caribbean. (DiMaggio's famous wife, Marilyn Monroe, separated briefly from the Yankee Clipper to spend a handful of days entertaining U.S. troops in neighboring Korea.) Maduro arranged for the Yomiuri Giants, the most popular team in Japan, to play three contests at Gran Stadium. The Cuban squads won two out of the three.[13]

In March, the much-traveled mogul set off for a tour of his own, through minor league spring camps in the U.S. Maduro was accompanied by Regino "Reggie" Otero, the Sugar Kings' newly appointed manager. The pair were on a last-minute talent search.

As the much-anticipated International League opener approached, Maduro also arranged for his league's Rochester brethren to play four tune-up games in Mérida, Mexico. The Sugar Kings had been conditioning in the locale beforehand. Otero's team took three out of four from the Red Wings in the April 8–11, extended weekend set.

Finally, the Cuban Sugar Kings opened their inaugural campaign at home versus the Toronto Maple Leafs on Tuesday, April 20, a day ahead of the other circuit teams. The paid attendance of 17,600 was short of Gran Stadium's baseball capacity of 24,600. Venezuelan right-hander Emilio Cueche tossed a complete game, winning 7–2, holding the visitors to eight hits. He also went three-for-four, with a pair of RBI, as part of a 15-hit Sugar Kings attack. IL president Frank Shaughnessy, Canadian ambassador to Cuba Harry Scott, and his U.S. counterpart, Arthur Gardner, participated in the pre-game ceremonial pitch toss. "Beautiful Gran Stadium was decked with flags in World Series style," noted one newspaper. "Monsignor Alfredo Muller, Archbishop of Havana, blessed the flag of the Cuban team in a ceremony at home plate. The band of the Havana orphanage played the national anthems of Cuba, the United States and Canada as the players stood on the foul lines."[14]

The home team wore white, pinstriped uniforms with red-scripted "Cubanos" on the chest, red stirrups and caps with the letter C. (In subsequent years, the club would utilize a white pinstriped cap with red bill.[15]) On their left uniform sleeve was the fixed outline of a heavy sugar bag with the imprint SUGAR KINGS under a stenciled crown, all inside of a C that resembled a horseshoe.

The highest-paid hurler on the squad with a reported salary of $7,000, Cueche was an established pitcher in his home country's winter league and had been lobbied for by manager Otero (who would go on to manage successfully in the winter circuits of Cueche's Andean nation well into the next decade). Nicknamed "Indio" because of his indigenous background, Cueche became a centerpiece on the mound for Maduro's franchise

On opening night, April 20, 1954, Monsignor Alfredo Muller blesses the Cubans' banner. Looking on, at far left, is Maduro. Holding the ends of the flag are manager Reggie Otero (next to Maduro) and coach Reinaldo Cordeiro. International League President Frank Shaughnessy admires the dedication (courtesy Ralph Maya).

in this and future seasons, as the only pitcher to perform for the team in each year of its existence. The 26-year-old hurler had reportedly turned down a $12,000 bonus contract from Cleveland Indians superscout Cy Slapnicka and similar monetary overtures from the New York Giants, citing the environment of racial inequality and lack of cultural assimilation help that confronted foreign-born players.

Playing center field, Angel Scull led off the game, the first Sugar Kings batter for posterity. Two years to the month earlier, Scull had been one of a trio of Miami Beach Flamingos to integrate the Florida International League. (Compatriot and winter league luminary Silvio García and former Negro Leaguer George Handy were the others.) Shortstop Juan Delís, a native of Santiago de Cuba—the island's second-largest city—hit second. Two former North American big leaguers followed Delís: five-season American League outfielder Ray Coleman batted third (rf) and former heralded New York Giants prospect Clint Hartung took his cuts as the cleanup hitter (lf). Julio Bécquer, only 22, manned first base and hit from the five-hole. Swinging from the sixth slot, Ray Noble, one of the biggest stars in the CWL, caught the slants of Cueche. Hitting next, another of Venezuela's finest, Luis "Camaleón" García, defended third base, while eighth-place hitter and second baseman Bob Ramazzotti rounded out the keepsake lineup card. Scull and Bécquer each swiped a base, although it is not clear who claimed the first steal in franchise history. Otero made no substitutions in the game. Except for Cueche, García and Scull, all the players in the starting lineup had been or would become major leaguers. All the starters collected at least one hit. Cueche's three bingles were the most by any player. The Sugar Kings played flawlessly in the field behind their winning pitcher. Time of game clocked in at two hours and 35 minutes. Fred Hahn suffered the defeat for Toronto. Maple Leafs center fielder Sam Jethroe, the National League Rookie of the Year in 1950, had the distinction of being the inaugural game's first hitter.

Hahn and Jethroe composed a Toronto starting nine that included eight former or future major league graduates, most notably among them cleanup hitter and catcher Elston Howard. The entire visitors' infield of Ed Stevens (1b), Loren Babe (2b), Héctor Rodríguez (3b) and shortstop Billy DeMars had spent time in The Show, as did right fielder Mike Goliat. Only Lew Morton, in left, checked in as a career minor leaguer. In a final historic tidbit, DeMars and the Kings' Julio Bécquer are the only surviving players from that first game's starting roll call.

DeMars, 91, currently resides in southwest Florida. In a telephone interview, 69 years after his major league debut, he sounded sharp and engaging.

From the Hotel Nacional you could hear the car horns tooting. They didn't have traffic lights in Havana. So whoever honked the horn loudest at the intersection had the right of way. The hotel staff always told us not to spend too much time at the hotel pool, warning us about getting sunburn. Funny, I remember that.

The stadium was loud and noisy, especially when they [Sugar Kings] were hitting. They used to have bands—not the greatest music—but a lot of noise. You couldn't hear the ball off the bat, couldn't get a good jump on defense. When we were hitting, the fans were silent. I'll never forget that. [Chuckles]

After the game, there were always a bunch of kids waiting for us [players]. There was one kid in particular. He couldn't have been more than eight or nine. He looked just like a miniature Sandy Amoros. He always had a big, bright smile. I would always give him a quarter or half dollar when I saw him. I took such a liking to him that I started to bring him clothes. I received a letter from his uncle once thanking me. I never answered it. But I always wondered what happened to that boy. It was sad to see what happened down there.

When you wrote me I remembered the name right away—Maduro. Bobby Maduro, I can't recollect meeting him, but he was a very nice man from what I heard people talk about him. I'm sorry he lost everything.

When I was with the Philly Athletics, we had a catcher, Fermín Guerra. He was a real good backup catcher and even better person. He was from down there.

My wife Catherine and I were married for 70½ years until I lost her in January of this year. We met in the service during World War II. We were together 72½ years. We were going together for two years before we married. She was two years older than me. She was born in 1923. We had a great life together. I have a daughter that lives in Tampa. My son, who lives in Denver, is coming to visit me next week. My grandkids are not close. I'm going to have to get through it like everybody else. I'll manage.[16]

Another ex-big leaguer, Julio Moreno, took the hill for the Sugar Kings in their second game, the following evening. He claimed the winning laurels, 4–2, hurling nine innings and dispersing the same number of hits. Moreno, Bécquer and Camaleón García collected RBI (the fourth run was unearned). García garnered a special place in team history, clubbing the first Sugar Kings home run—a solo blast in the fourth. García, by the way, had returned a $10,000 bonus to the Chicago White Sox a few years earlier, after being unable to acclimate to spring training in the States. He returned home to Venezuela, suffering from "homesickness," never to take another "plunge" at the major leagues. Less than half the previous day's total crowd turned out to cheer the triumph.

A scheduled doubleheader was rained out, forcing a Friday twin bill. In the opener, Carlos Pascual rode a five-run first inning to a 5–2 win. The right-hander allowed eight hits and struck out six. In his third game, Otero made his first managerial move—substituting Paul Smith in left field for Hartung late in the contest. The Sugar Kings fell from the undefeated ranks in the second game. Jim Melton, one of three Cubans pitchers who were in the Cincinnati Reds organization, started but was not involved in the decision. Among the seven hits surrendered by Melton in five innings of work were a home run and triple by New York Yankees draftee Elston Howard. Sugar Kings reliever Edward Varhely was the pitcher of record, on the losing side, in the 5–2 defeat.

On April 24, the Cubans began a new series when the Rochester Red Wings came to town. Chalking up a 4–3 victory, Cueche tossed his second complete game in a row, a five-hitter. The sparkling centerpiece of the Sugar Kings' fourth win in five tries came with a 400-foot home run off the bat of Clint Hartung, with a man on base. Hitting home runs would not be an easy feat at Gran Stadium, with foul line distances of 340 feet from home plate, and left and right center field power alleys measuring 110 feet farther away, as measured by one visiting reporter.

The first Sunday doubleheader, on April 25, attracted 8,400 spectators. Maduro missed the games to be with his ill son Felipe, who was still fighting his leukemia. Starting at 3 o'clock in the afternoon, the teams split, with the road club handily winning the opener, 9–3, and the home team squeaking out a 3–2, seven-inning second set. Moreno was roughed up in his second start in the first game. Saul Rogovin delivered a solid debut on the mound, gaining the complete-game win in the scheduled short program in the afternoon.

In a preview of the Monday series continuation, a local Rochester newspaperman noted that the game would start at 9:45 p.m. As no other information was given to explain the late starting hour, it may be assumed that most night games at Gran Stadium began around this time—at least during the nascent period of the club. The game, won by Rochester, 9–4, lasted an even three hours, as the Red Wings used three pitchers and the Sugar Kings six—or seven, technically, counting Emilio Cueche, who was used as a pinch-hitter.

In the series finale on April 27, Jim Melton bounced back from an inconsistent first outing and delivered a 6–2, complete-game win. Though touched for ten hits and three walks, Melton apparently made "out" pitches when he had to, in picking up the first of his team-leading 14 victories on the campaign. Angel Scull reached base all five times he came to the plate. This game and the Sunday doubleheader had been televised. Four thousand fans were present.

The first two series, hosting Toronto and Rochester, drew just over 50,000 fans for nine games, lower than initial estimates. The Sugar Kings won six of their first nine games before taking to the road. The Rochester and Cuban teams boarded a Colonial Airlines flight shortly after midnight on April 28. The DC-4 stopped in Miami and New York before dropping off the Sugar Kings in Toronto and the Red Wings in Rochester.

On April 29, the Sugar Kings played their first-ever road game and first in Canada. At Maple Leaf Stadium, the club broke in their new, non-pinstriped road flannels for the occasion. "Cubans" was scripted across the chest, with the bottom loop of the capital "C" extending under all the letters, and the spacing between the blouse buttons separating "Cub" and "ans." White stitching around the "C" of their red caps made the letter easier to discern. A capacity crowd of 18,012 turned out for the chilly Friday afternoon affair. Canadian Olympic figure skater Barbara Ann Scott handled the ceremonial first pitch. The 1948 Olympic gold medalist threw the pitch to her catcher, Cuba's ambassador to Canada, Alfredo H. Pupo y Proenza. Ontario's Lieutenant Governor, Louis Breithaupt, in the batter's box, purposely swung and missed. The tossed ball also escaped the Cuban ambassador in a bit of amusing pre-game hijinks. In the game, the Cubans fell short of a furious comeback when catcher Fermín Guerra lined back to the pitcher with one out and the go-ahead runs on base in the top of the ninth inning. Toronto reliever Jack Crimian wheeled and threw to second to double off the runner for the last out of the game. The final was 6–5; the Sugar Kings had scored twice in the frame.

The Cubans, with a 2–5 road record, returned to Havana having split their first 16 games. In their first action back in the Tropics and against the Buffalo Bisons, Emilio Cueche continued making a case as the team's best early starter. On May 8, Cueche became a four-game winner when Angel Scull scampered home with the winning run on a squeeze play in the bottom of the ninth inning for a 3–2 Sugar Kings victory. The speedy Scull, designated in one newsprint portrayal as the first "dark-skinned diamonder of the Washington Senators," had played spring exhibition games for the Senators before being sold to the Cubans. That season, it had been expected that the Matanzas-native would become the Washington franchise's first black player, and Topps issued a trading card with Scull in a Washington uniform. But Scull had to settle for recognition of his fine abilities in four seasons as a Sugar King, ten campaigns in the Cuban Winter League and an ultimately long-tenured minor league career of nearly two decades.

Cueche, who stood only 5'6", raised his record to 5–1 with another 3–2 win four days later over the same team. The right-hander allowed five hits, two more than in his previous outing. The Sugar Kings tied the Bisons for third place with the win. "Cueche has a heart this big," said his manager in an interview, spreading his arms wide. "I wouldn't take $50,000 for him right now. [He] has a nice fast ball, a fine curve, a passable slider and a good change of pace."[17]

The first Sugar Kings "shutout" was authored, two days later, May 14, by Maury Fisher. A Cincinnati-owned pitcher, Fisher tossed a seven-inning two-hitter against the Syracuse Chiefs. The 2–0 win preceded another Sugar Kings victory, 5–4, in the regulation-length nightcap. Syracuse took it on the chin twice more on May 16. Cueche won for the sixth time in seven decisions, cruising to a 9–2 win. Jim Melton followed with a 2–1 triumph in the seven-frame nightcap. The next day, Otero's club (17–10) swept the six-game series from Syracuse, behind pitcher Saul Rogovin, and moved into first place. Clint Hartung's two extra-base hits, including a homer, drove in three of the Sugar Kings runs in the 5–1 win. The victory, its seventh in a row, placed the start-up franchise in a first-place tie with Rochester, but percentage points ahead.

After a long, overnight flight to Ontario, Canada, the Sugar Kings won their eighth straight game, defeating the Ottawa Athletics, 11–7, in 12 innings, May 18. Julio Bécquer started the winning uprising with a triple. Moving into sole position of first place, the Sugar Kings pounded out 17 hits, and reliever Clarence "Hooks" Iott earned the win in the four hour and five-minute exercise. Prior to the game, manager Otero was gifted a hockey stick and a small box of packed snow by the locals.

The winning streak was snapped the following evening at Lansdowne Park. An 11th-inning single by the Athletics' Joe Taylor sent home the winning run as Ottawa prevailed, 5–4. Raúl Sánchez pitched the distance in absorbing the loss. In the third game of the set, Hartung and Scull homered to back Jim Melton's 7–2 winning effort. Before the contest, both squads were feted in a celebration of cultural interchange. "The A's and Kings attended a reception given by the Cuban ambassador at the [Hotel] Chateau yesterday afternoon, Cuban style, including a rhumba band," reported an Ottawa journalist. "The ballplayers left early to get to the game."[18]

The 19–11 Sugar Kings left Ottawa holding first place, but quickly dropped out of the top spot by losing eight of 13 games on their stops in Buffalo, Montreal and Richmond. During the Montreal encampment, Hartung slugged his tenth home run in 36 games.

Judged by the early results, the Sugar Kings performed better at Gran Stadium than away from it. Despite this, attendance was a slightly nagging drag, mostly because of the high pre-season estimates. Through 24 dates, the league listed 132,000 paid patrons for their southern-most franchise. And those patrons made their presence known. Otero referenced this as he summed up two weeks of travel time upon the team's return to Havana on June 1.

> Looking back over that road trip, we left behind our most valuable player—the horn-tooting, bell-ringing, drum-thumping, riotously partisan Havana fans. There's nothing in the States to compare with the fans who elbow their way into Gran Stadium to whoop and holler and dance and wave their handkerchiefs and otherwise urge on their heroes, unless maybe it's in Brooklyn.[19]

The fans whooped it up for Jim Melton on June 9, as the erstwhile Texas League pitcher tossed the first nine-inning shutout by a Sugar Kings pitcher. Melton (5–2) handcuffed the Montreal Royals on four hits, 2–0. Paul Smith, who had taken over as a starting outfielder for Ray Coleman, knocked home both runs with a double and triple.

Defying the actuarial odds, Melton is still going strong today, actively assisting his grandson in a home construction restoration company in northeast Oklahoma. "I was born September 13, 1928," he says in a voice strong with pride.

> I went to a couple of spring trainings but was never on a big league roster. The closest I got was in 1954 with the Reds. We had 37 pitchers in camp. It was Birdie Tebbetts' first year as manager. He had all these younger pitchers, like me, but he had decided to go with experience instead of youth.
>
> I didn't know I pitched the first shutout in Sugar Kings history. I was on option from Cincinnati, that's how I ended up in Havana. My first summer there, I was alone. I was pretty much confined to the hotel where we [players] stayed. It was the hotel to the ballpark and back for me. It was a nice ballpark, a nice, big ballpark to pitch in.
>
> My wife and two boys came later, when I stayed over and pitched in the winter league with Cienfuegos, which was managed by Reggie Otero. He asked me to stay. We brought our car over for the winter and had more mobility then. My oldest boy, he was six, he started school in Havana. We liked traveling outside the city. I remember seeing a farmer with a wooden plow pulled by oxen. The boys got a real kick out of that. We pulled over and walked right up to him. I had picked up some Spanish by then.
>
> We did not cater to the night life. I never drank a beer in my life, but that doesn't mean I frown upon those who do. *Arroz con pollo* was my favorite Cuban food. And for dessert, fresh *piña* [pineapple], three quarter-inch slices.
>
> I met Bobby Maduro ... not a whole lot, but more than once. He never came into the clubhouse that I can recall, but what I can say [about him] is that he was a gentleman and a scholar. He had a son, nine or ten-years-old [sic] who was ill.[20]

Less than a week later, the 30–27 Sugar Kings left Havana, following Emilio Cueche's ninth win on June 14. The 3–1 victory over the Richmond Virginians was hurled to completion, and Cueche singled in the tie-breaking runs in the eighth inning. The road trip started most promisingly, three days later, with double triumphs in Syracuse, which moved the Sugar

Kings into sole possession of third place. But things went south from there, to the point of dropping the team's record under .500. The Sugar Kings were nearly no-hit on June 25 by Buffalo Bisons pitcher Ken Johnson. In the one-hit, 2–0 defeat, Ray Noble's eighth-inning double averted the embarrassment.

Seeking offensive help to boost his team, Maduro signed one of the best-known players in Cuban Winter League history, Pedro Formental. A former winter league leader in every Triple Crown category, Formental met the club in upstate New York before the end of the month. In his first game in organized baseball, the 39-year-old Formental homered and drove in seven runs in leading the Sugar Kings to an 8–5, first-game win at Red Wing Stadium on June 29. Formental did not fare as well in the second game, going 0-for-4, but the Sugar Kings overcame the lack of production with a 5–3, ten-inning win over hosting Rochester. Pinch-hitting for winning pitcher Charles "Bubba" Harris, Roberto Ortiz—another former CWL star—delivered a clutch, two-run single that provided the winning margin. The addition of Formental may have been as much dictated by the loss of Angel Scull, who fractured his cheekbone in an outfield collision two days prior. He was lost to the team for several weeks.

Winning eight of the final 12 games of their long road trip, the Sugar Kings returned to Havana on July 6. The International League played a schedule of 154 games equal to the majors. Several games past the halfway point of the season, Maduro's franchise was in fourth place with a record of 42–39. Their 43rd win was obtained the same evening of their return, as Bubba Harris recorded his ninth win in 14 decisions, 5–4. The victory over the Rochester Red Wings was accompanied by some interesting side notes to the action in one of the next day's "foreign" newspapers:

> The three hour marathon was witnessed by an estimated 7,500 howling, chanting fans despite the fact that the game was televised ... in colorful military type ceremonies Cubans presented [manager] Harry Walker a Cuban flag and key to the city in appreciation of courtesies extended to the Sugar Kings in Rochester ... The Red Wings' George Baer and Theresa (Tess) Connolly mixed business with pleasure, beating the heat by watching from Cuban owner Bob Maduro's glass-enclosed, air-conditioned elevated box.... Listeners to recreated Red Wing broadcasts during this series have a treat in store. All the weird bell-ringing, bongo-drumming, chanting, singing and the hot trumpeting of the informal Mambo band are on the disc cut here last night. The parading, candle-lighting, banner-waving, marching and bandana-shaking must be left to the imagination.[21]

The Sugar Kings earned four wins in the six games played against Rochester. Included was Emilio Cueche's tenth victory and eighth without a defeat at home. Cueche whipped the Red Wings, 4–1, surrendering only three hits. The Venezuelan owned a 2–6 record away from Gran Stadium. The series concluded with unofficial indications that the Sugar Kings, nearing 200,000 in paid attendance, were leading all other clubs at the International League gate.

On July 15, a new, single-game regular season International League attendance mark maintained a strong prospect for the league. A night set aside to honor Roberto Maduro de Lima at Gran Stadium generated the elevated expectations. Maduro was bestowed with the Medal of Havana for distinguished service by the mayor of the city, Justo Luis del Pozo. Manager Otero was also given a trophy from the City Council. A heavy rain leading right up until game time kept the crowd to 24,139, short of the 28,038-turnstile record set by Baltimore's former franchise on July 28, 1946. (A Junior World Series game in Baltimore in 1944 attracted over 50,000 at what was primarily the city's football venue.) The evening's drawing cards, Toronto and the Sugar Kings, played to a seven-inning non-conclusion. The game was halted to allow Toronto time to catch their planned plane flight. With no other trips scheduled to Havana and the Maple Leafs holding a 3–2 lead, the suspended game would be completed in Toronto during the Sugar Kings' final visit there. Prior to the healthy turnout, the team had registered a rounded-off box office total of 238,000 fans, an average of 6,000 per game.

Melton won his tenth game against only three losses in a 12–2 laugher in Syracuse on July 18. Clint Hartung collected four of the Sugar Kings' 20 hits on the day. The 26-year-old Melton followed that up with another complete game outing, six days later at Montreal. At Delorimier Stadium, the right-hander subdued the Royals, 9–2, permitting six hits. The Sugar Kings broke the game open in the eighth, plating six runs on three hits, a hit batsman and four errors. The next day, July 25, the young "bonus baby" of the Brooklyn Dodgers, Roberto Clemente, had a direct hand in forcing one of two defeats upon the Sugar Kings. As a defensive replacement in the opening contest of a doubleheader, Clemente clubbed, in today's popular jargon, a walk-off home run in the tenth inning to elevate the Royals to 7–6, foot-stomping win. In the second engagement, Clemente doubled in a run, backing the five-hit pitching of Tommy Lasorda. The 26-year-old hurler tossed a 4–1 victory, upping his record to a fine 13–5.

During the Sugar Kings' next stop, also in Canada, Pedro Formental received a top hitting credit with a ninth-inning solo clout against the Toronto Maple Leafs. Benefiting from the blast, Ken Raffensberger, the third Cincinnati Redlegs pitcher with the Cubans, closed out his second victory of the year, 3–2, and snapped an 11-game Toronto winning streak.

Raffensberger, 37, was winding down his pitching career after more than a decade at the big league level.

In early August, Cueche righted a string of setbacks with another home win. This one, 7–2, against the Buffalo Bisons, came as his 12th. The following day, August 5, Melton (12–4) pitched 11 innings for 2–1 victory over the same squad. Formental drove home the game-winner with a single. The same day, an announcement from Cincinnati divulged that the Ohioans had signed a formal "working agreement" with Maduro's team for 1955. The player development pact was spearheaded by club general manager and repeat visitor (as recently as July) to Cuba, Gabe Paul. (As mentioned, several Cincy farmhands were already performing with the Sugar Kings.) Cueche dropped a rare home game on August 8. The 7–1 loss to Buffalo marked the final game of the homestand. Otero's men hit the road immediately afterward, in fourth place, owning a 60–57 mark and a one-game advantage over next-best Syracuse. Winning more than 60 percent of their games, 71–43 Toronto held a 2½-game lead over second-place Rochester. Third-seated Montreal (65–51) trailed their Canuck brethren by seven games while holding a five-game advantage over the Sugar Kings.

The quest to remain in the first division—and therefore secure a berth in the Shaughnessy playoffs—suffered a setback during the team's road excursion. The Sugar Kings went 2–9 in meetings with Toronto and Buffalo before coming back home to play—and lose to—Montreal on August 20. Ken Raffensberger absorbed the 8–5 loss, lowering his record to 6–5. In fifth place now, the Sugar Kings made a deal to obtain pitcher Willie Powell from Toronto. A day after joining the club, August 21, Powell, a 7–5 hurler with the Maple Leafs, provided a top-notch debut. The former Negro Leagues right-hander tamed the Montreal Royals at Gran Stadium, 4–1, defeating one of the league's best in Ken Lehman (16–8).

The following day, a saddening occurrence, hitting close to home, left everyone reflecting on life's priorities. On August 22, Maduro's leukemia-stricken son Felipe passed away. He was 12 years old, attending the prestigious *Colegio De la Salle* in Havana and an unquestionable baseball devotee like his father. The young man was especially proud of his photo collection of big league players, some with autographs he obtained himself. Over 1,000 people attended his funeral, a deferential nod to his father's stature and position in the community. "My memories of Felipe," says brother Jorge, five years his junior, "are of visiting him in the hospital and seeing tubes attached to him."[22] Understandably, the distressing sight has stayed with the 69-year-old younger brother.

Three—Birth of the Sugar Kings   49

Manager Reggie Otero congratulates pitcher Emilio Cueche for being named outstanding Cubans pitcher during the opening month of the inaugural 1954 campaign. Venezuelan compatriot Camaleón García beams his approval (courtesy Ralph Maya).

On the day of Felipe's passing, Jim Melton's record dropped to 12–8 after losing a tough 2–0 decision to the Royals' Glenn Cox. A two-run homer by Rocky Nelson spoiled an otherwise excellent outing. Contrary to script, the Sugar Kings played poorly following their return to Havana. The club lost nine of 14 games as the home team before putting together a five-game win streak to close out a 10–9 homestand. A 2–1 win over Richmond on September 4, hurled by Jim Melton, ended the final regularly scheduled game at Gran Stadium on a high note. Sacrifice flies by Pedro

Formental and Roberto Ortiz brought home the decisive runs. The positive streak brought the 72–75 Sugar Kings to within one-half game of Syracuse for the final playoff berth.

With seven games remaining, the Sugar Kings packed their bags for a season-concluding road trip. Raffensberger raked in his eighth victory and the Kings' sixth in a row on September 5. At Parker Field, the left-hander blanked the Richmond Virginians, 3–0, though reached for 11 hits. Taking two out of three from Richmond, the Cubans slipped into fourth place by half a game and moved on to Rochester, where they were met by Bobby Maduro. Accompanying the owner was his 13-year-old and eldest son, Roberto.

The idle Sugar Kings were tied by Syracuse, September 9, after the Chiefs stonewalled the Ottawa Athletics, 5–0. The next day, Friday, September 10, the Cubans took back sole possession of fourth place by racking up two wins over the second-place Red Wings. The first effort lasted only half an inning, as it was the completion of a suspended game from earlier in the season in Havana. Jim Melton retired all three men in the ninth, sealing an 8–6 advantage the Sugar Kings held. In the scheduled game, Raffensberger outpitched 18-game winner Jack Faszholz, 4–3. Outfielder Paul Smith, Ray Noble and Formental (two) accounted for the Sugar Kings' runs. Across the state, Syracuse won one game of a doubleheader against the league doormat Athletics, with the other postponed by rain. The Cubans then maintained their half-game lead with an 8–1 triumph on Saturday evening. The dominating effort was hurled by Pat Scantlebury, a recent pick-up from Dallas in the Texas League. An unexpected cold snap through the region combined with an already assured playoff slot for the home team limited the crowd to less than 1,000. (Scantlebury had won 42 games, pitching in the Big State and Texas Leagues, over the last two seasons.) Ninety miles away in Syracuse, the Chiefs again had their way with Ottawa, 8–1.

Scantlebury's victory forced Syracuse to win both games of a doubleheader on Sunday, September 12, if the Sugar Kings won their season finale the same day, to stand a chance at advancing to the post-season. The Sugar Kings trounced the Red Wings, 12–2. Spotting the home team two runs in the first inning, Otero's inspired crew scored 12 unanswered runs. Formental socked a pair of home runs, and Noble slashed four hits and scored as many runs. Jim Melton gained his 14th win, offsetting nine defeats. The four-game sweep by the Sugar Kings dropped Rochester to third place. Taking advantage of their weak competition, Syracuse lassoed two victories from Ottawa to finish 78–76, tied with the

Sugar Kings. Maduro, Otero and traveling secretary Miguel "Coco" Bacallao ensconced themselves in Red Wings general manager Bing Devine's office, listening to the disappointing results of the second game in Syracuse. The Sugar Kings then bussed over to Syracuse to play a one-game tie-breaker.

Otero named Willie Powell to be his starter in the special playoff. The game, designated for September 13, was rained out, which did not alter Otero's pitching plans. The selection of Powell remains controversial to this day, at least to one former team member. "Reggie had a bunch of pitchers he could have used," says Jim Melton. "He had Cueche, Moreno, Bubba Harris, Rafy [Raffensberger]—he had me. But he chose Powell."[23] (Melton implies that he could have pitched on one day's rest.) Perhaps the detected resentment lies with the fact that Powell had only been with the club for three weeks. He had won three out four starts during the short span. Otero, with good reason, had lost faith in Cueche, a hittable pitcher over the last two months of the season. Unlike Moreno, Harris was not a front-line starter. Powell had not pitched since September 6. Raffensberger had last started on September 5. The Cubans had the momentum, having won 11 of their final 12 games.

According to league rules, a coin flip would determine where the one-game playoff would be played. But Maduro waved it off, sparing both teams a potential long plane flight if the Sugar Kings owner won the coin toss. A compensatory coin flip was held prior to the tie-breaking game, instead. Maduro called correctly, and the Sugar Kings acted as home team at MacArthur Stadium. On September 14, the Chiefs, in their home whites, batted first—and scored five runs. Powell did not retire a batter; he was removed in favor of Raffensberger, who retired the side while allowing one run himself. The Sugar Kings closed the gap to 5–4, but following Raffensberger's removal for a pinch-hitter in the sixth inning, the Chiefs began pulling away. A five-run ninth destroyed any hopes for a comeback. The final was 13–4, as the Sugar Kings used five pitchers, including Moreno and Harris.

Fourth-seeded Syracuse stunned Toronto, four games to two. Montreal downed Rochester in six games. The Chiefs upset the Royals in a distance-extending series of seven games to claim the championship.

The Louisville Colonels won the Junior World Series, in six games, over the upstart Chiefs.

Thrust from Class B into Triple A, by most accounts Reggie Otero's team produced a better than expected first season. Although not an official award in the league until the following decade, Otero was named the circuit's outstanding manager in a sportswriters' poll. On his team, Paul Smith led the Sugar Kings in hitting with a .321 average, 12 points behind circuit leader Bill Virdon of Rochester. After a world-beating start, flychaser Clint Hartung fizzled and hit only four more long balls. His 14 home runs were the best total on the squad, but less than half the league's best power hitter. Montreal's Rocky Nelson clubbed 31 round-trippers for his second-place team. Without the benefit of playing for the first two months of the campaign, Pedro Formental slammed 13 circuit clouts. Despite also missing time due to injury, Angel Scull stole the third-most bases in the circuit (31), as the Sugar Kings led the IL in steals by a comfortable margin with 97.

Pacing the Cubans' pitching staff with 14 wins, Jim Melton trailed 18-game winners Ken Lehman of Montreal and Rochester's Jack Faszholz as the circuit's top winners. Melton threw 211 innings (most among Sugar Kings pitchers) with a tabulated ERA of 3.40. In his first year in organized baseball, after a 10–2 start, Emilio Cueche went 13–12 with a 4.80 ERA in 180 innings. He was apparently worn down by the unaccustomed length of the campaign.

1954 International League Final Standings

	W	L	T	PCT	GB	Manager	Major League Affiliation
Toronto Maple Leafs	97	57	2	.630		Luke Sewell	None
Montreal Royals	88	66	1	.571	9	Max Macon	Brooklyn Dodgers
Rochester Red Wings	86	68	0	.526	11	Harry Walker	St. Louis Cardinals
Syracuse Chiefs	79	76	1	.510	18½	Skeeter Newsome	Philadelphia Phillies
Cuban Sugar Kings*	78	77	2	.503	19½	Reggie Otero	None
Buffalo Bisons	71	83	1	.461	26	Billy Hitchcock	Detroit Tigers
Richmond Virginians	60	94	1	.390	37	Luke Appling	None
Ottawa Athletics	58	96	2	.377	39	Les Bell/ Taffy Wright	Philadelphia Athletics

*lost a playoff tie-breaker to Syracuse

Although their actual name was the Cuban Sugar Kings, because Maduro wanted the team to represent "all of Cuba and not just Havana," the foreign press, from the start, did not distinguish the country from the city when referring to the team. International League standings in newspapers in the U.S. listed "Havana," along with the other franchise cities of Buffalo, Syracuse, Ottawa, etc. The reason probably stemmed from the leftover of eight years of FIL play (Havana Cubans) and perhaps because of the subtle difficulty in translation the North American press did not deal with during this period. (Exceptions were *The Sporting News*, which used "Cubans" in their weekly International League standings block—except in the team's first year, when they listed "Havana." The annual International League schedules printed in the *Baseball Guide* remained faithful to using the antecedent "Cubans," per Sugar Kings chronologist John Phillips.) The *Cubanos Reyes del Azúcar*, as the team was known in Spanish, translated as the Cuban Sugar Kings. Informally, at home, *Azucareros* was also used—although lost in Spanish, as well as in the English translation of "Sugar Caners," is the original royalty aspect of the team's nickname. The club was incorporated by Maduro under the parent name *Asociación Cubana de Béisbol Internacional*.

Gran Stadium offered the lowest admission prices in the International League, driven primarily by the differences in wage standards and costs of living between the other countries and Cuba. Tickets for single games ranged from 60 cents to $1.20, with a price bump for doubleheaders from 80 cents to $1.50 (something not done in the U.S and presumably Canada). From an average ticket price of 75 cents, for example, Maduro paid the league office seven cents. The visiting club received 20 percent, three percent went to the Sports Ministry of the Cuban government, 16 percent in stadium rent (to himself and partner), and eight percent to the press. Paying the print media for coverage and promotion was an established tradition, including in the winter league. The club was not charged for advertisements in the newspapers.

There was also TV and radio money, estimated, by more than one source, at $20,000 for the small screen medium and $60,000 from four radio stations. (Not every game was televised, and later financial accounting concluded a lower grand intake for the combined radio and television broadcast rights in the team's first year.) Additionally, park concessions added to the revenue stream.

Regardless of the reproduction fees, the atmosphere for the ballgames at Gran Stadium, as typical throughout Latin American ballparks, was a festive level above most found to the baseball north. "To the Cuban customers, every night is New Year's Eve," one upstate New York writer concluded, following his team's initial visit. "They shake maracas and they beat on bongo drums. They grind sirens and sing and wave handkerchiefs. They encourage their heroes with 'go-go' cheers. They bring banners and stalks of sugar cane and parade around the stands. They mouth a weird jungle-type chant and perform weird, shuffling dances."[24]

But the conviviality, for all its genuineness, could not mask the troubling threat of fiscal peril caused by the burdening travel expenses absorbed by the team in its inaugural season. The Sugar Kings drew 295,493, slightly below the low-end expectation of 300,000. (This was roughly 12 times more than the destitute Havana Cubans had drawn in their final season.) Yet, placed alongside the other seven franchises, it was a total turnstile count to be viewed optimistically. "Only Toronto, which attracted 408,876, outdrew Havana," capsulized one scrutinizing history of the period. "By comparison, the 1953 Browns had drawn 297,238 in their last season in St. Louis."[25]

At the NAPBL owners meeting in November in Houston, Maduro more than hinted at wanting a change in his original travel subsidy-pact. He was also a staunch supporter of the Ottawa franchise's planned moved to Florida, preferring Miami as the relocation center. Maduro touted the city as having the ideal playing venue in Miami Stadium. Recently, the stylishly modern stadium had become a favored destination point for more and more annual Brooklyn Dodgers spring exhibition games. But a leasing agreement between Ottawa and stadium owner José Alemán, Jr., could not be reached. In his early 20s, Alemán, Jr., had become owner of the stadium following the premature death of his father a few years earlier; he harbored hopes of selling the stadium.

"A Florida shift would be of big help," Maduro said, still pushing for a Sunshine State location after the Miami deal fell through. "Tampa-St. Petersburg is the best choice. They aren't so large [as Miami], but they are great for baseball."[26] (According to a later disclosure, the young stadium owner seemed to have missed a golden opportunity. Maduro told Miami writer Jimmy Burns that Alemán, Jr., turned down a deal that would have guaranteed him $30,000, plus the cost of property taxes on the stadium (about $5,000), in order to option the stadium's use for Jai-Alai to another investment group.)

The Ottawa relocation fell far short of the peninsula state, however, landing in Columbus, Ohio, instead. Details were announced at the International League meeting January 29, 1955, in New York. The city of Columbus, a "pillar of the American Association" for more than half a century, became reborn as a new International League franchise. For their former Canadian affiliate, the Kansas City Athletics received $50,000 from nine Columbus businessmen, who combined to make the move possible. The same men additionally had to compensate the St. Louis Cardinals, who owned the old Columbus Red Birds and Red Bird Stadium, a whopping $450,000 for territorial payment (including the stadium). The fatwalleted Cardinals then resettled their minor league club in Omaha, Nebraska.

In addition, an agreement renegotiating Maduro's travel subsidy for the other clubs was reached. The new terms were not released, but there was expected sympathy from his peers after Maduro revealed that the agreed-to air fare costs had amounted to $40,000. (These are the mid–1950s dollars, which adjusted for inflation and other economic indicators projects to roughly $366,000 in 2018 money.)

How satisfied Maduro became with the new arrangement was not made clear. But there can be no question of the measure of satisfaction he felt a few days later. Several East Coast newspapers picked up the same commendation announcement out of Havana: "Minnie Minoso, Chicago White Sox outfielder, was voted outstanding Cuban athlete for 1954. Bob Maduro, owner of the Havana Sugar Kings in the International League, was voted the man who did the most for sports in Cuba last year. Minoso and Maduro will receive trophies emblematic of their awards at the annual Cuban Sports Writers dinner here, February 4."[27]

Six weeks afterward, the sophomore Sugar Kings began training camp. Keeping with the international outreach from last year, when they worked themselves into shape in Mexico, the team trained in the Dominican Republic, departing Havana on March 19. Jim Melton was part of the assemblage.

> We trained in Ciudad Trujillo [Santo Domingo]. The first day of training Reggie tells me, "I want you to run in the outfield with the pitchers." Well, I had just pitched over the winter and, of course, the summer, with little time off. I told Reggie, "I'm already at my playing weight. Do you want me down to 140 pounds?" The next day, Reggie tells me the same thing, "I want you to run in the outfield with the pitchers." I said, "Reggie, I don't need to run. If I lose weight, I'll be ineffective. Do you want that?" I could have gone nine innings that first week of camp. He says something like, "You know, Bill, we don't have to keep you here." I should have bit my tongue, I should have bit my tongue—but I didn't. I said, "Well, Reggie, you're not doing me any favors by keeping me." The next day, I was gone.[28]

And so the club, of its own volition, prepared to begin its second season without its best pitcher from a year ago. As the team went through the paces on Hispaniola, the forward-thinking Maduro initiated new methods for cultivating future talent for his team. This recapitulation by Cuban sportswriter Pedro Galiana very much resembles, in its text, the concept of baseball academies that the majority of major league teams established in Latin America in the latter part of the 20th century as a method of developing and honing prospects:

Maduro (*inset*) shares the cover of an International League program with Sugar Kings cartoon mascot "Beisbolito," sliding into a base. At the bottom is the team's slogan in Spanish of "One More Step and We'll Make It," referring to the major league aspirations of the franchise (author's collection).

A 15-day tryout camp now is operating in Maduro's Gran Stadium here. Some 500 boys have been scouted during the past year, with 250 of them being brought in from all parts of the island for final inspection by Florence Amando Llano, chief scout of the Sugar Kings; the Cubans manager Reggie Otero; Nap Reyes, ex–Giant; Tony Castaño, Emilio Cabrera, Tony Pacheco and Reinaldo Cordeiro.

Maduro estimates that he has spent approximately $25,000 on the year-round project, which included a summer clinic last year lasting about six months, scouting by the entire staff around the calendar and the current tryout camp.

Youngsters attending the tryout camp are provided with complete accommodations in Gran Stadium. They live right on the premises, sleeping in comfortable beds set up in the ballpark clubhouses, and take their meals in the Stadium Club restaurant. First class meals are served, with breakfast scheduled daily for 7:30 a.m., and the calisthenics workout at 9 o'clock. Bed time is 10 p.m.

All are supervised closely in their routine workouts featuring batting, fielding, running, throwing and circling the bases.[29]

Another person closely watching the progress of these youngsters had to be Paul Miller, who was named general manager of the Sugar Kings two weeks before the season. Assistant GM last year, Miller's promotion required him to resign as treasurer of the Cuban Winter League, a post he had held since 1939. A native of Pennsylvania, Miller also gave up his office job with a Havana shipyard company in order to dedicate himself fully to his new position.

In a position all too familiar to him from a quarter-century of contact, Cuban native Connie Marrero opened the Sugar Kings' 1955 season, April 19 at Gran Stadium. Signed by Maduro after five years with the Washington Senators, the extremely popular amateur and winter league pitcher hurled the first six innings against the Buffalo Bisons, allowing two runs. Outfielder Asdrúbal Baró's seventh-inning, three-run home run elevated the Sugar Kings to a 4–2 victory. Marrero's former Washington teammate, Julio Moreno, picked up the win in relief. Over 15,000 celebrated the Tuesday night return of the International League. Marrero and Moreno were two of nine Cuban players on Reggie Otero's roster. Five North Americans, five Venezuelans, and one native each from Panama, Puerto Rico and the Dominican Republic rounded out the multinational crew.

Last year's opening night starter, Emilio Cueche, took the mound for the second game. He took a 2–0 lead into the eighth inning when he apparently tired. The Venezuelan was removed and charged with three earned runs in the frame. With his team trailing, 3–2, in the bottom of the ninth, last evening's hero, Baró, did it again, blasting a game-tying home run against Bisons pitcher Hal Erickson. Cueche compatriot Camaleón García followed with a game-winning round-tripper for the spectacularly thrilling 4–3 victory. Moreno picked up his second relief win in as many nights.

Another Venezuelan pitcher hurled the Sugar Kings to a fourth victory in a row. In the second game of a doubleheader on April 21, Julián Ladera blanked the Bisons, 4–0, on five hits. Otero's club won the opener behind Ken Raffensburger, 5–1. Two days hence, in front of 7,000 spectators, the Azucareros suffered their first defeat, 6–1, to Montreal's Ken

Lehman, who would again top the league with 22 victories. Allowing half of the runs, Pat Scantlebury was hung with the defeat. The following day, April 24, the Sugar Kings swept a Sunday doubleheader, 6–4 and 9–6 (seven innings). Pedro Formental went deep in the opener. One thousand fewer fans than the previous day witnessed the double triumph over Montreal. Raffensburger tossed a near-shutout on April 25. The left-hander suppressed the Royals on six hits for eight innings. Bubba Harris nailed down the 4–0 final. The Royals nosed out a 4–3 win in the fifth-game series finale. Charlie Neal's seventh-inning, solo four-bagger was the difference.

In their initial road game of 1955, Willie Powell, in his first appearance as a starter, stymied the Buffalo Bisons, 5–0, on April 28. In a performance perhaps many Sugar Kings fans lamented as coming one start too late, Powell held his opponents to eight hits, spoiling the Bisons' home opener. Formental homered for two runs. The victory was anything but indicative of a successful road foray. The club, after reaping seven wins in nine home games, dropped nine out of 12 in their U.S. and Canadian travels, with owner Maduro accompanying the squad.

Back in Havana, it was a different story. In a homestand culminating on May 19, the Sugar Kings gained back eight victories in ten decisions for an 18–13 overall record (15–4 at Gran Stadium). While most teams play better at home, it is a small wonder that visiting clubs weren't even easier fodder for the Sugar Kings with all the "diversions" of the city away from the diamond. Targeted at the U.S. summertime vacationer, a travel write-up in a northern newspaper around this time detailed some of the excitement and allure of the Cuban capital.

> For the visitor ... long, lazy days are filled with swimming, yachting, golfing, tennis and other sports. In addition to La Concha Beach, there are numerous small beaches within one or two hours' drive from the city. There are famous old restaurants such as the Floridita, the Paris, la Zaragozona and the Palacio de Cristal, which serve the traditional fine food of Cuba and Spain. It's here one eats *paella* [rice and seafood], Moro crab, *congrí* [sautéed black beans and rice], and in-season tropical fruits such as mango and *aguacate* [avocado].
>
> For sports enthusiasts, Havana has a variety of attractions to offer, including boxing every Saturday night at the National Sports Palace, horse racing at the famous Oriental Park and dog racing in Marianao. An evening at the lightning fast game of jai-alai, played six nights a week at the huge fronton, provides a most revealing glimpse at native life and temperament. If the visitor gets homesick for a bit of good old Americana, there is always night baseball, with the Havana Sugar Kings competing for the International League pennant at the splendid Havana Stadium.
>
> Night time in Cuba is still the most enthralling time, with exotic spots to dine, dance and listen to the wild native rhythms. If brighter lights are preferred, there

are always the innumerable night clubs and cafes, including the "Big Three"—Tropicana, Sans Souci, Montmartre, all offering lavish entertainment, gambling rooms, and orchestras playing both Cuban and American music.[30]

After another underachieving road foray of five wins and seven losses, the Sugar Kings hosted—inhospitably—the second-place Toronto Maple Leafs on June 1. Connie Marrero flung a three-hitter, winning 8–0. Marrero, 44, retired the defending pennant winners on three pitches in the ninth inning, as Otero's charges crept within 5½ games of first place. The Cubans and Leafs split the six-game series with Emilio Cueche and Corky Valentine (seven innings) gaining the other victories on shutouts on the final day of the series. Valentine, a 12-game winner with the Cincinnati Redlegs last season, had, days earlier, been optioned to the Sugar Kings from the parent club. To make room for Valentine, Ken Raffensberger, who was being used less and less, was given his release—a desired one at that, as he shortly signed on to pitch in the Piedmont League with the York White Roses of his hometown, York, Pennsylvania. Later in the month, the Reds traded outfielder Clint Hartung, who had returned to Havana, to the Oakland Oaks for PCL standout Joe Brovia. Hartung had hit an unspectacular five home runs prior to the exchange.

The Sugar Kings used the twin bill shutouts as a springboard to reel off 12 straight wins, with ten more against Rochester and Richmond, to catapult them to within one-half game of first place. The streak was broken by a 6–5 loss to the Virginians on the final day of the homestand, June 15. It appeared the Kings had their 13th victory in a row in hand, but Richmond rallied for four ninth-inning scores.

A three-week-long, 10–11 road trip concluded on July 5 with a 4–2 setback to the same Richmond Virginians and a significant retreat from challenging for the top spot in the circuit. During the journey, manager Otero was suspended by the league president for a day for bumping umpire Bob Smith multiple times in a 3–2 defeat at Montreal. The incident was triggered by Smith's ejection of Pedro Formental for throwing his bat. Another game of unusual interest occurred June 29. With an Angel Scull single knocking home the ninth-inning deciding run, the Kings downed the Red Wings, 9–8, at Red Wing Stadium. Thirteen pitching changes were recorded—with more than half by two Sugar Kings hurlers. In the eighth inning, Otero brought in right-hander José "Carrao" Bracho and put current left-handed moundsman Pat Scantlebury at first base. The final five outs of the game were obtained by the two men as they swapped positions, alternating pitching to right- and left-handed batters. Scantlebury picked up the final out to gain his sixth win.

Opening a much-welcomed home stay on July 6, Connie Marrero surrendered only two singles to the Buffalo Bisons in a 4–0 blanking. Detroit Tigers signee and Bisons starting pitcher Jim Bunning took the loss, his fourth. Preceding the contest, a previously suspended game was completed in which the Bisons closed out a 4–0 victory of their own. By chance, Bunning had been the starter in that earlier, unfinished game, and he registered the final outs for an officially recorded two-hit shutout of his own, his eighth win. The next day, Bracho, a pitching giant in his home country of Venezuela, twirled a three-hitter against the same team. Formental slugged one out of Gran Stadium in the 6–1 whipping. Two more Venezuelan hurlers earned victories in the six-game set (counting the suspended game): Julián Ladera, his sixth (4–0), and Cueche, his eighth (3–2).

Cueche won a game—with his bat—for teammate Connie Marrero on July 13. Pinch-hitting (as he often did) for Marrero in the bottom of the ninth inning, Cueche slashed a single off Montreal Royals starter Tommy Lasorda, driving home the only run of the game. Allowing seven hits, Marrero (5–1) was credited with his third shutout in the second game of a doubleheader. The game followed a very similar 1–0 victory by the Sugar Kings, with Raúl Sánchez besting a turning 19-year-old Don Drysdale. Asdrúbal Baró delivered the winning run with a hit in the first extra frame of the intended seven-inning contest. The outfielder had been the hitting star a day earlier, as the Kings took a pair of contests from the same club. Registering the first of two walk-off hits in as many days—an eighth-inning single—Baró drove in the winning score in a 2–1 decision. In the nine-stanza, second-game tilt won by the Cubans by a 4–3 count, Baró's sixth-inning, two-run homer put the club ahead, 3–2. The second doubleheader sweep of the Royals in two days moved the Cubans a season-high 20 games over .500 (56–36) and past Montreal into sole possession of second place, two games behind circuit-leading Toronto. The schedule shortly dictated visits to other cities, which resulted in playing 13 games in ten days. Winning just three times, the Sugar Kings slipped back to third place.

Commencing another homestand on July 27, Marrero won his sixth and the Sugar Kings' 60th game, 4–0, with his fourth shutout. The whitewash came against last-place Richmond. The Sugar Kings then clicked off ten more wins in a row at Gran Stadium, nearly matching their earlier season-best streak of 12. The 11th game without a loss came against the Columbus Jets on August 4. It was realized by Marrero, who authored his fifth shutout in the back end of a doubleheader. (The five shutouts were a franchise record for a season—later tied by Cueche and Mike Cuéllar in 1958.) Pompeyo "Yo-Yo" Davalillo scored the only run of the game in the ninth inning on a wild pitch. Marrero allowed only one hit, to the Jets' Dick Kryhoski, as he earned the distinction of pitching the first one-hitter in team history. In the curtain-raiser, Pat Scantlebury became the first Sugar Kings pitcher to reach double figures in wins with a 9–0, seven-inning decision. The dual shutouts were the 18th and 19th recorded by the staff and brought Otero's hot team (70–48), once again, to the doorstep of Toronto's first-place mansion.

When the winning march was ended by Syracuse the next day, the Sugar Kings' home record stood at a remarkable 51–14. In the midst of such pleasing results, a special "Cubans Day" celebration was held August 1 at Gran Stadium. Havana fans paid tribute to their team like never before, and like never before in the history of the league. Jamming Gran Stadium to see the Cubans defeat the Columbus Jets, 9–5, a crowd of 29,917 established the largest, regular season single-game attendance in league history. In only their second season, the Cuban Sugar Kings had recorded a new, one-game spectator record in the United States' oldest minor league.

Perhaps hoping they would bring his team good luck, if not good public relations, Maduro sent Señorita Ofelia García, "Queen of the Sugar Kings," and the three-runner-up beauty contestants for the same title, with his club on their next northern sojourn. In Rochester, the queen and her court, consisting of Señoritas Gladys García Ledo, Nancy Martínez and Angela Hernández, were special guests of honor at a luncheon arranged by the Red Wings' front office, August 19. Two days earlier, in a twi-night doubleheader, José Bracho's eight-game unbeaten streak had been ended by Red Wings pitcher Ellis "Cot" Deal, 4–0. During the final stop of the four-city tour, in Toronto, Pat Scantlebury's 13th win, 2–0, gave the Sugar Kings' staff its (by a wide margin) league-leading 20th whitewash on August 21. Outfielder/first baseman Saturnino "Nino" Escalera's two-run home run supplied the difference.

The 80–58 Sugar Kings, a few days later, flew back to Havana to conclude the home campaign. Toronto maintained a tenuous half-game lead over Montreal and 2½ above the third-place *habaneros*. On August 28, the Kings, with their 83rd and 84th wins, pushed to a season-best 24 games above .500. The doubleheader sweep over Rochester was the 13th of the season (an unusually high number), and trimmed Toronto's advantage to two games. That set the stage for the first-place club's arrival the next day. The potential showdown turned into a letdown for the hometown fans. Managed by Luke Sewell, the Maple Leafs took it to the Sugar

Kings, winning four out of five, transforming Otero's team from pennant contenders to pennant pretenders. Havana native Mike Fornieles won both of his starting assignments for Toronto in the five-day set.

The Sugar Kings played their last four games of the season in Richmond, where the team won its 14th twin bill and lost its first on successive days (the team split two other doubleheaders). While in the "Mother of States," the International League Baseball Writers Association released the news that Otero was voted "Manager of the Year" for the second consecutive year.

At season's end, Greg Mulleavy's Montreal squad barely nosed out last year's pennant winners, Toronto, by one-half game. Both clubs lost 59 games, but a tie game couldn't be made up by Toronto, which cost them a first-place deadlock. Besides the top pitcher in the league in Ken Lehman, Montreal also boasted the best hitter. Rocky Nelson emphatically took the honors by capturing the Triple Crown at the conclusion of the season. Also one of the Cuban Winter League's favorite North American players, Nelson hit .374, clubbed 37 home runs and knocked home 130 runs.

Winning eight more games than last season, the Sugar Kings (87–66) easily cinched third place, 11 games ahead of fourth-slotted Rochester, as the other five teams in the circuit all finished with records below .500. The Cubans placed 7½ lengths behind Montreal. Pat Scantlebury (13–9) edged out Emilio Cueche (12–10) for most wins on Otero's club. The Panamanian also garnered the loop's ERA title with a 1.90 mark. In limited duty, 44-year-old Connie Marrero held his own, with a 7–3 record and 2.69 ERA in 16 games. Raúl Sánchez and José Bracho contributed with ten and nine wins, respectively. On the hitting front, third sacker Camaleón García showed surprising power, leading all hitters with a dozen home runs. Ray Noble and Asdrúbal Baro slammed ten each. Nino Escalera displayed fine hitting form, accruing a .297 average—the best among regulars—in over 500 at-bats. Pedro Formental hit .293, as he had last year, with eight homers and 55 RBI. Though this was the 40-year-old outfielder's final Sugar Kings campaign, his career average would go down as the highest by a Sugar Kings player with more than one year of service with the franchise.

Scantlebury opened the first playoff game in Sugar Kings history versus 94-win Toronto on September 7. He received a no-decision. Bubba Harris picked up a well-deserved win with 3⅔ innings of scoreless relief, as a 13-hit attack paced the visiting Sugar Kings to a 5–4 victory at Maple Leaf Stadium. The triumph bestowed a terrific 40th birthday present on field leader Otero. The next day, however, an eight-run fifth inning propelled the Maple Leafs to an easy, 11–2 triumph. Roughed up on the mound was Sugar Kings starter and loser José Bracho. The third contest was also played in Toronto, and the Maple Leafs used another single-inning outburst to take a two-games-to-one lead in the series. Putting up a six-spot in the fourth, Toronto doubled up the Cubans in an 8–4 decision. Otero used five pitchers, including starter and loser, Vicente Amor. Chalking up his third victory in less than two weeks over the Sugar Kings, Mike Fornieles pitched the distance for the victors and tallied three of his team's 17 hits in the game.

After an off-day, the series resumed in Havana on Sunday, September 11. In contrast to the liberal hitting of the previous contests, the pitchers for both clubs assumed control. A solo home run in the top of the tenth inning by Maple Leaf Mike Goliat decided the issue in favor of his team, 2–1. Johnny Hetki and Jack Crimian combined on a five-hit victory, putting the Cubans in a 3–1 series hole. Scantlebury valiantly pitched the route, also surrendering only five safeties, including the decisive blow.

Much to the chagrin of the home team's followers, Toronto wrapped things up the following day. Scoring three runs in the first inning, the Canadian club held on for a 4–2 win. Knocked out of the box in the first frame, Bracho absorbed his second loss in the series. Game Three's triumphant hurler, Eddie Blake, won his second decision with bullpen help from Ray Shore. Otero was ejected halfway through the game for rudely complaining about an umpire's refusal to comply with a request to examine starter Blake's baseball for possible "doctoring." In the third *and* fourth innings, opposing manager Sewell had asked for the ball, examined out of the palm of Sugar Kings pitcher Raúl Sánchez, and was appeased both times by the arbiters—the umpires found nothing suspicious. An uninspiring 5,000 fans witnessed the Gran Stadium defeat.

The Sugar Kings were defeated by the Toronto Maple Leafs in five opening round playoff games. Fourth-place and sub-.500 Rochester upended pennant-winning Montreal, four games to one, and then stepped forward to shockingly sweep four games from Toronto to win the International Baseball League's Governor's Cup.

The Minneapolis Millers ended Rochester's Cinderella season with a seven-game Junior World Series win.

For the Sugar Kings, analyzing their play on the field and from an economic angle, no one could categorize the season as anything but a success—their playoff loss notwithstanding. On April 13, almost a full week prior to the season opener, Maduro had held a press conference and outlined his two goals for his club to the gathered writers. They were: to give the fans a pennant contender, which undeniably occurred, and to crack the 300,000 mark in attendance. On the paid-rooting front, a final total of 313, 232 was superseded only by Toronto's loyal followers, numbering 350,742. Gran Stadium spectators accounted for one-fifth of the circuit's total attendance.

But with socio-political headwinds looming over the not too distant horizon, organized baseball reached its 20th century peak in Cuba with the last turnstile click of the 1955 campaign at Bobby Maduro's grand ballpark.

1955 International League Final Standings

	W	L	T	PCT	GB	Manager	Major League Affiliation
Montreal Royals	95	59	0	.617	—	Greg Mulleavy	Brooklyn Dodgers
Toronto Maple Leafs	94	59	1	.614	½	Luke Sewell	None
Cuban Sugar Kings	87	66	3	.569	7½	Reggie Otero	Cincinnati Reds
Rochester Red Wings	76	77	1	.497	18½	Harry Walker/ Lou Kahn/ Dixie Walker	St. Louis Cardinals
Syracuse Chiefs	74	79	1	.484	20½	Skeeter Newsome	Philadelphia Phillies
Buffalo Bisons	65	89	0	.422	30	Danny Carnevale	Detroit Tigers
Columbus Jets	64	89	0	.418	30½	Nick Cullop	Kansas City Athletics
Richmond Virginians	58	95	1	.379	36½	Luke Appling	None

Four

"Los Cubanitos"

The Havana Cubans did not have a single black player in their eight-year history. Professional baseball in Cuba had long been integrated, but due to segregation laws in Florida the team maintained an all–Caucasian composition. In the more tolerant International League, the Cuban Sugar Kings, under Maduro, promoted a diverse lineup of multiracial players from its inception.

In 1954, although the vast majority of their men of color were Latin Americans, the Sugar Kings' first African American player was veteran Willie Powell. The pitcher was acquired from Toronto late in the season and started the playoff tie-breaker against the Syracuse Chiefs. He worked mostly out of the Sugar Kings' bullpen in 1955.

Powell was not part of the Sugar Kings as the team entered the 1956 season, hoping to build on their most recent third-place finish and increased attendance figure of 313,232. Toronto and Havana were the only cities to attract over 300,000 people to their parks. While the Maple Leafs and Sugar Kings were the most envied clubs as far as ticket sales, on the other end of the spectrum were the Syracuse Chiefs. Only one year removed from their improbable Governor's Cup playoff run, their fan base had inexplicably deserted the team. The fifth-place club (74–79, –20½) drew the interest of only 85,191 customers during the most recent four and one-half month-long campaign.

A few months after the season, an ownership group led by St. Louis investment banker Sid Salomon and including former Cleveland Indians president Bill Veeck stepped in and bought the struggling franchise for $100,000, with the intent of relocating it to South Florida. The transaction was met with overwhelming approval in a meeting of directors of the reinvented league. "Officials of the other International League clubs heartily endorsed the move to Miami," declared a report of the gathering, "partly because they feel this rapidly-growing resort city will draw well and partly because the Miami location will break up the long trip from Havana to Richmond, the next southernmost city in the league."[1]

The new Miami Marlins would play at Miami Stadium, in a deal brokered between the new ownership group and the city of Miami, which currently held a short-term lease on the appealing, seven-year-old stadium. International League author Sam Zygner depicted much of the park's attraction during this era:

> At the time of its construction, Miami Stadium was considered the jewel of the [U.S. & Canadian] minor leagues and a state-of-the-art venue that was the envy of clubs everywhere. One of the most impressive features of the ballpark was the cantilevered roof that sported beamless supports and provided an unobstructed view of the playing field. The unique roof design covered the majority of the spectator area, unlike the traditional flat or sloping roofs of most ballparks, and wrapped around the infield portion of the playing field from first to third base. The arching roof protected fans from the rainy weather, as well as providing much-needed shade that is so important during the alternating sunny summer months in south Florida.[2]

Miami city fathers were hoping to purchase the park from owner José Alemán, Jr. through a revenue bond offering. Aleman, Jr. had set an $850,000 asking price to part with his inherited sports edifice. The park was unequivocally a key element in the move. "Miami Stadium, the spring training [exhibition] home of the Brooklyn Dodgers," underscored another print review, "is considered by Veeck to be the finest baseball plant for its size in the country. It has 9,500 permanent seats and can handle another 5,000 customers in bleachers."[3] The rental fee was fixed at five percent of the team's gross revenues.

The owner most elated over the league's new announced look had to be Bobby Maduro, especially after a concurrent unanimous resolution carried by the circuit directors stated that each team would be responsible for its travel costs to Havana. Although his travel reimbursement commitment involving the rest of the franchises had been reduced in its second year, he still had absorbed a $64,000 out-of-pocket expense over the first two years of the onerous accord. (That's the buying power of nearly $600,000 in today's dollars.) Last season, the highest revenue-generating teams in the league, determined by attendance, agreed to chip in to offset some air travel bills to Havana. Moreover, Maduro had been a proponent of a franchise for South Florida, believing a rivalry could be easily started between the geographically close clubs.

Meanwhile, as the spring conditioning period approached for the Sugar Kings, another estimable facet of Maduro's wholehearted dedication to the game surfaced. Expanding on the baseball academy idea, Maduro borrowed from the concept of sponsored youth organizations in the United States that for years had been healthy outlets for youngsters to participate in recreational baseball activities. The Maduro-led Little League program was called *Los Cubanitos* and had its own league commissioner, Nap Reyes. Its early success gained attention in the North American press. One such write-up began:

> Baseball in Cuba is being used as an incentive to get boys to attend school. Kids in the 8–13 age group must certify that they attend school and are of good behavior if they want to play baseball.
> "We have 36 teams in nine Little Leagues in Cuba," says Bob Maduro, president of the Havana Sugar Kings. "They are sponsored by the Havana team and small business on the island."[4]

Reyes touched on the social value the program offered, resonating with a broader theme. "There are many poor people in Cuba," he said, "and the Little League gives them their only chance to play sports."[5]

Another printed excerpt pointed to another Maduro associate who appeared to have exerted substantial influence during initial stages of the worthwhile organization: "Maduro's interest in player development extended as far as the children's ranks.... A man named Mako Pérez, who was an instructor at the Miramar Yacht Club, was the driving force behind the league. The program covered the entire island and kept roughly 5,000 children occupied."[6]

The Cubanitos were three-quarters of the way through their season when the Cubans commenced their third campaign on April 18, 1956. As was the custom, the Sugar Kings opened at home. The Rochester Red Wings provided excellent competition as participants to a smashing home opener viewed by 18,700 spectators, topping the two previous inaugural games.

French crooner Maurice Chevalier, who was headlining the Havana cabaret circuit, threw out the first pitch, after Cuban soprano Alba Marina sang the U.S., Canadian and Cuban national anthems. Third-year skipper Reggie Otero presented a lineup card listing: Don Nicholas, rf, Angel Scull, cf, Nino Escalera, 1b, Woody Smith, 3b, Ultus Alvarez, lf, Amado Ibáñez, 2b, Pablo Bernard, ss, Dutch Dotterer, c, Vicente Amor, p. The starting nine represented players from four countries: Cuba, Panama, Puerto Rico and the U.S.

The future major league hurler Amor matched up against former major league pitcher Cot Deal. Tied 2–2, the game appeared headed for extra frames when Deal retired the first two batters in the ninth. Woody

Nap Reyes hands his signed contract as manager to general manager Paul Miller prior to the 1957 season. Following this season, Maduro, in the white jacket, would call upon Reyes twice more to manage his club, including part of the uprooting 1960 campaign (courtesy Ralph Maya).

Smith then stepped up to the plate and socked a home run over the left field wall for a joy-jumping finish. The pulsating solo shot was the sixth hit allowed by Deal, and the first for extra bases. Amor went the distance, allowing no earned runs, as his team scratched back from a 2–0 deficit. "Long after the lights were doused tonight," observed one writer, "parading, trumpeting, bongo-banging fans celebrated outside Gran Stadium."[7]

Blissfully impervious to the reverie of the moment was one Reggie Smith, toddling son of the home run hero. "My dad Forest 'Woody' Smith played for the Sugar Kings in the 1956 season," said the now 63-year-old. "He had 15 home runs for Havana and ended up with 19 for the year. He played the first 113 games for Havana and then was bought by Miami, playing the next four years with them and accumulating numerous franchise records. I was only two years old that summer in Havana so I don't remember anything."[8]

The exhilarating opening night triumph was not a portent of immediate things to come. Following the inaugural victory, the Sugar Kings endured their worst homestand since joining the IL. The team dropped ten of its next 14 games on home soil, including a four-game sweep, April 24–27, to the Montreal Royals. It marked the first time the Sugar Kings had ever been swept in a series in Havana. The club tumbled into the basement of the three-country league. Maduro's team did receive what turned out to be a pitching boost when Rudy Minarcin, a Cincinnati farmhand, was reassigned to the Cubans prior to the Royals series. A right-hander, Minarcin won his first start on April 29, snapping a five-game Sugar Kings losing streak. The victims were the Toronto Maple Leafs, 9–2.

The following month, the Sugar Kings met the newest relocated IL entry for the first time. The initial square-off took place at Miami Stadium on May 28. Don Cardwell pitched the Miami Marlins to a 7–3 victory in front of 5,173 fans. Returning starter José Bracho absorbed the loss. The Marlins took three out of four games in their home park, including a Decoration Day doubleheader sweep, May 30. Inimitable pitching relic Satchel Paige saved both games in relief. The almost 50-year-old pitcher tossed the final 2⅓ innings of a seven-inning, 3–2 win in the opener. In the nine-inning nightcap, Paige obtained the final out to preserve a stellar 4–1 pitching outing by Marlins starter Jack Spring.

The home and home series began its Havana portion the next evening. The Sugar Kings rebounded with an 11–1 stomping of the International League's "newest" team. Nino Escalera's two-run home run led a well-balanced offensive attack. On June 1, Cardwell, the future Philadelphia Phillies hurler, beat the Cubans for the second time in four days. But he needed extended help from Paige. Relieving Cardwell with the bases loaded in the sixth inning and extinguishing the Sugar Kings' attempted rally, the venerable right-hander was nicked for a run in the eighth before wrapping up the contest. With the 7–2 decision, the 20-year-old Cardwell improved to 5–0, and he clubbed a home run for good measure. Miami shut out their Havana "cousins" the following day, and then Paige started the fourth and final game of the series. The ancient pitcher claimed the victory, 5–2, though requiring aid in the sixth. Reliever Seth Morehead clamped down the Marlins' sixth win in eight games over the Sugar Kings.

The next day, June 4, Reggie Otero resigned as dugout leader, initially citing "poor health." Otero's sudden illness coincided with being at the helm of a last-place team. He was allowed to save face by voluntarily leaving on his terms instead of being fired. He remained with the organization in a front office capacity, the kindness owing to Maduro. Replacing the only manager the Sugar Kings had known was former New York Giant and Los Cubanitos commissioner Nap Reyes.

The team responded in a big way in their new skipper's debut, trampling the Buffalo Bisons, 10–6 on June 5 at Gran Stadium. It was only the Sugar Kings' 18th victory in 49 games. In his second game, Reyes recorded a rocking chair win, 13–0. Pat Scantlebury, sent down on "24-hour recall" by the Cincinnati Reds, corralled the Bisons on four hits. The suitcase-packed pitcher, Hal Bevan and Juan Delís all drove in three runs. Reyes received his first taste of reality the following game—a 5–4 defeat at the hands of Buffalo.

"Even the mambo bands are in a slump," quipped one North American visitor to Gran Stadium, following Rochester Red Wings pitcher Bob Blaylock's two-hit shutout over the Cubans on June 8. A two-run home run by Blaylock's batterymate Dick Rand off starter Vicente Amor sunk the Sugar Kings (19–32) deeper into last place.

Shortly afterward the club departed on a road trip, almost definitely without their team owner, who was awaiting the birth of another child. On June 16, the day his team defeated the Rochester Red Wings, 5–4, in ten innings, the Maduros became proud parents of a son, Alberto. Appropriately, it was Fathers-Sons Night at Red Wing Stadium. The familial promotion disappointingly attracted fewer than 2,800 fans. But far away in Havana, the new addition to the Maduro clan must have been viewed as a special blessing, not two years removed from the loss of Felipe.

In a character reversal, the Sugar Kings won six of nine games on the road. Then the club escaped the basement following a four-game sweep of fifth-place Toronto in Havana; Reyes' squad climbed into sixth place with a 30–37 mark. The team was still 11½ games behind first-place Montreal, but only four games out of the first division. Montreal had defeated the Sugar Kings nine straight times when the teams took the field for a Sunday doubleheader at Gran Stadium, June 24. The Sugar Kings gained some measure of payback with two come-from-behind victories. The home team erupted for nine runs in the sixth inning of the opener against starter Fred Kipp and two relievers, leading to a 10–5 win. A left-hander, Kipp had shut out the Sugar Kings, on four hits, in his last start against them in Montreal. He was cruising along until he walked pitcher Raúl Sánchez with one out in the fateful frame. The Sugar Kings batted around from there. In the seven-inning nightcap, infielder Owen Friend delivered the big blow—a three-run, third-inning home run—to help carve out a 6–3 victory.

All these many years later, Kipp has settled in his home state of

Kansas. A far-travelled man, thanks to baseball, the former pitcher also spent several winters playing ball in Venezuela and the Dominican Republic.

> I started in the Dodgers' organization, in Ashville [Tourists], then Miami [Sun Sox]. Then I went into the army. When I got out I was sent to Mobile [Bears].
>
> There was no room for me in Brooklyn, so I was sent to Montreal. That was 1956. I was 24. Everyone read the newspapers back then, everyday; I still do, to this day. In spring training, Dick Young [NY sportswriter] wrote, *Kipp has about as much chance of making it to Brooklyn as the Holland Tunnel.* [Chortles] But I got a call-up in September 1957. I went up there as a green rookie, I'll tell you.
>
> I played two seasons with Montreal—'56 and '57. I pitched well one year [20–7] and not well the other [8–17]; we had a lousy team. We flew commercial to Havana. Wives never went on road trips, this was the minor leagues. I remember always bringing back cigars and all types of flavored rum—peach rum, banana rum. Everybody in Montreal would ask you to bring back something. You could bring back four or five bottles without duty charge. They were pretty cheap, about a buck a piece. I remember going to a cigar factory and watching them make cigars.
>
> The Hotel Nacional was very nice. There was an old skinny guy always waiting outside to jump on our team bus. He would sing a song or two on the way to the ballpark. We took turns tipping him. In the stadium clubhouse there were a couple guys that would do anything for a price [tip]. I'll never forget the hottest day I ever spent was a Sunday afternoon game. I was pitching. The visitors' dugout was on the first base side. The sun hit there in the afternoon. The dugouts weren't very big, and only about two feet deep. There was no relief. On the other side, they were used to it [the heat]. There was a mariachi [sic] band, I vaguely remember. Of course, they played really good ball in the winter down there, you know.
>
> We had a guy on our team in Montreal, Bobby Dolan, he was a career minor leaguer. He always liked to tell the story about how after a series in Havana, they landed in Columbus, Ohio. Well, a bunch of the guys and him decided to go to confession. They went to a church, and there were two confessional lines. Bobby was the first to go in. Suddenly, in a loud voice, the priest says, *You did what?* All the guys on the team then moved together into the other line. [Laughs]
>
> I'm managing okay, although my stamina isn't very good. I'm getting a stent put in near my heart next month. I still do my bit. I get up early, sometimes I go to Mass, read the paper.[9]

The second encounter with Miami came about on July 10. Playing in Havana first this time around, the Sugar Kings handed nine-game winner Don Cardwell only his third defeat, 6–1. Nino Escalera was the batting star with four safeties, three RBI and a sixth-inning steal of home. The next evening, the starters for each club would have grabbed the fancy of any geriatrics club or their sympathizers. "It's a good bet that last night's Miami-Havana game matched two of the oldest pitchers in captivity," read one story. "Creaking Satchel Paige, who is rumored to be anywhere from 46 to 56-years-old, and Conrado Marrero, who will never see 45 again, were the principals in the battle of aching bones. Paige showed that young whippersnapper a thing or two about pitching, tough, getting credit for his sixth victory in a 1–0 effort."[10] Neither hurler was around after the sixth inning. Allowing five hits, Paige required relief help from Angelo LiPetri in the combined shutout. Taking home the distinct memory were 4,500 fans.

Miami had turned into the hottest club in the league, as the Sugar Kings found out in their next meeting in South Florida. The Marlins swept a three-game weekend set, July 20–22, gaining their 15th win in 18 games. Managed by Don Osborn, the Marlins had surged into a second-place tie with Rochester. In the Friday contest, Sugar Kings coach Reinaldo Cordeiro's misbehavior got him suspended for the remainder of the season for spitting multiple times on umpire Frank Guzzetta, following an altercation. In handing down the ruling several days afterward, league president Shaughnessy indicated that Cordeiro could apply for reinstatement next season.

In late July, the Sugar Kings agreed to take on Sandy Consuegra, following his release from the Chicago White Sox. Less than two years removed from a 16–3 campaign with Chicago, the veteran right-hander went 3–4 for his new team, matching Scantlebury's team-low 2.57 ERA, albeit in fewer (63) innings. He would be traded to the Baltimore Orioles on the last day of August for cash and the 1957 re-assignment of minor league hurler Bill Diemer to the Sugar Kings. On the final day of July, the Sugar Kings swept a road, twi-night doubleheader from the third-place Rochester Red Wings, 2–1 and 6–0. Tossing the whitewash, Rudy Minarcin—who had pitched a one-hitter during his rookie tryout with the parent Reds last season—scattered 11 hits, with two walks. In the seven-inning opener, Ultus Alvarez smacked his second two-run homer in three days in the visitor's half of the sixth, the deciding blow. Former Dodgers and Cubs lefty Joe Hatten picked up the shortened, complete-game victory.

In his first season with the club, Alvarez, 23, paced the team in homers with 16. In the past CWL season as a member of Cienfuegos, he had tied for the lead in longs balls with ten, in his first full season in the circuit. Alvarez was a Maduro find during the pre–Sugar Kings days. The backstory comes from the *Wilmington News-Journal*:

> Bob Maduro spotted Alvarez as a teenager on a trip to Cumanayagua, a southern Cuban town about 300 miles from Havana. Maduro took Alvarez to the Brooklyn training camp at Vero Beach, Fla., and after appraisal by scouts, Alvarez was signed. That was 1952.
>
> Maduro, now owner of the Cubans, bought the redhead's contract from Brooklyn and optioned him to Columbia in the South Atlantic League for the 1955 season. He trained with Cincinnati in the spring of 1956 before reporting to Havana.[11]

Four—"Los Cubanitos"

The development of Alvarez may have let Maduro more easily part ways with opening night hero Woody Smith. As previously indicated, he had been sold to the Miami Marlins for $15,000 on July 26. Three days later, facing the Toronto Maple Leafs, Alvarez temporarily made the fans forget the loss of Smith as he duplicated the third sacker's heroic feat. The first baseman bashed a one-out, walk-off, two-run homer against reliever Lynn Lovenguth, to carry the Sugar Kings to a 2–1 win. Emilio Cueche was awarded the victory in relief of starter Jehosie Heard.

As his sixth-place team tried to gain some traction in the standings, a news brief announced a new Maduro venture which displayed more of his visionary talents: "For the first time in Latin-American broadcasting history, a new radio station—Radio Deportes—scheduled to devote 24 hours a day to sports news and events was opened in Havana, Cuba, August 16. A group of Cuban sportsmen, headed by Bobby Maduro, is associated with the enterprise. A cocktail party to launch the affair was held at Gran Stadium, August 14."[12]

A couple of weeks later, one International League player deserved a special toast all to himself. Curt Roberts accomplished what few minor or major league players ever have on August 27. Playing for the Columbus Jets against the Sugar Kings, Roberts swatted four home runs in the first game of a doubleheader against three Sugar Kings pitchers. At Jets Stadium, Roberts, who in 1954 became the first African American player for the Pittsburgh Pirates, tagged starter Jerry Lane and relievers Raúl Sánchez and Jehosie Heard (twice) in leading Columbus to a 10–7 win. Making the accomplishment all the more remarkable was the seven-inning duration of the contest. Driving in six runs, Roberts became the fourth International League player to slug four round-trippers in a game and the first to do it in a seven-inning fray.[13] The Sugar Kings came back to win the regulation-length nightcap, 5–2. Emilio Cueche improved to 6–2, with a relief assist from Joe Hatten. Roberts collected a hit in four at-bats. The Kings, at this point under Reyes, had failed to make any type of striking turn-around. At 63–75, the club was firmly in the second division, 16½ games behind perennial league leader Toronto.

During the first week of September, the pitching staff exhibited some of its glory from last season, shutting out the Miami Marlins four times in five games, while winning all five. On September 3, the Kings took a pair of 3–0 decisions. Heard tossed seven shutout innings in the abridged first game. Satchel Paige (11–4) started and was pinned with the defeat. The nightcap nearly lived up to its nocturnal billing, taking 15 innings to complete. Starters Emilio Cueche and Don Cardwell tossed 13 and 14 innings, respectively. Three Marlins errors, including one by the tiring Cardwell, led to the Sugar Kings' first scoring. Cardwell was relieved in the last frame as the pitcher of record on the losing side. Keeping the Marlins off the board for two innings, Connie Marrero picked up the victory after spelling Cueche. Rudy Minarcin wielded the whitewash brush again at Miami Stadium the next day. The 2–0 triumph was the right-hander's 15th and his fourth shutout. In the series finale on September 6, Jerry Lane and Raúl Sánchez combined for a 1–0, ten-inning blanking. Nino Escalera scored the deciding run on a Danny Morejón base hit, after tripling.

Joe Hatten closed out the Sugar Kings' season, three days later, with a 1–0 win over the Marlins in Havana. In sixth place, with a final record of 72–82, the team finished well out of playoff contention. Pitching, which had buoyed the team last season, did not carry over (with the exception of the last week of games). Minarcin headed the mound staff, assuming the heaviest workload with 234 innings, going 15–12 with an ERA under three. Raúl Sánchez won ten games and Joe Hatten nine, as other significant mound contributors. Pat Scantlebury, in between recalls to the Reds, contributed five wins in ten decisions. He posted a sharp 2.57 in 105 innings. On the hitting side, Hal Bevan's .302 average topped all hitters on the team, though he suited up for only 113 games. Playing in 150 contests, Escalera stood out as the most dependable Sugar King; he hit .281, though his slugging dropped off, with only six home runs. Rookie Ultus Alvarez slammed the most Sugar Kings home runs with 16, albeit a paltry number in comparison to the 35 of circuit champion Luke Easter. Owen Friend, who was picked up from Louisville in late May, socked 12 balls out of the park, behind Alvarez's and Woody Smith's 15. But apparently, it was all or nothing for the former Chicago Cubs infielder, as he hit a measly .202 in 94 games. Montreal's Clyde Parris, one of several outstanding players unable to crack the Brooklyn Dodgers' deep infield corps of that decade, topped all IL hitters with a .321 average.

The first-year Miami Marlins (80–71) not only bested their regional neighbors in the standings but at the box office as well—288,582 to 220,357. Their attendance was immensely boosted by a special, IL record crowd of 51,713 at the Orange Bowl on the evening of August 7.[14] (Notwithstanding, the Miami team would still have edged the Sugar Kings.) Of side note interest, Satchel Paige displayed his idiosyncratic skills in the attendance-shattering game against the Columbus Jets and came away with a 6–2 win. The winning hurler pitched 7⅔ innings and helped his cause with a three-run double. Versatile bandleader Cab Calloway and film comedienne Martha Raye headlined the pre-game entertainment. Net proceeds from the nationally promoted game were donated to charity.

Turning to an oft-repeated quote in newspapers during the campaign, Nap Reyes said of the ageless Paige: "He pitched in the gas light age, and now he's pitching in the atomic age."

In the first playoff round, Toronto defeated Montreal, four games to one, and Rochester ousted Miami in the same number of games. Rallying from a 3–2 deficit on the road, Rochester upended the Maple Leafs to win the IL championship.

The Governors' Cup champions were dumped in four straight games by the Indianapolis Indians in the Junior World Series.

1956 International League Final Standings

	W	L	T	PCT	GB	Manager	Major League Affiliation
Toronto Maple Leafs	86	66	1	.566	—	Bruno Betzel	None
Rochester Red Wings	83	67	1	.553	2	Dixie Walker	St. Louis Cardinals
Miami Marlins	80	71	0	.530	5½	Don Osborn	Philadelphia Phillies
Montreal Royals	80	72	1	.526	6	Greg Mulleavy	Brooklyn Dodgers
Richmond Virginians	74	79	0	.484	12½	Eddie Lopat	New York Yankees
Cuban Sugar Kings	72	82	0	.468	15	Reggie Otero/ Nap Reyes	Cincinnati Reds
Columbus Jets	69	84	2	.451	17½	Nick Cullop	Kansas City Athletics
Buffalo Bisons	64	87	0	.424	21½	Phil Cavarretta	None

In January 1957, Maduro flew to Caracas, Venezuela, to scout players in the Venezuelan Winter League. The ten-day ivory hunting expedition also took him into the interior of the country. The most significant result of the ten-day trip was the announced working agreement between the Sugar Kings and the Oriente club, owned by Joe Novas and John Cruz.

On March 9, Cincinnati Reds owner and industrialist Powel Crosley, Jr., and his wife hosted the Reds' annual "family" dinner for club officials, players, writers, sportscasters and their significant others at the Columbia Restaurant in Tampa, Florida, the team's spring training site. Among the 80 or so invited guests were Mr. and Mrs. Bobby Maduro. At the dinner, Crosley made clear that he preferred the "Reds" nickname over "Redlegs," leading to an eventual return to the original nickname, as the Communist hysteria which produced the change began to wane. The Maduros took in the first two games of the Reds' exhibition schedule, March 9 and 10, before flying back to Cuba.

Just three days later, the Maduros' homeland was shaken by a violent, political uprising targeted against the illegitimate government in place since 1952. "Havana was outwardly calm today and business normal," detailed one of the many dispatches flying out of the Cuban capital, two days after the March 13 incident.

> The government withdrew four tanks, guarding approaches to the palace, this morning. Army machine-gun detachments were also withdrawn from the palace entrance, but a reinforced military guard continued on duty. Forty persons were killed in the abortive attempt to kill President Fulgencio Batista and in scattered gunfights against police throughout Havana and its suburbs.[15]

As the autocratic Batista struggled to maintain a sense of overall control, Maduro engaged in a different type of crisis management. The Sugar Kings owner, who had turned 40 last August, was called upon by the Baltimore Orioles to intervene with holdout Willy Miranda. The slick-fielding shortstop had broken off contract talks with the Orioles' front office and had been fined $1,000 for being three weeks late reporting to spring training in Arizona. The Cuban baseball executive convinced Miranda to fly to Scottsdale, where he finally negotiated and signed his 1957 contract.

There were no holdouts on the Sugar Kings when the players gathered in Mexico again for spring camp. The roster boasted its broadest contingent of international players. Athletes of the Americas included natives of the United States, Mexico, Panama, Venezuela, Puerto Rico and Cuba.

The following month, the Cubans jaunted over to Key West for a scheduled three-game exhibition series against the Miami Marlins, April 10–12. The Sugar Kings won the first contest, 6–0, behind pitchers Vicente Amor and Orlando Peña. The second game was called after four innings due to rain, with the third game, the next day, also washed out.

Days later, with the other six clubs not kicking off for two more days, the Sugar Kings opened the IL schedule in Havana on April 15. And what an opening it was, at least in terms of pomp and ceremony. From his press box seat, Cuban sportswriter Máximo Sánchez dispensed this fetching report:

> The most spectacular inaugural ceremonies ever witnessed here marked the International League opener between Montreal and the Cubans. The pre-game show was featured by a novel introduction of the Sugar Kings. As a band pirouetted around the field and passed the scoreboard in deep center field an artistically lighted truck drawn by a jeep appeared with ten girls aboard. A gigantic simulated cake was on the truck. When the cake was cut, the entire Cubans squad sprang out one by one.

The show reached its climax when, with the Stadium lights still off, the national anthem of Cuba was rendered and firecrackers began exploding in front of the left and center field walls. The firecrackers were in the form of the Cuban flag and later depicted the symbol of the Sugar Kings, a huge king wielding a bat with the lettering: "Saludos Amigos" ("We welcome you, friends!")[16]

Circuit chief Frank Shaughnessy threw out the first pitch and watched Royals pitcher Connie Grob command the day, or evening—as did a home viewing audience in the televised inaugural. The former Washington Senators right-hander cruised to a six-hit, 7–2 win. Baltimore Orioles slugging prospect Jim Gentile belted a solo home run in the Royals' 11-hit assault against four Sugar Kings pitchers. The third hurler was Miguel Angel "Mike" Cuéllar, who hurled two scoreless innings in his Sugar Kings debut. Surrendering six runs in five innings, starter Emilio Cueche took the loss in front of 12,000 fans. A threat of rain dissuaded a larger gathering.

Home runs by infielder Witremundo "Witty" Quintana (a grand slam) and Oscar Sierra led the Sugar Kings to a 5–2 win the following evening. Vicente Amor tossed a four-hitter. For the second straight game, the Sugar Kings fielded an all-Hispanic lineup to begin the contest: Scull, cf, Bernard, 2b, Escalera, 1b., Alvarez, rf, Morejón, lf, Quintana, ss, Enrique "Hank" Izquierdo, 3b, Sierra, c. A crowd of 15,000, larger than opening night, showed up and were glad of it.

Rain and an off-day kept the Sugar Kings from playing again until April 21, a Sunday doubleheader versus the Toronto Maple Leafs. After dropping the seven-inning opener, 2–1, Francisco "Panchillo" Ramírez and Orlando Peña combined for a 4–1 victory in the nightcap. Ramírez had been the top pitcher in the Mexican League the prior summer, posting a 20–3 record for the Mexico City Red Devils. The following day, Maduro treated Maple Leafs manager Dixie Walker to a fishing excursion on which Walker landed a seven-foot, 100-pound sailfish. Walker put the special hospitality aside and guided his club to a 5–1 win later in the evening. The Leafs grabbed three out of four games from the Cubans.

The Buffalo Bisons followed Walker's Maple Leafs to Havana and took two weekday games from the home team. The finale of the three-game set was rained out, as was the Saturday game with the new team in town, the Rochester Red Wings. A doubleheader the next day, April 28, placed two Sugar Kings hurlers in the limelight. Vicente Amor, in his third year with the Sugar Kings, tossed a 2–0, seven-inning shutout, allowing just two hits and walking one. Pancho Ramírez outdid his moundmate with a 3–0, seven-hit, regulation-length whitewash in the second game. Fewer than 2,000 fans witnessed the fine exhibition of pitching. The Red

Wings gained their revenge quickly, winning a twin bill the following evening from the home favorites, and the Sugar Kings closed the homestand with a 4–6 record as April expired.

Expectedly, with the less than mediocre showing on display, the team did not initially draw well at home. Early rainouts and persistent soggy weather had not helped. But there were other factors behind the dwindling attendance apart from a lack of winning baseball and threatening skies, as one IL writer documented:

> Havana, the capital of Cuba, has a humid, sub-tropical climate. But so far as International League baseball is concerned, the island city is not so hot. The Cubans seem to be more occupied with bomb-throwers than baseball-throwers. Uneasy residents, apparently fearful of violent political eruptions have turned to the radio and television mediums for their beisbol. Home games are aired on three stations, Union Radio, Circuito Nacional and Radio Deportes, and televised three times a week over CMQ.[17]

Some Northern writers joked that Molotov cocktails were being flung more often in Havana than sharp-breaking curves. In the midst of the political unrest at home, the undaunted boss of Cuban baseball pushed through a proposal to keep expanding the reach of organized baseball in Latin America in conjunction with promoting his team. In early May, Frank Shaughnessy announced an "epochal date" in the history of his league, whereby its territorial dominion would extend, at least temporarily, to a second continent and fourth country. "The Sugar Kings will play a three-game series with the Columbus Jets in Caracas, July 16–17," it was broadly reported. "Cornellian Bob Maduro doesn't expect the situation [in Cuba] to be abated this season and at next winter's session may ask the International League to let him take games deeper into the Southern Hemisphere. Thus a plan in effect this season may be expanded. Maduro indicated that he would have games in Panama, Venezuela and Puerto Rico another year."[18]

If Nap Reyes had not already been managing the Sugar Kings, it was a good bet Maduro would have done all he could to put the Santiago native in the Cubans' dugout. At the helm of the Marianao Tigers, Reyes had led the team to the most recent Cuban Winter League title, and then to a Caribbean Series victory at Gran Stadium two months earlier. He defended his team's stumbling start. "We are far from an eighth-place club," he said, while addressing potential weak spots. "I have too many rookies at this time. I could use another pitcher, a good first string catcher and a long ball hitter."[19]

Reyes had lost starting catcher Oscar Sierra to a broken finger, but pointed to one of his other players, outfielder Danny Morejón, as being off to a tremendous start. Reyes was also surprisingly pleased by Cuban-Venezuelan shortstop Elio Chacón's performance, both in the field and at the plate. Chacón had pushed Witty Quintana over to third base. The displaced Quintana and Morejón keyed a 3–1 Sugar Kings win, May 14, in Richmond. Morejón doubled in one run and Quintana powered one over the wall for another to support Pat Scantlebury's complete-game victory. It came as one of the few wins achieved on a 5–12 road trip that dropped the 9–18 Sugar Kings into last place.

Back home, Jerry Lane, in his second season with the Cubans, pitched eight hitless innings on his way to a one-hit shutout of the Columbus Jets on May 19. Shining with the bat, the 26-year-old Morejón doubled in the only run of the contest in the first inning, the second game of a Sunday double bill. He topped that in his previous at-bat, unloading a three-run home run off Bob Kuzava in the first game's bottom of the eighth inning to give the Sugar Kings a 4–1 win.

On the road trip that followed, a young Sugar Kings pitcher previewed the talent that would eventually summon him to the big leagues and future stardom. A day after recording a 1⅓-inning save against the Columbus Jets, Mike Cuéllar pitched a shutout in his first International League start. Of the seven-inning variety, it came on May 26, versus the Jets; the score was 1–0, in a doubleheader's afterpiece. The two-hitter gave the Cubans a split of the day's action, after the club dropped the opener, 6–4. Four days hence, Cuéllar, who had just turned 20, combined with Orlando Peña on another two-hit, seven-inning blanking. The victims were the Miami Marlins. Rain washed out the nightcap, additionally disappointing the holiday crowd of 6,000 at Miami Stadium. Escaping the basement, the Cubans scaled into sixth place.

It seemed Cuéllar was specifically relegated to seven-inning contests when in his third start, on June 7, he blanked the Buffalo Bison, 5–0, in the first of two scheduled games. He permitted four singles and extending his scoreless innings string to 22. Three Sugar Kings pitchers continued the goose-egg parade in the regulation-length nightcap, taking a 4–0 victory. A left-hander, Cuéllar picked up his fourth unblemished victory on June 8. In ninth-inning relief of starter Jerry Lane, Cuéllar became a winner when the Sugar Kings rallied for two last-at-bat runs against the Buffalo Bisons. Nino Escalera's single brought home the winning tally. Two nights later, the young southpaw saved another game, pitching the bottom of the ninth at Montreal. Trailing by five runs, the Royals had rocked Sugar Kings starter Pat Scantlebury for a pair of two-run home runs, tightening the contest to 6–5; Cuéllar was summoned to record the final three outs. With the win, the now fifth-place Sugar Kings bettered their record to 26–28, a game out of the first division.

Cuéllar had been discovered by one of Maduro's scouts in the island's centrally located Las Villas province. A native of Santa Clara, the provincial capital, Cuéllar had been pitching weekends for an army team. He had enlisted in the army, the story goes, to avoid having to cut cane. "The army captain threatened to throw our scout in jail if he even talked to the boy,"[20] said Maduro, who was given credit for arranging Cuéllar's release to the Almendares club. As a 19-year-old, Cuéllar had his professional baptism with the Scorpions the prior winter, appearing in five games, winning his only decision with a complete game.

An exciting comeback victory on June 13 at Delorimier Stadium, kept the Kings clawing toward .500. An Ultus Alvarez three-run blast in the eighth inning tied the game at seven-all. The Sugar Kings came away win-

Two of the Sugar Kings' best hurlers, Orlando Peña and Mike Cuéllar. Peña, left, missed the 1959 championship season, toiling for the Cincinnati Reds. Cuéllar posted the best ERA (2.86) in franchise history and tied with Emilio Cueche for most lifetime shutouts with ten (courtesy Ralph Maya).

ners, 8–7, on a bases-loaded walk in the next stanza, for a split of their four-game series with Montreal.

At the end of June, Vernon "Lefty" Gómez visited Havana as part of a promotion involving Los Cubanitos. The Spanish-Irish Gómez appeared on local radio and television shows and was seen sharing pitching tips with a legion of the Cuban Little Leaguers. Gómez, who had managed Cienfuegos in the winter league in 1947–1948, attended as a guest of honor at a Cubanitos luncheon, where he was joined by Maduro, among others.

A commercial revelation in *The Sporting News* following the Gómez visit offered a snapshot into a Maduro-involved side business. Branch Rickey's American Baseball Cap Company reported hefty profits, as more and more ballplayers began accepting the wearing of plastic helmets, in one form or another. Among the stockholders in the manufacturing firm, *TSN* reported, were home run king Ralph Kiner, hitting giant George Sisler and Roberto Maduro.

A public revelation on July 3 cast a pall over Cuban baseball. Sixty-six-year-old Adolfo Luque, the major leagues' first Hispanic star, died of heart failure in a Havana hospital, to the sorrowful loss of an entire nation. The Sugar Kings were in Columbus. It was the second passing of a Cuban diamond great within ten weeks. On April 25, Lázaro Salazar shockingly suffered a cerebral hemorrhage while managing a game for the Mexico City Red Devils, and died the next day. He was only 45 and, apart from being an outstanding former player, had already won over 1,100 games piloting teams in Mexico and Venezuela.

The week of Luque's passing, Fred Jones, president of the Columbus Jets, announced that he planned to fly the team's directors in his private jet to Caracas for the club's groundbreaking series against the Cubans. But shortly thereafter, the two-day face-off was called off due to a conflict in scheduling dates with the *Pequeña Copa del Mundo de Clubes* (Little World Cup). The soccer tournament consisted of two European teams (Barcelona and Sevilla) and two from South America (Brazil and Uruguay). The deflating declaration left many scratching their heads at the lack of calendar purview by Venezuelan officials. A modern baseball park called University Stadium had opened in Caracas in 1953. Like Gran Stadium, it was a multi-purpose facility. The stadium was commandeered for the soccer games, leaving the Sugar Kings and Jets without an adequate place to play.

The series was rescheduled to Havana. As it took place, *Atlanta Journal* sports editor Furman Bisher authored a provocative piece indicating that the Atlanta Crackers would be climbing up the minor league ladder to take the place of the Sugar Kings in the International League next season, due to lack of fan support currently being experienced in Havana. Bisher hedged his story by saying that if the move into the IL failed, the Crackers would have the option of replacing Wichita's American Association franchise.

Maduro categorically denied any opinion of the Sugar Kings not operating in 1958. Gabe Paul also assured fans: "Havana is a solvent operation, and has no intention of moving."[21]

"I have heard absolutely nothing about such a move," minor league head George M. Trautman stated from Columbus, Ohio. "Our Havana club is well operated by Bob Maduro. Atlanta has long been a keystone of the Southern Association and I know of no reason why it should not remain there."[22]

From Montreal, Harry Simmons, the IL's secretary, labeled the report baseless. "There has never been any talk of moving the Havana franchise, nor any intention," he said. "It is common knowledge that Havana has been hurt by the situation there, but no one has ever suggested moving the team, nor has anyone from Atlanta made approaches as far as this office knows."[23]

Like many far-reaching announcements, it turned out to be nothing but wild speculation. As far as the standings were concerned, it was still anybody's guess whether the Cubans would make the playoffs. Reyes' band had entered July with a deflating 33–43 mark. But playing its best ball of the season and winning 20 games in the month, the sixth-place squad would roll into August with a still-tattered record of 53–58, yet only three games out of playoff contention.

The Sugar Kings picked up an experienced pitching commodity from the Buffalo Bisons to help them in their playoff push. Burdened with an 0–5 record, José Santiago, who the prior season had been pitching in the major leagues, was sold to the Cubans by Buffalo. Nicknamed "Pantalones" ("Pants"), Santiago threw a shutout in his first start for the Cubans on July 28. Taking only an hour and 40 minutes, he blanked the Montreal Royals on four hits in the back end of a doubleheader at Gran Stadium. Orlando Peña twirled a seven-inning, 2–1 decision in the lid-lifter. Time of that game was 1:51.

The Montreal Royals were a last-place club with little chance of making the post-season. Their visit to Havana was made in a spirit at odds with the usual sense of eagerness or expectation that filled most visiting teams who touched down in the Cuban capital. The reason, typified in the following report, was one that would interminably entwine itself with the sport into the next century—politics:

> Bobby Maduro, president of the Havana Sugar Kings, assured President Frank Shaughnessy of the International League that the anonymous telephone calls and death threats received by the Royals were of "no importance." Each Montreal player received airmail leaflets, postmarked Havana, warning him not to go to Cuba for the scheduled weekend series. The players met after last night's game against the Miami Marlins and agreed to fly here this morning "under protest."
> Maduro assured Shaughnessy by telephone that "nothing has happened here and nothing is going to happen." Havana has been rocked by political unrest in recent months.
> Montreal players spent the day today calmly wandering about the lobby, swimming pool and gardens of their luxurious hotel.[24]

Maduro's assurances proved correct. The series was conducted without incident. But the next team to come to town, the Rochester Red Wings, were also harassed beforehand. Eleven "warning letters" were received by Red Wings players during a layover in Miami on August 5. The country's political strife could no longer be ignored. Neither could its effect on the Sugar Kings' attendance. In an atmosphere of eerie emptiness, few fans were regularly braving their way to Gran Stadium to see their team. "Braving" clearly was the operative word, judged by the first-hand account by a Rochester sportswriter:

> On the day the Red Wings landed in Havana [August 6] a bomb exploded in a Woolworth five and ten store. A woman lost her arm and was reported near death. Six other civilians were injured seriously.
> In the press box in Gran Stadium, the first night of the series, this reporter typed sidebar notes about the bombing ... about the wife of club owner Bobby Maduro and one of his children having been in a store across the street at the time of the bombing ... about warnings to avoid certain downtown areas and other places at various hours ... about warnings to players not to answer anonymous phone calls to the Nacional Hotel ... about censorship and suppression of news in the capital city Havana.[25]

Amid the suppression of civil liberties for the first time in Cuba, the Sugar Kings carried on. The game of August 6 was won by Red Wings pitcher Gary Blaylock, 2–1, in 11 innings. A home run by Gene Green in the decisive frame handed Blaylock the run he needed for the well-earned victory. A visiting writer estimated the Gran Stadium crowd as the smallest he had seen in four years of travels to Havana. The next day, José Santiago responded splendidly to his new pitching environs with another whitewash in his next start. Again as a doubleheader's nightcap hurler, the right-hander silenced the bats of the Rochester Red Wings, allowing three singles, to collect a 2–0 victory. The Sugar Kings did not fare as well in the first game, bowing 4–2 in eight innings. Outfielder Gene Green repeated his home run heroics from the previous evening, stroking a deciding, two-run home run in the extra frame, in what one northern writer dubbed as "boiling Gran Stadium" because of the heat.

Someone used to a steamy climate, José Santiago is one of the last of a dwindling breed of "golden era" winter and summer league players. He has resided in one of San Juan's best-known residential high-rise condominiums for more than 30 years, the last few without his deceased wife Matilde, to whom he was married for 65 years.

> I can never lie about my age because I was born nine days before Hurricane San Felipe, a devastating storm that hit Puerto Rico in September of 1928. I was brought to New York from Puerto Rico by my father when I was 27 days old. It was San Juan with a stop in Port-au-Prince, to Miami, and then a train to New York. It took five days back then to get from Puerto Rico to New York! I returned to Puerto Rico because my father wanted me to learn Spanish—but I came back to the U.S. as a teenager. I went to Seward Park High in lower Manhattan, near the Williamsburg Bridge.
>
> I was signed by the Cleveland Indians, but they had so many good pitchers. Yet I made the team coming out spring training in 1954. And you know what kind of pitching staff they had that year—Feller … Lemon … Mike García … Early Wynn.
>
> I really believe I was obtained by Maduro because of the success I had pitching against Cuban teams in the Caribbean Series. I later recommended Tite Arroyo to Maduro. I did not pitch well with Buffalo. After I was signed by the Sugar Kings, I rented an apartment in Havana, and my wife and two little girls came to live with me. I was paid well, I guess because I was a veteran. That was 1957. I had hurt my arm the year before pitching a game I wasn't expecting to pitch. I was with the Kansas City Athletics then. I told Lou Boudreau [manager] I wasn't feeling up to pitching. But in those days, if a manager told you to do something he didn't take no for an answer.
>
> I remember my first year with the Sugar Kings after one game in Montreal, Napoleón Reyes was the manager. We were not playing well. Reyes came into the clubhouse and looked at us and said, "Many of you will not be here next year." I thought I may have been one of them. But then in 1958, I was back with the Sugar Kings and started the first game the team played outside Havana—in Morón.
>
> Maduro had an organizational set-up like organized baseball. He had scouts all over Cuba. Fidel [Castro] used what Maduro had set up in the provinces, that infrastructure, for developing players for all those years [later].[26]

League-leading Buffalo followed the Red Wings into town. In the most eventful day of the series, a Sunday diamond duet on August 11, the clubs broke even. In a pitchers' duel in the first contest, the Sugar Kings gained a 1–0, 15-inning victory, the only run scored by Yo-Yo Davalillo. Mike Cuéllar hurled the first 13 frames and combined with Orlando Peña on a seven-hitter. In the process, the pair kept the Bisons' Luke Easter, who was having a monster slugging year, under wraps. Lou Kretlow pitched into the tenth inning before he was relieved by loser Ray Herbert. The second game score was 4–2, Buffalo plating two late-inning runs on errors.

Cuéllar won his seventh decision against four setbacks on August 17 at Montreal. Erupting for eight runs, on seven hits, in the tenth inning, the sixth-place Sugar Kings gained their 59th victory by an unusual extra-inning score of 11–3. The next evening at Delorimier Stadium, the International League All-Star Game was held. In only its second year, the showcase game matched the IL's best against the reigning National League champion. Coincidentally, Montreal was the host city, and the Brooklyn Dodgers, the Royals' parent club, were the opponents. Cuéllar and Orlando Peña were the only Sugar Kings selectees for the game, although three other Cuban nationals throughout the league were also chosen: infielder Héctor Rodríguez, pitcher René Valdés, and former Sugar Kings catcher Ray Noble. Nap Reyes served as a coach. Although Cuéllar had pitched ten innings two evenings earlier, IL All-Star manager Dixie Walker called on him for one inning of work. Trying to protect a 1–0 lead, the left-hander surrendered the tying run to the Dodgers in the eighth inning. The big league club pushed across a run in the top of the 11th against the Red Wings' Lynn Lovenguth for a 2–1 victory. Hurling four scoreless relief innings, Sandy Koufax notched the win. The Dodgers flew into town for the Monday exhibition on their 44-passenger, twin-engine Convair 440 airplane and left the same day.

The Sugar Kings scratched to within a game and a half of fourth place, following dual road wins over the Columbus Jets on August 25. Cuéllar emerged victorious, 9–4, benefiting from eight runs the Sugar Kings scored over the final three innings. In the seven-inning second game, Ultus Alvarez clocked the big hit, a grand slam. The final was 10–4.

At Gran Stadium, Cuéllar saved José Santiago's fourth win since joining the Sugar Kings, on August 29. One out shy of a 2–1, complete-game victory over the Richmond Virginians, Santiago pulled a muscle. Cuéllar came in to claim the 27th Virginian victim. The seemingly revived team had received some disheartening news two days earlier, when Frank Shaughnessy confirmed that he would not permit any of his International League teams to travel to Havana, in the event the Sugar Kings reached the post-season. Shaughnessy pointed to the economic disadvantages involved with the unstable political climate.

As it turned out, any fanciful hope for a Nap Reyes championship trifecta slowly dissipated in the final two weeks of the campaign. The

Cubans, 72–82, were passed in the standings by the Rochester Red Wings and had to settle for sixth place, 3½ games out of the first division. Defeating the Sugar Kings, 7–2, in Havana, the Miami Marlins clinched the final playoff spot in the next-to-last game of the season.

Miami reached the championship finals after beating the Toronto Maple Leafs in six first-round games. But the Florida team was defeated in a series of five contests by the second-seeded Buffalo Bisons. The Governors' Cup champions possessed a powerful hitting duo in batting titleist Joe Caffie (.330) and league home run and RBI champ Luke Easter (40/128).

Phil Cavarretta's team stumbled in the Junior World Series, winning only one game against the American Association champion Denver Bears.

For the Sugar Kings, Danny Morejón's team-leading .296 batting average was good enough to crack the top ten of International League hitters. Ultus Alvarez enjoyed his best slugging season with 18 home runs. The Kings undeniably suffered from the loss of Nino Escalera, who was struck with hepatitis in late June and missed the rest of the season. Another starter, Panamanian Pablo Bernard, was purchased by the Indianapolis Indians on July 15. From the mound, Mike Cuéllar, who won his first five decisions, posted an 8–7 record with a fine 2.44 ERA (tops in the league) in 155 innings. Orlando Peña and Pat Scantlebury tied for most wins on the club with 12. Vicente Amor, an 11-game winner, was recalled by the Cincinnati Reds on July 24. José Santiago went 4–2, in a promising turnaround from his winless Buffalo record.

The attendance nosedived to only 84,320, a more than 130 percent decline from last season's 220,357 total.

1957 International League Final Standings

	W	L	T	PCT	GB	Manager	Major League Affiliation
Toronto Maple Leafs	88	65	2	.575	—	Dixie Walker	None
Buffalo Bisons	88	66	0	.571	½	Phil Cavarretta	Kansas City Athletics
Richmond Virginians	81	73	1	.526	7½	Eddie Lopat	New York Yankees
Miami Marlins	75	78	2	.490	13	Don Osborne	Philadelphia Phillies
Rochester Red Wings	74	80	0	.481	14½	Cot Deal	St. Louis Cardinals
Cuban Sugar Kings	72	82	0	.468	16½	Nap Reyes	Cincinnati Reds

Four—"Los Cubanitos"

	W	L	T	PCT	GB	Manager	Major League Affiliation
Columbus Jets	69	85	0	.448	19½	Frank Oceak	Detroit Tigers
Montreal Royals	68	86	1	.442	20½	Tommy Holmes/ Greg Mulleavy/ Al Ronning	Brooklyn Dodgers

Five

Championship Glory Amid Political Discord

Belying the box office collapse at Gran Stadium, Havana, at least in one broad commercial sector, was humming along. "Nineteen hundred and fifty-seven was one of the best years in the economic history of Cuba,"[1] stated the U.S. Ambassador to Cuba, Earl E. T. Smith, a few years later to a U.S. Senate Subcommittee. Backing Smith's claim were the grand inaugurations of three luxury hotels within a few months of each other. In November 1957, the $5 million Hotel Capri opened; the following month the Hotel Riviera, with its $10 million price tag, flung open its doors for the first time; and on March 28, 1958, the 650-room, $22 million Havana Hilton welcomed guests for the first time, as the largest hotel in Latin America.

The same month as the Capri's launching, Bobby Maduro passed out cigars for the eighth and final time, celebrating the arrival of daughter Isabel. The previous month, Maduro had quelled a speculated rebirth, of sorts, for his franchise. The announced abandonment of New York by both of the city's National League teams to the West Coast reopened the Jersey City, New Jersey, territory for the International League. Jersey City had been one of the original 19th century franchises in the IL until the parent New York Giants sold the club in 1950 to the Philadelphia Athletics, whose directors moved the team to Ottawa. Both Maduro's Sugar Kings and the two-year-old Miami Marlins were singled out as the most viable candidates for relocation to the Northeast population center. Miami, perhaps not by coincidence, along with the Sugar Kings, had endured a sharp attendance decline of more than 100,000 fans from its inaugural season. (Although if the special Satchel Paige–Orange Bowl game from 1956 were removed from the equation, the drop for Miami was nowhere near as steep as Havana.)

"We are not interested in transferring our franchise to Jersey City or anywhere else," Maduro clearly stated. "The Sugar Kings will remain in Havana."[2]

"We are quite happy with Miami and would like to stay there,"[3] Marlins general manager Joe Ryan said, in an attempt to dispel any notions to the contrary.

Talk of the potential move of the Sugar Kings, for valid reasons, would not go away throughout the winter and spring months.

In January 1958, part of a *New York Times* story projected to the Northern Hemisphere the welcome news most of the island's populace had already received: "Guarantees of constitutional rights were restored to the people of Cuba, with the exception of Oriente province, early today by President Fulgencio Batista. This means that censorship of press and radio is ended in five [of Cuba's six] provinces. The constitutional guarantees had been inoperative since the start of this year and during most of 1957."[4]

As Batista, more and more, resorted to brutality to keep his hold on power, the sports page focus veered toward the Cuban Winter League, where another American League pitching hopeful was making a significant mark. "A Cuban sugar king who touted Detroit on Jim Bunning last winter and turned out to be a true prophet, is tabbing Bob Shaw as the hottest pitching prospect in the Tigers organization," publicized *AP* writer Joe Reichler. "Bob Maduro, owner of the Havana club in the International League and one of the most respected men in baseball, told Tiger officials recently that the 24-year-old Bronx-born right-hander is a cinch to make it big in the majors. 'Remember I gave you Bunning last year,' Maduro said. 'This year I'm telling you that Shaw can become one of your regular pitchers in a year or two. He's the best in Cuba right now.'"[5]

Maduro had furnished Detroit's organization with a ringing endorsement on Bunning the previous winter, after the Kentucky native had distinguished himself with the Marianao Tigers. Following his Cuban campaign, Bunning, in his first full major league season in 1957, had won 20 games for the Tigers of Detroit. Although Shaw would not pan out as broadly as Bunning, the New Yorker did spearhead the Nap Reyes–led Marianao Tigers to a second straight Caribbean Series victory. A 14-game winner in the winter league, Shaw hurled a 2–0 victory in the Caribbean Classic's championship game, February 13, versus the Caguas Criollos in San Juan.

A few weeks before Shaw's championship gem, the Sugar Kings and Maduro sustained more dubious publicity.

> President Frank Shaughnessy of the International League said tonight the Havana Sugar Kings may have to move to another city if the club fails to get official aid promised it. Shaughnessy said Bob Maduro advised him that he is disappointed because the official aid promised has not materialized. Shaughnessy did not say what official aid constitutes but added that the club also is having a difficult time in getting advertisers interested in paying for broadcasting of the Cubans' games.[6]

A month earlier, Maduro had had a sit-down with the Cuban government's strong-armed leader, Batista. It was reported that the right-wing dictator had pledged to Maduro that he would "extend all possible aid." Apparently, that assistance was currently lacking or not forthcoming.[7] Maduro turned to Havana's civic leaders for support.

Bernard J. Berry, former Jersey City, NJ, mayor and current park commissioner, tried to take advantage of a viewed opportunity and traveled to Havana the first week of February to meet with Maduro. He sailed home on February 7, offering no comment to the inquiring press. Maduro's steadfast remarks of the same day may have accounted for Berry's reticence. "As long as I continue to get the support of Cuban fans to help the team financially," Maduro said, "there is little possibility I would move the squad northward."[8]

With the start of the 1958 IL season three weeks away and his team conducting training exercises in Trinidad, Maduro invited Rochester community baseball club president Frank Horton and head honcho Frank Shaughnessy to spend two days at his home in Havana. The pair spoke to newspapermen, ambassadors, city officials and common citizens; they attended a jai-alai match and passed several movie theaters, concluding that reports of a disruptive city life were exaggerated. They did, however, mention a striking lack of movement around hotels, recognizing a suffering tourist industry. "Why there's less violence in Havana than there is in New York," said Shaughnessy upon his return. "You can say definitely that we will start our season April 16 with the same eight teams we had last year. Havana is one of those teams."[9]

Inviting the IL executives to his home was a strategic move by Maduro that not only paid off but went a long way in reassuring important others who harbored concerns over the continuance of baseball in the Cuban capital. "There was talk that the trouble in Cuba might make it wise to move the Havana franchise to Tampa and I even suggested it to Bob Maduro," Shaughnessy added. "He talked me into going down there and seeing for myself. I'll tell you, some of the stories I have been reading in the papers are a joke. Most of the trouble is way up at the other end of the island but at Havana it's all right."[10]

Maduro's dilapidated waterfront home today (side view). Mostly hidden by the guest house behind the seawall, part of the main two-story residence is seen with the old water tank on its flat roof. Photograph is taken from the property line of the former Havana Biltmore Yacht & Country Club (renamed Club Havana). At the extreme left, a beach recreation area is partially visible. The author was not allowed on the property as the zone is for the exclusive use of military personnel and their families (author's colection).

But Havana was not all right—at least not to the complete satisfaction of the teams that were required to travel there. Ten days before the scheduled curtain-raiser in the capital, Shaughnessy yielded to pressure from the circuit's owners to reevaluate, if not reconsider his earlier position. "The league has scheduled a meeting in Miami, Fla., next Sunday [April 6] to consider the possibility of moving the Sugar Kings franchise to another site," read a troublesome *UP* affirmation from Havana. "President Frank Shaughnessy said that some league teams are 'scared' to come here because of the current political unrest. Among cities mentioned as possible relocation sites are Jersey City, N.J. and Tampa, Fla."[11]

"I've never run into anything this tough," admitted Shaughnessy on the eve of the meeting, expressing the touch-and-go nature of the volatile situation. "Everything is so damned indefinite now I'm not sure what we will do. I think the newspapers are magnifying this thing in Cuba.... I was in Havana two weeks ago and it was as quiet as Fort Lauderdale. But with all these teams frightened, something has to be done."[12]

The Los Angeles Dodgers' announced canceling of a three-game exhibition between the Montreal Royals and Sugar Kings in Cuba, the day before the special meeting, did not further the Sugar Kings' cause. Instead, the Cubans trekked to Cienfuegos, 150 miles southeast of Havana, and played a game in front of 4,000 fans.

The awaited outcome from Miami resulted in a positive and undisruptive move forward. From at least one print account, it could be gathered that one man's influence had clearly been responsible for the status quo: "The Sugar Kings of the class AAA minor league got the green light to open as scheduled against the Buffalo Bisons on April 16. Club owner Bob Maduro, in an hour-long speech, assured the league that baseball in Cuba will not be affected by the political strife.

"The eight league representatives voted unanimously to permit the Sugar Kings to remain but attached a condition. In the event the situation 'deteriorates,' and by that Shaughnessy meant 'some actual shooting takes place,' the franchise would be moved to another city."[13]

In a nightmarish plot twist, the firearms caveat laid down by Shaughnessy came to pass all too quickly. On April 9, eight insurgents were killed and three policemen wounded in separate incidents in the capital. Shaughnessy was on the phone to Maduro the next day. To his credit, the 74-year-old league president did not commit to a knee-jerk reaction, even when *United Press* later upped the loss of life to 15. The violence was a culmination of an anticipated day of revolt that rebel leader Fidel Castro had called upon some of his dissatisfied fellow countrymen to undertake. A massive general strike on the part of the populace had been urged by Castro's revolutionary lieutenants but failed to materialize. In the end, Maduro convinced Shaughnessy to hold off on a final decision until the weekend.

That weekend the Sugar Kings hopped over to Key West to play a couple of tune-up games. Maduro resisted an overture by a local city commissioner and ardent baseball fan to make the resort town a temporary home for the Sugar Kings. "We are going to play in Havana and that's definite," Maduro emphasized from the United States' southernmost city. "We just played three games in Morón, 250 miles into the interior of Cuba and rumored to be a troubled spot," he added. "We had no incidents whatsoever."[14] The practice games at Morón, located in the central part of the island and much closer to perceived rebel stronghold areas, were obviously arranged by Maduro to placate the watchful eyes of organized baseball.

Convening another "special owner's meeting" in Miami on Sunday, April 13, Shaughnessy showed he was not without doubts. The action may have been forced by the previous day's fracturing announcement by the Buffalo Bisons that they were *not* going to go to Cuba. Nevertheless, the owners reaffirmed their prior decision to open in Havana as scheduled—with the one dissenting vote. "One life saved is worth all the franchises and money in the world," stated Buffalo Bisons president John C. Stiglmeier. "We're not so mercenary as to risk having one of our players killed or kidnapped."[15]

"After speaking to the American ambassador [Earl E. T. Smith], I decided that things in Cuba had not materially changed [for the worse],"[16] Shaughnessy commented.

"We are going to be in Havana on the 16th," the unwavering Maduro said. "If Buffalo isn't we win four games."[17]

It took a pledge from the league to assume responsibility for all traveling players' safety (in the form of a $1,000,000 insurance indemnification policy) and a personal phone call from Ambassador Smith to Stiglmeier to convince the Buffalo owner not to disrupt the planned commencement of the International League's 75th season. "If children play in the streets, why can't men play in the stadium?"[18] said Smith, who was scheduled to throw out the first ball at the home opener.

Maduro used a child of his own—literally—to make a similar point. The Cubans owner and his young daughter Rosario met the Buffalo Bisons team plane from Miami at Havana International Airport on April 16. "What are the Buffalo Bisons?" responds Rosi Chica (née Maduro) 59 years later, when asked if she recollected the occurrence. "I was five years old, and don't remember anything about that."[19]

"A [police] escort rode behind the bus to and from the hotel," recorded one Buffalo sportswriter, "[and] there were plainclothesmen on the bench behind the dugout. 'But I'm sure now,' said Buffalo manager Phil Cavarretta, 'that the situation was magnified and we did not need any protection. After the second day, the plainclothesmen didn't show up, and we did not ask any questions. They knew we were convinced.'"[20]

As implied by the preceding overview, the inaugural occurred without extraneous incident. A crowd topping 10,000, including Frank Shaughnessy and Ambassador Smith, witnessed an uplifting, comeback win by the Sugar Kings, who plated three ninth-inning runs to register the 6–5 success. Catcher Sam Calderone lined a bases-loaded, two-run single to bring home the winning runs, after Danny Morejón had singled in Yo-Yo Davalillo with the first scoring of the inning. With an inning of scoreless relief, Rodolfo "Rudy" Arias, the last of five Sugar Kings pitchers on the evening, gained the win. (An amusing aside involving the 29-year-old Davalillo, who stood 5'3", occurred when he brought his diminutive younger brother Vic to the Sugar Kings' training camp the prior month.

"Is that your brother or your son?" Maduro responded when asked by Davalillo to give his sibling a tryout. The elder Davalillo was on his way to earning a distinctive place in Sugar Kings history. The undersized player would play in more games than any other franchise member, 641, and would record the most at-bats, 2,215, hits, 610, doubles, 93, and runs, 268.)

In their next game, pinch-hitting for starter Mike Cuéllar, Rogelio Alvarez (no relation to Ultus) whacked a game-tying, two-run home run in the bottom of the eighth inning. Four frames later, a bases-loaded walk to Elio Chacón forced in the Sugar Kings' third and winning run. Bisons starter Harry Taylor lost the arduous, 12-inning effort. On April 19, a day after his 20th birthday, Rogelio Alvarez crashed two more home runs and drove in four runs, leading the Sugar Kings to a 5–3 victory, the team's third in four tries against the defending Governors' Cup holders.

The first Sunday doubleheader brought out around 5,000 spectators on April 20, but did nothing to promote higher team expectations. The Rochester Red Wings knocked off the Cubans twice on the afternoon. The next day, long balls from Morejón and Witty Quintana helped clip the Red Wings, 6–2. In relief of Cuéllar, Raúl Sánchez earned his second victory.

Taking the starter's hill for the first time on April 23, Orlando Peña utilized four first-inning runs by the Sugar Kings to carry through to a 5–1 decision over the Toronto Maple Leafs. The Cubans and Maple Leafs split the next two games of the three-game set.

The first game of another Sunday twin bill, on April 27, saw Mike Cuéllar pick up his initial win, 3–1. Against the Montreal Royals, first baseman Jack Daniels doubled home Nino Escalera and Elio Chacón in the fourth frame of the seven-inning contest for the deciding scores. The Royals nabbed the nine-inning afterpiece, 3–2. The Royals' Clyde Parris singled home the game-tilting run in the seventh. Designated in the dual role as Montreal's pitching coach and starting staff component that season, Tommy Lasorda, 30, put on an attention-grabbing exhibition on the art of hurling for his entire staff the following evening. Coming off a one-hit shutout over the Miami Marlins in his previous start, Lasorda blanked the Sugar Kings on three hits. The winning score was 5–0; the Kings closed their first homestand splitting 14 games against four visiting teams.

Another Sunday doubleheader, this one at the outset of the Sugar Kings' first road trip, previewed the type of season in store for the Havana club. The Kings were unable to dent the plate in either game of the May 4 Sabbath duet in Montreal. Opening the festivities, Lasorda threw his second shutout against the Cubans, and third overall, permitting six hits. Royals batters battered four Sugar Kings pitchers for 14 runs. Babe Birrer authored the second blanking, 10–0, in the (merciful) seven-inning second game. Sugar Kings hitters managed only ten hits on the day, while their counterparts teed off for 32.

The 15–21 Cubans reached the quarter pole of the season, May 24, boosted by an unusual 13-hit shutout engineered by José Santiago over Rochester. At Red Wing Stadium, the right-hander pitched around ten singles, a pair of doubles and a triple to pull in a 5–0 win. He walked one. A two-run homer by countryman Nino Escalera provided some of the backing for Santiago.

The second-division club showed they were not complete pushovers, battling—in more ways than one—to a 6–5 win versus the Buffalo Bisons a few days later. Ahead by one run, Vicente Amor decided to push the bounds of competitiveness and whizzed a fast pitch behind the head of Luke Easter in the bottom of the eighth inning. The Bisons slugger had won the first game of the Offermann Stadium series with a ninth-inning single. He had homered earlier against Amor and had collected eight hits in three games. Easter threw his bat in the direction of Amor, who avoided the lumber and then swung a left hook into the face of Hank Izquierdo as the backstop attempted to intercede. Both benches cleared, and when order was restored Easter had been ejected. (Seemingly getting off lightly, the star player was fined $100 by Shaughnessy, but not suspended for the bat throwing or fighting.) Morejón and Davalillo went deep for the Sugar Kings, as Amor, finished the contest to record his first win.

The next night, May 29, a carbon copy incident provoked another brawl between the two teams. After surrendering a circuit clout to Tony González, Bisons pitcher Dave Newkirk sailed a high hard one over the head of the next hitter, Witty Quintana. The Sugar Kings infielder dropped his bat and raced out to the mound, where both men engaged in fisticuffs. Quintana was expelled. Two home runs by González and one each by Rogelio Alvarez and Escalera forged a 10–4 victory for the road team. Reached for nine hits, four bases on balls, and striking out 11, starter and finisher José Santiago won his third game in five decisions in the high-pitch-count effort. (Coincidentally or not, Shaughnessy would soon implement an "anti-duster rule," which automatically ejected any pitcher who threw at a batter immediately following a home run.)

Nap Reyes again, the manager of the fifth-place team, remained optimistic, pointing out to an IL writer a camaraderie that existed on his club, which he evidently felt would translate into more wins. "Reyes," wrote the scribe, "who has to deliver his clubhouse oratory in both Spanish and English, says current squad has best spirit of any club he's managed in the International. In the past, the Sugar King squad has been noted for splitting into nationalized cliques. 'This year,' says Reyes, 'Jack Daniels is at first base and he has great team spirit. He keeps my infield together, and off the field my guys are together, too, for the first time.'"[21]

Buffalo, which had initial trepidations about commencing the season in Havana and had sunk to the bottom of the standings, became the first IL team to engage the Sugar Kings in Cuba outside the capital. Morón was a town of about 35,000, located in the eastern province of Camagüey. Morón's notoriety stemmed from being a railroad hub that had facilitated the expansion of Cuba's centralized sugar mill commerce. A new municipal stadium had been constructed there the prior year with a seating capacity of more than 6,000. Gladdening the hearts of city fathers, Maduro had taken out a ten-year lease on the park, which had been installed with lights and was the only stadium in Cuba with an electric scoreboard. On June 6–8, four games were conducted, attracting 17,000 baseball enthusiasts. The first contest (started by José Santiago) ended in a 6–6 tie because of a late first pitch and league curfew. The game did not start until 10:40 p.m. because of travel delays encountered by the visiting team due to rainy weather. The Cubans then swept a low-scoring doubleheader, 3–0 and 2–1. Orlando Peña tossed the seven-inning shutout, while Mike Cuéllar made two first-inning runs hold up in pitching a four-hitter in the second contest. Buffalo salvaged the rain-shortened, Sunday finale, 4–3, to the complete disapproval of 6,000 fans. Catching for the Bisons, Ray Noble's seventh-inning, two-run home run preceding the rains delivered the game to the last-place New York team. Residual significance to the series manifested itself quickly afterward with the announcement that the Sugar Kings had topped last season's woeful attendance mark of 87,000.

Although the Sugar Kings struggled at several games below .500, games like the one on June 23 went a long way in continuing the demonstrable reversal of last season's turnstile misfortunes. In the most dramatic fashion, Danny Morejón ended an extra-inning game in the Cubans' favor, 6–4. Putting the 11-inning, home win in the books, Morejón blasted a two-run bomb against former Sugar Kings and current Toronto Maple Leafs hurler Pat Scantlebury. Intended for seven innings as the first of two games on the day, the extended game forced the nightcap to be halted after seven frames because of curfew with the Sugar Kings ahead, 3–0. A Monday crowd of 4,500 attended. A three-run circuit clout by Morejón had also been the difference in a 5–2 win over Toronto two days earlier. Jose Santiago (4–5) pitched a six-hitter. It was the Puerto Rican hurler's last win for the Sugar Kings. After successive losses, the Kings sent the pitcher to the Texas League's San Antonio Missions.

The long-term lease on Morón Stadium had been part of a three-point plan of Maduro to not only win back the absent followers of his club but broaden its base of appeal. Back in February, he had verbally staked his team's future on "the support of Cuban fans." That same month, Maduro instituted a "Fans Club." Membership fee of six dollars included entry to every Sugar Kings game at the general admission level. Everyone had the unrestricted option of upgrading to reserve or box seating by paying the difference in price at the games of their choosing. Maduro had been pleased by 10,000 memberships sold, considering the short marketing period available prior to the season and the sidetracking foreign press coverage of the Sugar Kings. A newspaper advanced the impression that Maduro used hometown media coverage as a tool to his advantage whenever possible and that the initial success of the "Fan's Club" could be derived as a reflection of that business acumen: "There are 17 newspapers in Havana, a fact that provides wide publicity for baseball clubs. Roberto Maduro, Cubans (International League) owner, is adept at getting along with the press."[22]

The third point of action enacted by Maduro came by way of an accented call-up of the young talent the Sugar Kings had been developing in their established baseball schools, tryout camps and scouting programs. Rogelio Alvarez (nicknamed "Borrego," or "lamb" in English) had developed into an unexpected slugger at only 20 years of age. Another 20-year-old, Luis Zayas, had worked his way into the Kings' starting lineup as an infielder and outfielder. Also a flychaser, Andrés Antonio "Tony" González, 21, appeared to be the best of the three youths regularly contributing to the Sugar Kings. González, a future 12-year big league veteran, hailed from the same Central Cunagua sugar mill town where Maduro's father established his initial, lucrative Cuban holdings.

Alvarez homered on July 8 at Miami Stadium, as did catcher Hank Izquierdo. His batterymate, Vicente Amor, won his third game with a four-hit, 4–0 shutout over the Miami Marlins. Prior to the game, Diosa Costello and her Mardi Gras Revue performed for the 4,600 fans in attendance, which included consuls from 17 Latin American countries. (The Puerto Rican–born Costello, whose real name was Juana de Dios Castrello, was considered one of the original "Latin Bombshells." A few years earlier, in the part of Bloody Mary in James Michener's *South Pacific*, she became the first Hispanic woman to perform in a significant role on Broadway.) The win bumped the Sugar Kings record to 38–47.

In their first home series of July, the Sugar Kings celebrated "Fans Night." The evening of appreciation included a ticket promotion and the awarding of "numerous prizes." The largest crowd of the season, just under 15,000, turned out for the July 15 encounter with the Columbus Jets. Nino Escalera drew the most cheers with two hits, including a triple, and three RBI. Playing in his final season with the Cubans, the fourth-year Sugar King also stole a base. (In his four campaigns, Escalera topped all franchise players with 28 triples. He also placed second all-time in runs, 250, and doubles, 82.) Throwing the first seven innings, Rudy Arias capped the special night with a 6–2 victory, his fourth in a row. A couple of days later, Escalera and Elio Chacón were named to the IL All-Star Game versus the Milwaukee Braves, slated for July 28 in Toronto.

In their recent series in Miami, the Sugar Kings had missed Satchel Paige and were not sorry. The ancient wonder had won nine of ten decisions against the Havana team since joining the Marlins. On July 20, it took a considerable effort by Raúl Sánchez to loosen the debilitating grip. In a seven-inning battle of lanky right-handers, Sánchez came out on top with a 3–1 victory. Chuck Essegian reached Sánchez for the only Marlins hit of the game—a home run. In the second contest, Rudy Arias kept up his pleasing pitching with a nine-inning, route-going win, 2–1. A lower than expected home crowd of 2,200 showed up for the Sunday double feature.

Three days hence, rather unexpected, if not shocking news, came out of Havana. It had nothing to do with civil discontent, but more narrowly speaking, the discontent of one man. "Napoleon Reyes was fired as manager of the seventh place Cuban Sugar Kings in the International Baseball League," notified an *AP* wire. "He was replaced by Tony Pacheco, chief scout of the club."[23] Before the axe fell, the Cubans had won five out of six. (A little after Reyes' firing, it was leaked that the colorful former manager would maintain his post as head of the Cuban Little League program and work as both a scout and "troubleshooter" for the Cincinnati Reds in their close working relations with the Sugar Kings.)

A former Havana Cubans player in the early 1950s, Antonio Pacheco had been a charter member of the 1954 Sugar Kings. But after being struck in the head by a pitched ball, his season was curtailed after only ten games played. A second beaning, while playing in the Colombian Winter League in 1956–1957, had ended his minor league playing career. Surprisingly, he had no managerial experience, though one non-specific report stated that he had previously managed in winter ball. Pacheco could consider the appointment as an early birthday present. Two and a half weeks away from his 31st anniversary of life, the Cuban became the youngest manager in the IL. Pacheco's first game as benchmaster (July 23) was not only memorable for himself but for two other players. In a complete annihilation of the Toronto Maple Leafs, the Sugar Kings pounded out 18 hits and *17* runs. Borrego Alvarez and Nino Escalera set a Sugar Kings record for most hits in a game with five each. Outshining Escalera, Alvarez smashed two home runs and knocked home seven runs. The Pinar del Rio native, who had been discovered as an 18-year-old, set a single-season team mark with his 19th fence-topper. Orlando Peña added insult to injury by keeping the Maple Leafs from scoring for the entire game. The runs-scoring bonanza delighted 1,900 Gran Stadium attendees.

Proving the old adage that momentum is only as good as your starting pitcher, the Sugar Kings were nearly no-hit the following evening. Facing a new opponent in the Montreal Royals, Pacheco's team was held to one safety—an eighth-inning triple by Hank Izquierdo. The Royals' Charlie Rabe coasted to a 9–0 victory. Prior to the game, Bobby Maduro was presented with the National Association's trophy in recognition of being the first minor league club to surpass its prior year's attendance. The hardware, also donated by *Sporting News* publisher J.G. Taylor Spink, was handed to Maduro by U.S. Ambassador Smith in an on-field ceremony. On July 26, Rabe's moundmate, Tommy Lasorda, beat the Cubans for the fifth time, 6–0. It was Lasorda's third humbling of the Havana nine by shutout.

On August 10, assuming the one-day role of David over Goliath, the Sugar Kings finally defeated the future Hall of Fame manager. But it took a stellar undertaking by Mike Cuéllar to achieve the hard-earned victory, occurring in the first game of a doubleheader at Delorimier Stadium. The all-left-handed confrontation concluded with a 2–1, eight-hit Cuéllar triumph. Lasorda suffered only his fifth loss against a sumptuous 17 wins. In the seven-inning encore, Orlando Peña blanked the Royals, 1–0, as the Sugar Kings swept manager Clay Bryant's first- place club.

In a Sunday doubleheader a week later at Gran Stadium, Pacheco decided to throw an all-lefty starting hill combination at the visiting Rochester Red Wings. Rudy Arias and Cuéllar rewarded their manager's faith and achieved shutout victories—with Arias hurling a seven-inning no-hit, no-run game. The no-safety effort by Arias, a 27-year-old pitcher in the Chicago White Sox organization, became the first no-hitter in Sugar Kings history. *Bohemia*, the biggest selling magazine in Latin America, did not quibble with the game's shortened duration and paid off on their standing promotion of $1,000 to any pitcher who hurled a no-hitter in Cuban professional baseball. Two base runners reached, via a walk and error, on Arias, who spent part of the second game walking through the stands, his infant son in his arms. In that game, Cuéllar took the nine-inning measure of the Red Wings, while permitting four more hits than Arias had, and no runs. The 6–0 victory was his eleventh.

Arias followed up his no-no with a three-hit suppression of the Richmond Virginians on August 21. The 7–0 home triumph temporarily lifted the 59–74 Sugar Kings out of the basement. But the team quickly dropped back into the cellar. The Sugar Kings closed the season with three games in Miami. Prior to the set, Marlins manager Kirby Ferrell was fined $300 by minor league president George M. Trautman for comments in which he had accused the Sugar Kings of "handing" four games to Miami's playoff rival, the Columbus Jets, a week earlier. Ferrell tried to retract the comments by saying they were made in jest. Columbus reached the playoffs as the fourth seed, but were dismissed (with difficulty) by the pennant-grabbing Montreal Royals.

Montreal outlasted the Jets in a fully extended seven-game, opening round series. Toronto had an easier time beating Rochester in five games. In an all-Canadian final, the Royals triumphantly raised the Governors' Cup, defeating the Maple Leafs, four games to one.

The Royals were summarily stymied in the Junior World Series, losing four straight to the Minneapolis Millers.

The Sugar Kings played more poorly under Pacheco (19–33) than they had under Reyes. The 65–88 combined managers' records left the Cubans with a .425 winning percentage, the worst in their short history. Borrego Alvarez set a single-season team record for homers, 25. (Playing two more seasons, Alvarez would claim the most home runs (64) and RBI (225) by a franchise player.) Elio Chacón's .290 hitting mark led all other Sugar King regulars. Mike Cuéllar (13–12) pitched 221 innings and was the only starter to post an ERA below three (2.77). Emilio Cueche logged a bounce-back year to lead the staff in wins (14–13). Orlando Peña contributed 11 victories, with ten setbacks. No-hit rookie Rudy Arias chipped in with a 7–7 record, after starting the season in the bullpen.

The home attendance rebounded to 178,340, well behind Buffalo's 286,480, which placed at the top of the league—but better than Miami's 161,042 paying customers.

Five—Championship Glory Amid Political Discord

1958 International League Final Standings

	W	L	T	PCT	GB	Manager	Major League Affiliation
Montreal Royals	90	63	2	.588	—	Clay Bryant	Los Angeles Dodgers
Toronto Maple Leafs	87	65	0	.572	2½	Dixie Walker	None
Rochester Red Wings	77	75	4	.507	12½	Cot Deal	St. Louis Cardinals
Columbus Jets	77	77	1	.500	13½	Clyde King	Pittsburgh Pirates
Miami Marlins	75	78	0	.490	15	Kerby Farrell	Philadelphia Phillies
Richmond Virginians	71	82	1	.464	19	Eddie Lopat	New York Yankees
Buffalo Bisons	69	83	0	.454	20½	Phil Cavarretta	Kansas City Athletics
Cuban Sugar Kings	65	88	1	.425	25	Nap Reyes/ Tony Pacheco	Cincinnati Reds

Perception became reality on January 1, 1959, for Cuba and the rest of the hemisphere. The fraudulent, corruption-ridden, six-year-old government of Fulgencio Batista was toppled by revolutionary forces headed by Fidel Castro Ruz.[24] The Castro rebels had adopted wearing olive green fatigues and growing out their beards like their leader, who in the decades that followed would turn the grungy look into a kitschy symbol of oligarcharian defiance. The Cuban Winter League suspended play for five days. When it resumed on January 6, Gran Stadium threw open its gates to the soldiers and everyone wearing a beard, which caused one U.S. newspaper to cheekily accuse the circuit of becoming a real "bush league."

Mock trials followed by summary executions by firing squad occurring throughout Cuba for deemed "war crimes," without regard to world opinion, overshadowed the International League's annual owners meeting in Montreal on January 30. Prior to the gathering, Buffalo Bisons executive John C. Stiglmeier had gone on record as being a proponent of moving the Sugar Kings to Jersey City. "I hear people are stockpiling weapons down there and it's still a dangerous situation,"[25] he declared.

Knowing they were facing at least one detrimental vote, Maduro and Sugar Kings GM Paul Miller rendered what might today be called a PowerPoint presentation on why the league should maintain its presence on the turbulent island. The key, meant-to-be-convincing points of the six-hour meeting were: (1) Castro expressed to Maduro his cooperation for the upcoming season; (2) Castro would toss out the first ball on opening night, scheduled for April 14, and was invited by Toronto Maple Leafs GM Rudy Schaeffer to do the same in their initial home meeting with the Sugar Kings, April 29; (3) Public declarations of support for all sports from the appointed President of Cuba, Manuel Urrutia; (4) Non-salaried job offer to Maduro as the coordinator of all amateur sports in Cuba by the country's new military Sports Director, Captain Felipe Guerra Matos (Maduro accepted the post in an advisory capacity); (5) Guerra's first official act was to inquire on the situation of the Sugar Kings' season; (6) Anticipated larger baseball crowds as fear from civic turmoil had dissipated; (7) The new government's crackdown on the "numbers racket," a drain on citizens' income, especially the lower class. "This will give Cubans more money to spend and we hope a lot of it will go toward attending baseball games,"[26] Maduro said. (The national lottery was temporarily spared.)

Shaughnessy and the other owners needed no more persuading. The league president did not even call the matter to a vote. "International League delegates agreed last night baseball would continue in Havana," reported one sports journalist. "There was a day long discussion yesterday around moving the Havana franchise to the United States until things become more settled down there."[27]

"The league directors admire and respect Bob Maduro as a gentleman and as a great Cuban patriot," said Shaughnessy following the meeting. "We are solidly behind him. He has carried out every promise and agreement to the very letter."[28]

"I never said Batista was good, or Castro was bad," Maduro told the press afterward. "I don't say now whether Castro is good for Cuba or bad for Cuba, because I am not in politics. I am not a Castro man. I am a Cuban citizen. I always have kept out of politics because I have worked only for the good of Cuba, not for any particular government."[29]

Maduro also revealed how far the commercial situation had deteriorated and implied that without the rebel victory, he would have been forced to sell his team. "I had to close my bus lines, and five other businesses in which I have an interest were about ready to fold," he said. "My father owns the largest insurance company and he, too, was preparing to lock doors. I couldn't have kept from going broke another month the way things were going."[30] Perhaps an exaggeration at face value, Maduro may have been trying to paint an optimistic picture for others, going forward, by inserting his personal assets into the economic landscape.

That finances were weighing on him was indisputable, however. Shortly, he would disclose how much so. For now, in a one-on-one interview with the *Associated Press*, he went as far as to place a time limit of "two or three more years" of continued commitment. "No, I can't say I'm glad to be able to support the game to the extent [I have]," he said. "The Americans take more money out of Cuban baseball that they put in. For instance, we guarantee each team $800 per game. That's the equivalent to 4,000 persons per game. That's more that we get when we play in such fine cities as Buffalo or Richmond. We just don't draw there."[31] As he had last year, Maduro guaranteed a minimum $800 per diem to all the visiting clubs for 1959. In an era when gate receipt splits were the driving source of revenue for clubs, Maduro endured the recurring financial hardship whenever home attendance dipped below 4,000, which, in the recent past, had occurred more often than not.

While Fidel Castro would generate a great deal of fanatical myth-making in the years to come, it was during this period that the germinations of his false athletic prowess on the baseball field were planted. Hand in hand with the Sugar Kings' avoided dilemma, one newspaper story after another commented, or identified, Castro as being a former pitcher, usually at the amateur level. "Paul Miller assured newsmen [at the IL owners meeting] that Castro had played baseball at the University of Havana about 15 years ago," documented author John Phillips. "'He loves the game,' Miller said."[32]

Bobby Maduro, history reveals, unwittingly played the principle, perpetuating part in the long-enduring pretense as well. One writer's report, released at the time of Miller's statements, not only casts suspicions on Maduro's previous connection with the future despot but indicts him as the fabricator of the entire Castro baseball connection. "Maduro recalled frequent conversations with Castro three years ago, when the Sugar Kings trained in Mexico, and Castro was exiled there," wrote a Rochester newsman. "'We sat together through exhibition games. He used to be a semi-pro pitcher.'"[33] The Cubans opened spring training in Guadalajara on March 21, 1956, a time frame that does coincide with Castro's being in the country (July 1955–November 1956.) However, historical accounts have placed Castro's base of operation as Mexico City, 290 miles from the Sugar Kings' camp. Consumed by other priorities, such as fund-raising trips to New York, Philadelphia, Miami and other U.S. cities, as Castro was during his time in the Mexican capital (including a stint in a Mexico City jail for illegal weapons possession), it is questionable whether the situation would have aligned itself as Maduro described—unless the Sugar Kings visited Mexico City. But why would Maduro, who stated that he was not political, be seen sitting "through exhibition games" with the exiled rebel? And given Maduro's knowledge of the amateur and professional game in Cuba, it is even more improbable that he could have been duped into believing Castro had been a semi-pro pitcher as he expressed to the press (which ran with the unsubstantiated tale).

Comments by Maduro as the season neared place more doubt on his past relationship with the now self-appointed Premier of Cuba. "He [Castro] really loves baseball," Maduro told the *AP*'s Frank Eck. "I recall in 1954, our first season in the league, I used to go to the radio station when our team was on the road. I'd watched the teletype machines and Castro would be there. He had a half hour radio program in Cuba devoted to politics. We'd talk about baseball and everything else."[34] Fidel Castro was in a Cuban jail through all of 1954. Albeit with the best of intentions, and obviously for the sake of the Sugar Kings and Cuban baseball, it is clear that Maduro and Miller (who used practically the same "he loves baseball" quote) collaborated to build up perhaps not more than a modest appreciation for baseball by Castro into an untrue, ardent devotion to the game. A shrewd political manipulator, Castro quickly came to view the international spotlight which the game of bats and balls provided as a useful self-promotion tool.

Back on the team's marketing front, the season ticket membership to the "Fans Club" was increased from six to seven dollars, remaining still a bleacher seat bargain per ticket (including doubleheaders). The premium seat upgrade privilege, of course, remained unchanged.

The Sugar Kings stayed at home to train, setting up conditioning camp in Cienfuegos. The players would be put through the paces by a new manager. Showing his usual resolve and self-assurance, Maduro had named a new Sugar Kings bench boss two days *before* the owners' conference in January in Quebec. Pedro "Preston" Gómez, manager of the Mexico City Red Devils for the past two seasons and scout for the Los Angeles Dodgers, was the new Maduro appointee. Former pilot Tony Pacheco was hired as manager of the Palatka Redlegs, a Florida State League affiliate of the ubiquitous Cincinnati Reds.

While the Sugar Kings were preparing for the season in the east, Havana accommodated a pair of baseball clubs intent on pre-season intramurals. Excessive rain in Tampa, training home of the Reds, had canceled three straight exhibition games. The weather in Vero Beach, the spring haunt of the Los Angeles Dodgers, was not much better. Reds GM Gabe Paul and his Dodgers counterpart, Buzzie Bavasi, arranged for their teams to fly to Havana to play a couple of games of hardball. The Dodgers flew to Tampa, to drop off part of their team, and then to Havana. Dodgers owner Walter O'Malley then sent his team plane back to Tampa for the

Reds the next day. After playing an intrasquad game on March 19, the Dodgers faced off against their National League rivals for a pair of games on March 20 and 21. The two Gran Stadium exhibitions brought in over 11,000 fans. O'Malley's club won both contests, by one run each. O'Malley accompanied his men, but manager Walt Alston stayed with a "B" team in Tampa to play the Reds' second-team players, leaving coaches Pee Wee Reese and Greg Mulleavy in charge during the trip. Under the pair's care was pitcher Fred Kipp. "There were barefoot kids maybe 16-years-old carrying machine guns," he recalls. "Havana was a wide-open city."[35]

Los Angeles Times staffer Frank Finch was part of the press escort. His musings captured the current state of the Cuban metropolis:

> Several scores of pistol packin' rebels were in the stadium today.... Walter O'Malley made a big hit bantering with Cuban fans in the stands.... Behind the grandstand there is a private club, air-conditioned and complete with bar and restaurant.... To bring the team here for this series cost the Dodgers approximately $4,500, yet they turned a small profit.... In Havana there are 39 radio stations, 12 daily newspapers and five TV stations.... Bob Maduro hosted the press at his seaside mansion.[36]

Maduro had recently moved into the waterfront home, "with sliding doors facing the ocean 50 feet away and several levels of terrazzo floors,"[37] in an exclusive enclave of the Playa district of west Havana, after residing with his family in his father's home in upscale Vedado.

Two other U.S. baseball teams visited Cuba before the regular season. The Memphis Chicks of the Southern Association competed against the Sugar Kings in three games at Morón. The Miami Marlins also engaged the Sugar Kings at Morón in an exhibition series of four games over three days. Prior to the series, which drew 3,600 fans, the Marlins were given a parade, and manager Pepper Martin was handed a gold key to the city in special ceremonies. It was reported that the former "Gashouse Gang" leader was so moved by the gesture that his eyes watered.

It was expected that new dimensions at Gran Stadium this season would bring tears to the eyes of pitchers much more often than in the past. In a calculated move to increase offense, Maduro brought in the fences at his ballpark, the stingiest in the league for scoring runs. The foul line distances were reduced from 340 to 325 feet, and center field was slashed to 385 feet from home plate from the previous cavernous range. Last season, only 88 home runs were recorded in Gran Stadium, lowest of any IL ballpark.

Borrego Alvarez picked up where he left off last season and hit the first Sugar Kings' home run on opening night. He delivered a clutch, solo shot in the bottom of the ninth inning to send the contest versus the

Toronto Maple Leafs into extra innings. But the Leafs' Héctor Rodríguez hit a two-run, inside-the-park four-bagger in the top of the 11th, to propel the visitors to a 6–4 win. Many of the 14,106 in attendance surely felt mixed emotions watching Rodríguez circle the bases, as the Havana product was one of the most admired and accomplished players in the Cuban Winter League. Ted Wieand became the first North American hurler to pitch a home opener for the Sugar Kings; he went seven innings and allowed three runs, two earned. Prime Minister Castro threw out the first pitch. The next night, April 15, Preston Gómez chalked up his first managerial win, 8–4. Vicente Amor recorded the team's initial victory, with three-inning relief help from Luis Arroyo. The left-handed reliever had been obtained by the Cincinnati Reds in an off-season trade with Pittsburgh and was assigned to the Sugar Kings. Octavio "Cookie" Rojas smacked the second Sugar Kings homer in as many nights. Rojas was one of two young, 20-year-old infielders the Cubans had "brought up" that season. The other was Leo Cárdenas, and both were destined to have extended major league careers.

Three other Sugar Kings players cleared the more hitter-friendly fences on April 18, the start of a series with Montreal: Tony González, Chuck Coles and Walt Craddock. Coles, a South Carolinian and the Sugar Kings' left fielder, and Craddock, a southpaw pitcher, were part of a contingent of seven U.S.–born players on the Sugar Kings' opening roster. A circuit-high, 18-game winner with Buffalo two seasons ago, Craddock capped a memorable evening by tossing a six-hitter and easily winning, 10–1. The next day, González homered again (his fourth in three days) in the third game of the four-game set. It came as a grand slam in the second session of a Sunday doubleheader, powering the Kings to a 6–2 triumph and a draw on the day's work. Ted Wieand lost a 1–0, seven-inning decision to the Royals' Babe Birrer in the first game. A crowd of around 8,000 paid their way into the Havana park. The Royals won the Monday wraparound, 2–1, in 14 innings. Pitching nemesis Tommy Lasorda hurled 13⅓ frames for the win. Taking over for Lasorda, reliever Jackie Collum induced a game-ending double play from González. Luis Arroyo suffered the loss.

The Sugar Kings and their two opponents socked 17 home runs in seven games, constituting the extent of the first homestand. Tony González appeared to be the reincarnation of Babe Ruth, slugging five big flies, with 11 RBI, in those games. The Sugar Kings produced a 3–4 record. While the early performance could not have pleased Maduro, he became more unhappy over the 2,500 average attendance for the games—excluding the inaugural. Unwilling to wait to see if things would improve for his

Five—Championship Glory Amid Political Discord 107

fiscally embattled team, Maduro issued a general alarm and opened his books to the public.

> According to Havana Radio, the only hope for the Havana Sugar Kings lies in public subscription or a government dole. Directors of the International League team said last night the franchise may be moved to Jersey City, New Jersey unless financial help arrives.
>
> In a statement read over Havana Radio Station CMQ, the directors said the club has lost $133,387 since the franchise was acquired in 1954. Failure to sell television rights, low attendance and a slash in radio revenue have added to the financial burden, the statement said. Radio rights this year brought in only $10,000, some $60,000 less than the lowest previous annual radio gross.[38]

In 2018 dollars, $133,387 in 1959 amounts to approximately $1,138,000, the majority unquestionably from the pockets of the high-profiled owner. For the second year in a row, Maduro had failed to obtain a television sponsor for home games.

While his team was in Rochester, Maduro flew to New York City to confer with Fidel Castro, who was in town at the invitation of the American Society of Newspaper Editors. Maduro was forthright afterwards about his April 23 meeting with the self-installed Cuban leader, who was soaking up the star treatment given to him by the international press. Maduro said that he had not asked for a handout of government money. Rather, he had asked Castro to consider intervening with the sugar, tobacco and alcohol conglomerates to provide support for his club using mutually beneficial advertising practices. He also requested a Castro specialty—for him to make an oratory call to the populace to come out and help lift the box office count at Gran Stadium. (Castro never did.)

Maduro came out of the tête-à-tête expressing assurances that the Sugar Kings would not die and even renewed talk that his franchise would be a viable inclusion in the William Shea–Branch Rickey–backed Continental League—a proposed third major circuit under discussion. (Maduro later changed his position on the Continental League and came to see it more as a pipe dream venture.) A possibly sooner than expected financial shot-in-the-arm Maduro received less than a week after his conversation with Castro brought cause for more optimism. "The Cuban Sugar Stabilization Institute announced today it is donating $20,000 to the Cuban Sugar Kings baseball team as a contribution from the sugar industry," read a *UPI* bulletin on April 29.[39]

After 30 games, it could be said that the Sugar Kings themselves were in need of stabilization, sinking into the bottom position of the league with a record of 11–19. The Kings had 19 home-grown players farmed out to lower U.S. classification teams, a fine harbinger of the future, but there was a pressing need to win now. A week-long homestand in the middle of May brought better results. All-Star Elio Chacón, out of action due to a liver ailment, had seemingly been displaced in the infield by the 20-year-old tandem of Cárdenas and Rojas. On May 15, Cárdenas homered and Rojas went 4-for-4, with a stolen base, to lead the Sugar Kings to a 7–2 victory over the Columbus Jets. Old friend Emilio Cueche dispersed nine hits to the opposition in obtaining his third win. Having been with the club every year since inception, Cueche and coach Reinaldo Cordeiro were the last remaining original Sugar Kings from 1954. (Except for the entire 1957 season he spent with the Cincinnati Reds, veteran Raúl Sánchez was also an enduring member of the minor league team. His six career seasons are second all-time to Cueche's seven.) The next evening, Mike Cuéllar picked up his first victory by a 3–2, route-going score. In his third start, the southpaw hurler copped his first win when the Cubans pushed across a run in their last at-bat. Cuéllar had made the Cincinnati Reds coming out of spring training but had been sent back to Havana after only two appearances with the big club, both in relief.

During the 4–3 Gran Stadium stay, the team received a further injection of capital. "In mid–May," wrote John Phillips, "it was reported that Castro gave Maduro a $40,000 governmental subsidy. It's unclear if this included the $20,000 the Sugar Stabilization Institute donated April 29. The Sugar Industry had collected those funds."[40]

The Cubans embarked on their best road trip in franchise history, accruing an 11–3 mark through four cities, including eight wins in a row. The repetition of victories raised the team out of last place and tightened the IL standings to a degree that had league officials digging through their record books for a comparable situation. None was found. On the morning of June 1, five teams were within four games of Buffalo and Rochester, both tied for first place. The Sugar Kings had climbed to a game over break-even, at 25–24, and trailed the top-positioned clubs by only 1½ games. Toronto slotted last, six games behind the New York squads.

A precisely reported crowd of 12,491 welcomed the reenergized Sugar Kings home from their successful travel on the first of June. Breezing along into the eighth inning with a 4–0 lead and only two hits allowed, Mike Cuéllar and reliever Raúl Sánchez surrendered the advantage as they were reached for hits by six consecutive Buffalo Bisons, three pinch-hitters among them. After tying the game against the pair, the Bisons' Joe Caffie hit a solo home run in the tenth, against bullpen man Pedro Carrillo, for a 5–4 triumph. In the next meeting between the clubs, Borrego Alvarez, whose three-run shot had bolstered the lead in the game won by Caffie, blasted a home run, his tenth. Winning pitcher Walt Craddock and Luis Arroyo combined for a 1–0 triumph. The low-scoring affair entertained 3,700 fans. The next day, June 3, Arroyo's contract was purchased by the Cincinnati Reds. On June 6, Alvarez launched another one over the fence, in left center, against Rochester. Those in the know, including Maduro, said the king-size wallop, which sailed out of the park and over the side street into a parking lot, was the longest home run ever hit in Gran Stadium. Dick Ricketts, who surrendered the gargantuan blast (measured at over 500 feet by a civil engineer), was shortly thereafter called up by the St. Louis Cardinals, with perhaps more than a little jiving in store from his new teammates. Craddock raised his record to 5–2, as attendance topped 5,000.

The Sugar Kings interrupted their Gran Stadium dealings for an eight-game trip to Montreal and Toronto. On the trip, Vicente Amor, the club's winningest pitcher, registered his ninth victory—a relief-assisted 9–4 besting of the Toronto Maple Leafs. A day earlier, June 12, Ted Wieand improved his pitching ledger to 4–6 with a 6–3 win at Maple Leafs Stadium. Former Texas League outfielder Larry Novak lent a big assist with three hits, including one that left the ballpark, and four RBI. Wieand, a right-hander, had pitched better than his record indicated. In four of his starts, the Sugar Kings had failed to score a single run, and he had lost a startling three games by hard-luck 1–0 scores.

Preston Gómez's nickname was derived from his Oriente-province birthplace of Central Preston, an important sugar mill town that was home to the United Fruit Company. Employing the time-honored strategy of issuing a free pass with men on second and third, to attempt to turn a double play or obtain a force at any base, backfired on Gómez in an unusual way, on June 16 at Gran Stadium. Reliever Emilio Cueche's apparently unfocused first delivery to the Royals' Mike Goliat did not move far enough from the plate. Goliat swung and connected, depositing the lackadaisical throw over the wall. The three-run homer carried Montreal to a 7–5 win and nullified two circuit clouts by Larry Novak.

Through their first 65 games, the Sugar Kings had slugged 56 home runs; only Buffalo and Rochester had swatted more. However, the Cubans owned the worst team hitting mark in the circuit at .238. The Royals' Tommy Lasorda exploited the team's weak hitting, spinning a seven-inning, 5–0 shutout over the Cubans on June 19. The four-hit calcimining was his second in a row and eighth victory on the campaign. In the second tilt, the Kings came out mashing—belting four home runs for a 7–3 win.

Winning pitcher Ted Wieand got into the long ball act, along with batterymate Jesse Gonder, Tony González and Borrego Alvarez. The Friday twi-nighter was viewed by 4,300 fans.

A couple of days hence, Alvarez culminated a doubly satisfying day at the ballpark for Sugar Kings fans, crashing a two-out, tenth-inning, bases-loaded home run. The game-ending grand slam wallop, the first baseman's 15th fence-topper of the year, came against Toronto Maple Leafs pitcher Al Pehanick and lifted the Sugar Kings to a 7–3 victory. The Kings had snared the first contest, 7–5, in seven innings. About 6,300 turned out for the Sunday bargain bill. Two days later, the 35–35 Sugar Kings embarked on a 22-game road trip that would provide a great deal of insight into the true mettle of their team. Prior to the journey, Maduro turned down a proposed trade for Leo Cárdenas. The St. Louis Cardinals offered four players from their organization for the youngster.

The road trip was anything but successful, producing only six wins in 20 games. The Sugar Kings returned home on July 11 in a last-place tie with the Columbus Jets. The poor performance, the lagging home attendance (improved but still disappointing), the constant financial pressure over the years, all may have all conspired to crack the normally imperturbable façade of Maduro. The owner let out his frustration in an interview with the *Miami Herald*. "I will try to sell the franchise, if I lose money," Maduro stated. "But we will finish out the season. My home is in Cuba, I wouldn't leave here. I'd want to sell the franchise and get out of baseball. But I'm not going to give it away."[41] In the article written by *Herald* journalist Luther Evans, more light was shed on the $40,000 government subsidy the Sugar Kings had received—and nearly burned through already, according to Maduro. Apart from the $20,000 from the Sugar Institute, the chief of the army, Camilo Cienfuegos, had purchased $10,000 worth of tickets for distribution to his soldiers and other parts of the populace (a smart PR play). The balance came from the Cuban Tourism Commission.

The dire message from Maduro was received loud and clear by Fidel Castro, who—at best—could be said had only indirectly responded to Maduro's earlier plea for aid through his army chief's bulk tickets purchase. Within days of the *Herald* interview, the bearded seditionist summoned the Sugar Kings boss for another conference. "Castro reportedly told Maduro his regime is prepared to carry out his promise of last April to give the Cuban ball team any assistance it needs," read a newspaper report. "The Sugar Kings are part of the Cuban people," the sources quoted Castro. "It is very important to Cuban sports fans to maintain the team in a Triple

A league and we must battle if necessary to keep it there. Our revolutionary government will take steps to assure the Cubans on the team have no economic problems now or in the future."[42]

Yet it was Castro who exploited the delicate situation, asking for and receiving a handout soon after promising aid. On July 24, prior to the game between the Rochester Red Wings and Sugar Kings, a two-inning exhibition between teams of *"Barbudos"* ("Bearded Rebels") and Military Police was conducted. The pre-advertised spectacle featured Castro, in a baseball uniform, as a pitcher, and drew more than 26,000 people to Gran Stadium. "Castro was presented with a check for the proceeds of the gate receipts by Bob Maduro of the Havana Sugar Kings, for his agrarian reform fund," a wire report stated. "Several Cuban firms also gave him checks for the fund."[43] The Sugar Kings won the game that followed, 4–2, behind Raúl Sánchez and Luis Arroyo, who had been returned to the Sugar Kings after a month with the Reds.

Maduro, hands at his sides, receives an apparent unsettling look from future dictator Fidel Castro prior to the July 24, 1959, "Barbudos" exhibition contest at Gran Stadium. Castro benefited from the baseball infrastructure Maduro had in place to reap powerful, "amateur" international teams that Cuba produced in the decades that followed (courtesy Maduro Family).

The next evening, an unnerving incident occurred which left more than one ballplayer grateful to have avoided serious injury and an entire ballclub evacuating the city. A previously suspended game that was scoreless after seven innings, from the last visit by the Rochester Red Wings, was resumed, starting at nine p.m., prior to the regularly scheduled contest. The same two pitchers—for Rochester, Bob Keegan, and Ted Wieand for the Sugar Kings—reengaged their interrupted duel from June 7. The Sugar Kings scored a run in the eighth, following a Leo Cárdenas single, stolen base, and Yo-Yo Davalillo's double. Wieand, now 12–8, retired all six Red Wings he faced for the 1–0 win.

In the scheduled game that followed, Borrego Alvarez unleashed his late-inning, home run bludgeon again, this time with a man on base, in the bottom of the ninth inning, to tie the contest 3–3 and force additional play. The Red Wings went ahead in the top of the 11th on a Billy Harrell solo homer, only to have the Sugar Kings push across a tying run in the lower half of the frame. In the top of the 12th, before anyone could complete an at-bat, the clock struck midnight, ending the action—but not by curfew rule or other predetermined arrangement. The official start of a new day released an undisciplined barrage of celebratory gunfire from in and around Gran Stadium by the mostly bewhiskered, olive green-garbed military personnel. The significance of the new day, July 26, which unleashed the indiscriminate firing, dated to the day, six years earlier, that launched the Cuban Revolution.[44] One errant bullet tore a hole in Leo Cárdenas' uniform sleeve, but spared any type of laceration to his person. Another wayward projectile struck Red Wings third base coach Frank Verdi on his cap liner, knocking him to the ground. He recovered quickly and left the field on his own power. Red Wings manager Cot Deal refused to continue the game, with home plate umpire Frank Guzzetta in agreement. In surely a baseball first, the game was halted—on account of gunfire. The Red Wings refused to return to the ballpark the next day to complete the interrupted game or to play the remaining game of the series.

Verdi, who was manning the coach's box because Deal had been tossed from the game the prior inning, said afterward, "If that bullet had been two inches to the left, all the team would have had to chip in five bucks apiece for flowers."[45] Verdi stated the next day that he felt as if he had been hit by a blackjack and that his ear was burned and shoulder sore. He went as far as to say that his cap's rubber and plastic liner had saved his life. A widely distributed photo appeared in newspapers of Verdi sticking his finger through the bullet hole of his cap. Umpire Guzzetta found the spent bullet on the ground, which Verdi identified as appearing to be a .45.

Both Maduro and GM Paul Miller were upset at the Red Wings' decision to skip town and publicly said so, even as reports of 17 people being injured by incidents of gunfire that night trickled out. Maduro questioned, perhaps unwisely, the character of the Red Wings players and management, pointing to the throes of a losing slump the Red Wings were in as the basis for their decision to bolt. Frank Shaughnessy backed Rochester's decision. The abandoned games marked the end of the Sugar Kings' homestand, avoiding more potential bad publicity if the next scheduled club also balked at taking the Gran Stadium field.

The Sugar Kings brass could take some solace in the fact that their club had taken 12 out of 16 games during their home stay and had vaulted into the first division. Buffalo was securely out in front of the pack by 7½ games, but incredibly only two games separated the seven trailing clubs.

The improved play was sustained by the Sugar Kings on the road. Against the backdrop of Toronto's Civic Holiday celebrations, August 2–3, the club hauled in four victories—three in one day—all versus the Maple Leafs. In the August 2 doubleheader's opener, the Kings grabbed a 2–1, 16-inning nail-biter. Luis Arroyo (5–5) hurled five scoreless innings in relief of starter Walt Craddock for the win. In the nightcap, play was stopped by curfew after four innings, with the Cubans ahead, 3–0. Not to be dissuaded, starter Ted Wieand (13–8) came back out the next day, August 3, prior to the scheduled holiday twi-night double bill, and threw three more shutout innings to record the seven-inning victory, his eighth in a row. In the first scheduled twilight game, Arroyo saved Raúl Sánchez's eighth win, 5–4, obtaining the last six outs of the contest. Mike Cuellar (7–9) followed with an efficient 5–2, seven-inning decision. With the flurry of victories, the 59–56 Cubans moved into second place, eight games behind Buffalo but 1½ lengths in front of the third-place team.

Wieand had his winning streak stopped in his next start, August 7. He dropped a 2–1 contest to the league-leading Buffalo Bisons. Having emerged as the ace of the staff, Wieand was named to the IL All-Star squad. Teammates Leo Cárdenas and Tony González (as a starter) were also selected. Borrego Alvarez, though he had put up fine slugging numbers, was excluded due to a low batting average (in the low .200s).

While registering his public displeasure over the Red Wings hightailing it out of Havana, Maduro had said that he would not make up the games unless they were played in Havana. Frank Shaughnessy visited Havana and Maduro in August. Shaughnessy let it be known that he had found nothing in the city to consider stopping any future trips of IL teams. He also announced that the missed Red Wings games would be played in

Rochester on September 4. As much a fence-mending trip as an exploratory one, Shaughnessy's main purpose was to get across to all concerned local parties that machine guns at ballparks during ballgames are not a good mix.

There was no denying, meanwhile, that the fusion of talent nurtured by Preston Gómez had become a quality brand. The Sugar Kings captured five of eight games upon their return to Havana, against Montreal and Toronto. The club now had 26 victories to its credit in the last 37 games played. The rejuvenated team even knocked out arch-foe Tommy Lasorda in the second inning of one game, while Wieand tied Rudy Minarcin's 1956 club record for wins in a season with his 15th in another.

Franklin Delano Roosevelt Wieand had pitched one game in the major leagues so far with Cincinnati, and his performance with the Sugar Kings boded well for another opportunity with the Reds. Around the time of Shaughnessy's visit, Wieand volunteered some positive views about his Cuban experiences. "I've never worked for a finer man than Bob Maduro," said the 26-year-old right-hander, "and I've been happy in Havana. My wife and three children enjoy the life in Cuba. We have a home near the beach and the youngsters thrive in the sun. Everyone in Cuba has been wonderful to me and the other American players."[46]

The Kings completed not only an extended homestand on August 26, having hosted five IL teams, but also their home schedule of games. The home team whipped the Miami Marlins, 10–0. Winning his 11th game, Raúl Sánchez displayed exceptional pitching skills, yielding but five hits, in front of 4,100 spectators. Cárdenas drilled his 13th round-tripper. The club's record of 73–67 kept them in second place, barely ahead of Columbus and Richmond. Ancillary numbers of interest at this point were the 104 home runs hit as a team, well above the record of 86 set last season, and a figure above 200,000 in home attendance. The ticket sales, though, were sixth-best in the league, with only Miami (140,384) and Montreal (136,340) drawing more poorly. (The International League, the minors' best-supported circuit, barely missed drawing 2,000,000 fans for the first time in 1959.)

Entering September, the Kings had compiled a 38–25 mark since their July 4 turnaround. The team took four out of seven games from Columbus and Richmond, before having to use their off-day on September 4 to play out the two scrapped games from July with the Red Wings. The July 25 game was not ruled suspended, to be picked up at the point of the "shooting interruption," but rather a tie game to be replayed in its entirety. The Cubans were forced to pay the unexpected trip expenses out of the

50 percent gate split the club received at Red Wing Stadium. A minimum of 4,000 fans were required to attend the 6:30 p.m. twi-night doubleheader for Havana's team not to lose money in the exercise. Gómez started Pedro Carrillo, who was used primarily in relief on the season, in the seven-inning opener. Carrillo pitched and hit his way to a 5–4 triumph. The rookie right-hander homered with a man on base and scored the decisive run in the seventh inning after singling. It was all Rochester in the second game, as Gómez decided to use recent team addition Bob Moorehead to start. Moorehead was followed by another lower classification hurler, also new to the club, Gilberto Clark. The Red Wings collected 14 hits against the overmatched pair in what turned into an 8–2 trampling of the road team. A crowd of 3,939 was on hand for the stalemate outcome.

Having been pushed out of second place by what would become a season-ending ten-game winning streak by the Columbus Jets, the Sugar Kings flew overnight to Miami to finish the campaign. The Kings, who had already assured themselves a playoff berth, played and lost a 15-inning encounter with the Marlins on September 5 (7–6). The team finished the season, splitting a doubleheader the next day, in a grueling travel whirl of five games in three days. The 89-win Buffalo Bisons copped the pennant by 5½ games over the hot Columbus Jets. The 80–73 Sugar Kings placed nine games back, and 4½ lengths ahead of fourth-place Richmond.

Borrego Alvarez, who had received a gold-inscribed bat to commemorate his tape-measure home run of June 6, could not better his home run totals from last season, settling for 22. The 21-year-old free-swinger's average dropped precipitously to .193 in over 500 at-bats. All-Star Tony González hit an even .300 (fifth in the league), with 20 home runs and a team-high 81 RBI. Leo Cárdenas, who set a team record for most games played in a season with 154, hit a respectable .254. His youthful infield legionnaire Cookie Rojas had been struck down by jaundice, reducing his rookie season to 99 games and a .233 hitting mark. Elio Chacón, on the sick list at the start of the campaign, returned with a stabilizing effect on the infield, following Rojas's malady. The strong up-the-middle glove tandem of Chacón and Cárdenas, plus González in center field, fortified a Sugar Kings team defense that was near the top of the league, and compensated for the second-worst team hitting mark of .239.

Front-line starters Raúl Sánchez and Mike Cuéllar pulled in 11 and 10 wins, respectively. Veterans Emilo Cueche and Vicente Amor posted nine victories each. Although saddled with a losing record of 8–9, Luis Arroyo performed superbly out of the bullpen, possessor of a 1.15 ERA in 117 innings. At the vanguard of the Sugar Kings pitching, however, the

North American duo of Ted Wieand (16–11) and Walt Craddock (12–9) reigned supreme.

The Columbus Jets, the Sugar Kings' first-round playoff opponent, owned an even better pitching 1–2 punch in 16-game winners Joe Gibbon and Al Jackson. Both lefties, Gibbon and Jackson had tied for most shutouts with four. The Sugar Kings' new single-season wins leader faced Gibbon on September 9. At Jets Stadium, Wieand and the Sugar Kings snapped the Jets' double-digit winning streak, grinding out a 5–3 victory. Wieand, who had suffered from stretches of poor run support throughout the season, preventing a glitzier record, received two timely insurance runs in the ninth inning from his teammates. Holding a 5–2 advantage, the Sugar Kings ace started the final inning but needed Arroyo and Pedro Carrillo to obtain the final outs as the Jets scored once, charged to Wieand. With a few games left in the season, the Sugar Kings had suspended outfielder Carlos Paula for public actions following a missed team flight. The league allowed the short-handed team to call up Nashville Volunteers flychaser Ray Shearer from the Cincinnati Reds' Southern Association affiliate. Shearer homered and drove in two runs.

Gómez rearranged the pitching pecking order by starting Mike Cuéllar in game two the following evening. The future major league, four-time 20-game winner was marvelous, shutting down the Jets on three hits and 14 strikeouts. Retiring the last 12 batters he faced, Cuéllar earned a 5–1 victory, in which five different Sugar Kings players drove in runs. A much cooler night than the previous one reduced attendance by more than 1,100, from the 3,040 paid crowd of game one.

The seven-game series continued the next night in the same ballpark, with little improvement in the weather and greater deterioration by the home team. Sugar Kings starter Craddock was given a six-run lead prior to throwing his first pitch. Pelting 15 hits against five Jets pitchers, the Kings scored ten runs (all in the first three innings). In the non-slugging attack, Danny Morejón cranked the team's only two extra-base hits, a double and triple. Craddock was touched for three runs on nine hits and four walks, but completed the series-commanding, 10–3 victory.

The teams flew to Havana and, with little down time, continued the series on September 12. Facing the almost insurmountable challenge, Jets manager Cal Ermer called on Joe Gibbon. The league's strikeout king (152) matched zeros with Sugar Kings starter Raúl Sánchez for four innings, until he was reached for several hits and three runs in the fifth. Borrego Alvarez, Tony González and Sánchez knocked in runs in the frame, in which the Sugar Kings tacked on two more scores against Gibbons' reliever, Don Williams. Ermer resorted to the last-ditch measure of using Al Jackson in relief, to no avail. Sánchez spun a five-hit shutout (6–0), the staff's third straight complete game. Topping the three-game attendance totals in Columbus, 7,607 fans witnessed the Sugar Kings' first home playoff victory and series clincher. Although the Jets had won ten in a row coming into the series, the Sugar Kings (playing their first home game in 2½ weeks) clearly showed why they had been the best team in the league since July 4 (48–31, including playoffs).

While a series victory by either the Sugar Kings or Jets would not have been viewed as surprising, the sub-.500 Richmond Virginians' ousting of the league champion Buffalo Bisons was an outcome few could have predicted. One of the keys to Richmond's upset series win could be traced to its pitchers' successful clamping down on Triple Crown winner Francisco "Pancho" Herrera (.329/37/128). The Cuban slugger did not drive in a single run in the five-game encounter. Another key was the ballistic slugging of Vees third baseman Deron Johnson. On the cusp of a long major league career, Johnson drilled six homers and knocked home 11 runs, on 9-for-17 hitting.

The Cubans, merited by their better record, hosted the Virginians in the first game of the Governor's Cup championship round. On September 15, Wieand and Arroyo combined to stop the Virginians cold, 1–0, in 11 innings. Tony González singled home Yo-Yo Davalillo with the winning run. Arroyo secured the final seven outs for the victory. Gonzalez's hit was the Sugar Kings' tenth, compared to six for Richmond. Nearly 13,000 fans cheered the auspicious result. Rain prevented the second game from being played until September 17. Cuéllar received the opening nod from Gómez. The left-hander did not commence with his best stuff, surrendering a first-inning, three-run home run to Richmond's Fritz Brickell. The blow set the tone for a 5–3 road team win. Cuéllar was tagged for a second four-bagger by Jim Pisoni and another run, before being sent to the showers in the fifth inning. The Sugar Kings were held to only five hits by Richmond starter Bill Short and Johnny James, who picked up a five-out save.

A venue shift to Parker Field in Richmond for the next three games came about with no off-day, due to the rainout. Gómez came back with right-hander Sánchez on September 18, instead of Walt Craddock, as he had done versus the Columbus Jets. A tight pitchers' duel ensued between Sánchez and the Vees' Zack Monroe. The 28-year-old Havana native held a 1–0 advantage entering the last inning. Davalillo doubled home, as it turned out, a much-needed insurance run in the Cubans' last turn at bat. The Virginians scratched across a run in their final shot to make things interesting, but Sánchez prevailed, 2–1. He yielded four singles and only one extra-base hit, a ninth-inning triple; he walked none and struck out five, in a second consecutive masterful effort.

Following the fourth game, the Virginians could not have been blamed for feeling a sensation of déjà vu. Wieand and Arroyo again combined to smother the Virginians in a low-scoring contest, ending in a repeat 2–1 score from last evening. González sent home one run with a single, and Elio Chacón scored the other on an error. Arroyo pitched a perfect ninth after Wieand was removed for a pinch-hitter in the top of the inning. The Cubans' first error of the series resulted in an unearned run charged to the presidentially-christened right-hander.

Emilio Cueche, 9–8 with a 3.95 ERA on the year, had pitched 4⅔ scoreless innings in relief of Mike Cuéllar in game two. The one-hit-allowed performance plainly influenced Gómez enough to start the veteran against the backs-to-the-wall Virginians in the September 20 fifth game. Holding a 3–1 lead in games and knowing the next two contests were scheduled for his home park must have also factored into the manager's selection. That Gómez had Cueche on a short leash became apparent with his removal in the bottom of the fifth inning in favor of Pedro Carrillo, after Cueche had surrendered his only run of the game in the prior frame. Two innings later, 12-game winner Walt Craddock made his first appearance and served up Deron Johnson's first home run and RBI in the five games. Former American League pitcher Bob Wiesler kept the Cubans off the board until the eighth, when he was relieved by Johnny James, who brought home the 5–1, series-surviving victory.

A travel off-day allowed Raúl Sánchez to pitch game six on three days' rest in Havana on September 22. Sánchez, with help, garnered his third playoff win as the Sugar Kings captured the International League's coveted championship prize as its undisputed best team. A second-inning infield hit by Ray Shearer, followed by singles by Leo Cárdenas and Hank Izquierdo, plated the Cubans' only run. Though Sánchez had been splendid throughout, another Sugar Kings hurler reaped the more deserved platitudes. "Luis Arroyo turned in another remarkable performance last night as the Sugar Kings edged Richmond, 1–0, to clinch the best of seven series, four games to two," recapped one news source. "With Prime Minister Castro, former college pitcher [sic], cheering him on, the relief pitcher blanked the Virginians on one hit after relieving starter Raul Sanchez in the sixth inning."[47] Arroyo had figured prominently in three of the four wins, saving two and winning another in relief. He had pitched 7⅓ innings without allowing a run. Accompanying Castro, a crowd of 13,023 pushed attendance over 44,000 for the four playoff games held at Gran Stadium. An encouraging number, especially in comparison to those played in Buffalo, Columbus, and Richmond. The fandom for 11 games in those three cities averaged about 5,000 per game.

Beginning a decades-long propensity for imposing himself on the

Cubans outfielders Ray Shearer and Danny Morejón. Had there been an MVP awarded in the 1959 Junior World Series, Morejón, at right, would have won it. The Sugar Kings' left fielder delivered one ninth-inning, game-tying safety and two walk-off hits, including the Game Seven championship clincher. Shearer, a late-season addition, provided the clutch, game-winning hit in Game Three of the championship series versus the Minnesota Millers (courtesy Ralph Maya).

successes of his country's sporting achievements, Fidel Castro visited the Cubans clubhouse after the game.

"This is a happy day for Cuba,"[48] said the cigar-smoking Castro.

1959 International League Final Standings

	W	L	T	PCT	GB	Manager	Major League Affiliation
Buffalo Bisons	89	64	0	.582	—	Kerby Farrell	Philadelphia Phillies
Columbus Jets	84	70	2	.545	5½	Cal Ermer	Pittsburgh Pirates
Cuban Sugar Kings	80	73	1	.523	9	Preston Gómez	Cincinnati Reds
Richmond Virginians	76	78	0	.494	13½	Steve Souchock	New York Yankees
Rochester Red Wings	74	80	1	.481	15½	Cot Deal	St. Louis Cardinals
Montreal Royals	72	82	1	.468	17½	Clay Bryant	Los Angeles Dodgers
Miami Marlins	71	83	2	.461	18½	Pepper Martin	Baltimore Orioles
Toronto Maple Leafs	69	85	1	.448	20½	Dixie Walker/ Lou Kahn	None

The Cubans beat the Columbus Jets, four straight. The Richmond Virginians upset the Buffalo Bisons, four games to one. The Cubans defeated the Virginians, in six games, to win the IL championship, and earn the right to meet the American Association's repeat champion Minneapolis Millers in the Junior World Series.

Junior World Series

"The government has helped by getting us a radio sponsor. There is no more violence in Havana. The fans only have baseball to think about now,"[49] Bobby Maduro optimistically said on the eve of the annual series matching the playoff winners from two of the three highest-ranked minor leagues in the country. The American Association, with its collection of Midwestern teams, had faced off against the International League for more than 40 years in a best-of-seven "post-playoff championship" to decide the best minor league club in the country. At least two-thirds of the country—the Pacific Coast League held an "open" classification grade recognized above Triple-A status. Instead of being called the Minor League World Series, the inter-league clash was named the Junior World Series, also referred to for a time as the "Little World Series."

Five—Championship Glory Amid Political Discord 121

The Sugar Kings had to wait a few days to find out who their JWS opponent would be. Based on the following news snippet, none it seemed was more anxious to know than their enthusiastic owner: "When the Minneapolis Millers defeated the Ft. Worth Cats 4–2 Friday for the American Association playoff championship, news of the game was wired play-by-play into Bob Maduro's home and then transmitted to a Havana radio station."[50]

The Junior World Series opened on September 27, a raining Sunday afternoon in the Bloomington suburb of the Twin Cities of Minneapolis/St. Paul. Frank Shaughnessy, who had endured five straight post-season series losses to his American Association counterpart's league, was in attendance, along with 2,486 other fans, a slim total kept down by the wet weather. Delayed half an hour by rain and played mostly in a drizzle, the adverse conditions did not affect Ted Wieand, who kept the Millers off the board for eight innings, as the Sugar Kings headed off on the right foot with a 5–2 win. The Millers cracked Wieand for a pair of ninth-inning runs, but by that time his team had built a five-run lead with some timely hitting and a pair of runs forced in on bases-loaded walks. Borrego Alvarez knocked home two runs in a four-run third inning for the Cubans, which ended the afternoon for Millers starter Ted Bowsfield.

A damp, raw night followed, resulting in a meager attendance of barely over 1,000 shivering fans at Metropolitan Stadium for Game Two. The Millers broke out their long ball lumber, cracking four home runs, two each against Mike Cuéllar and Luis Arroyo, to spark a 6–5, come-from-behind win. Roy Smalley hit the Millers' first four-base hit versus Cuéllar to tie the score at 2–2. (Smalley's namesake son would reach the major leagues in the 1970s and bat against Cuéllar.) After the Sugar Kings regained the lead, 5–2, a two-run homer by Lou Clinton just about ended Cuéllar's evening in the eighth. After he retired the next batter, Arroyo relieved. He promptly surrendered a game-tying blast to Millers third baseman Red Robbins. In the bottom of the ninth, catcher Ed Sadowski slammed a leadoff home run to win the game. While all the winning team's runs came via the long ball, the Sugar Kings relied on RBI-producing hits by Alvarez, Danny Morejón and Leo Cárdenas for their scoring. Murray Wall procured the win with a two-inning relief stint.

With colder weather expected in the forecast and rain that could turn into snow, the minor league commission canceled the scheduled third game in Minneapolis and redirected the venue for the remaining games. The first minor league international championship series involving a Latin American team had been structured as a 3–4 format, eliminating any back-and-forth travel. Taking into account fan and player comfort—and even the players' wallets—the three-person minor league commission decided to conclude the series in Havana, with five games if necessary. Representing himself, AA president Ed Doherty, Shaughnessy and minor league czar George M. Trautman, Doherty released the official memorandum: "The commission unanimously agreed to make the move in fairness to the players. It is simply too cold here to play ball or watch it and since they share in the gates of only the first four games, they are entitled to a break. There is great enthusiasm in Havana and we are certain of good baseball weather there."[51]

Perhaps not anticipating an extended series, Millers manager Gene Mauch did not seem to mind the loss of the home game. "We are all right," he said. "I don't think home park edge for just one more game was vital. The boys have an increased financial incentive now and that could be important."[52]

Asked about the Millers' game two home run barrage, Maduro said, "We don't have the power to match some teams in smaller ballparks. But it's hard to hit the ball out of our stadium. Our pitching, defense and speed are good there."[53] His team would illustrate just how good in the games than followed.

The Cuban capital rolled out the welcome wagon for both teams the day they arrived:

> Sirens squalled, auto horns blared, a band played and fans cheered as Havana welcomed home its Sugar Kings and said hello to the Minneapolis Millers. A cheering throng greeted the teams at the airport. A band played both national anthems and a noisy cavalcade whisked the long way to Marianao city hall.
>
> There in an amphitheater seating some 2,500, players and officials of both clubs were introduced to a standing room crowd. Also Marianao mayor Efren Gonzalez presented plaques commemorating the 1959 Series to general manager George Brophy of Minneapolis and president Bob Maduro of the Sugar Kings.[54]

The Minneapolis Millers had repeated as playoff champions in 1959, making Gene Mauch the first manager in six years to lead an American Association team to back-to-back playoff titles. (The Millers had won last year's JWS.) Admirably, Mauch accomplished the feat despite losing his top two right-handed pitchers, Earl Wilson (10–2) and Nelson Chittum (11–5), to late-summer call-ups by the Boston Red Sox. Prior to the first pitch of game three on September 30, Mauch and his players received billfolds as presents, and Sugar Kings players accepted unspecified gifts. All were given handshakes by Fidel Castro, who had entered the stadium through the center field bleachers to rousing cheers and a sea of white handkerchief-waving that made it look like it was snowing in the stands, according to one northern writer. A paid crowd of 24,938, along with several thousand "security personnel," crammed the big ballpark. "There were an estimated 3,000 of Castro's soldiers on the premises, some bearded, others long-haired, and nearly all armed with sub-machine guns or carbines,"[55] detailed one pressbox eyewitness. (The same eyewitness later quipped that this JWS had to be the only one ever played in which the sub-machine guns outnumbered the bats.)

Raúl Sánchez was the logical choice for Preston Gómez. Mauch went with his third left-handed starter in a row, Tom Borland. The Millers' winningest pitcher on the year at 14–8, Borland carried a 2–0 lead into the eighth inning, one of the runs a long solo home run by Millers second baseman Carl Yastrzemski. In that frame, the Sugar Kings rallied, helped by a controversial hit-by-pitch on Yo-Yo Davalillo (Mauch argued that he had swung at the pitch). Davalillo took second on a wild pitch and scored on a Tony González single. Having retired one batter in the inning, Borland was removed in favor of Billy Muffett. The right-hander gave up consecutive safeties to Danny Morejón and Ray Shearer to even the contest, before getting out of the inning. Sánchez had been removed after seven innings, with two runs allowed. Gómez used Mike Cuéllar for two outs in the eighth and Emilio Cueche the rest of the way, including an extra frame, to keep the Millers from any more scoring. In the bottom of the tenth, after Muffett had set down the first two hitters, González, who led the league in triples with 16, stroked his third hit. Morejón was struck by another fateful pitched ball, pushing up González, and Shearer delivered again with a game-winning hit to right field, setting off wild celebrations on the field over the 3–2, extra-inning win. Fitted with the game's laurel wreath with his two run-producing hits, right fielder Shearer also cut down Yastrzemski trying to advance from first to third on a single in the ninth inning—which turned into a double play when the batter rounded first too widely and was caught off the base by a heads-up return throw by third sacker Davalillo.

On Thursday, October 1, several hours after the first game of the World Series was completed in Chicago, the fourth game of its minor league equivalent commenced at nine o'clock local time, 8 p.m. in Minnesota. Mauch did not hesitate to bring back southpaw Ted Bowsfield (10–5) as Ted Wieand's mound opponent in a rematch of Game One starters. With a regular starting lineup consisting of only one left-handed batter (González), the Sugar Kings appeared to be competing with an upper hand. Gaining the advantage in the game itself proved more difficult for both teams, until the Sugar Kings' fourth run—and third lead change of the game—in the bottom of the 11th inning decided the outcome. Danny Morejón's third hit and third RBI of the contest brought in Elio Chacón, who scored three of the Sugar Kings' four runs, in the winning stanza. Down by a run, the Kings had tensely forced extra innings, with one out in the ninth, stringing together three straight singles—the last by Morejón. Bowsfield was compelled to withdraw prior to the seventh, due to nausea from the heat. The Millers' fourth pitcher of the game, Vito Valentinetti, absorbed the loss. Mike Cuéllar, in his third appearance, two as a reliever, picked up the victory, recording the final two outs of the 11th. Succeeding Wieand, pitchers Arroyo, Pedro Carrillo and Cuéllar supplied four innings of hitless relief. A crowd of 14,155, pared-down from the previous night's gala, went home deliriously happy.

With his back to the proverbial wall, Mauch stuck to his left-handed guns and tapped the Game Two starter, Ted Wills (9–10), to try to keep his team alive the next evening. It was a great choice as the southpaw hurled a 4–2, Series-prolonging victory. Wills, who had been sent down to the Millers by the parent Red Sox earlier in the summer, allowed seven hits, one a two-run homer by the hot Morejón. He struck out 12 and walked four. In his first Series sighting, Walt Craddock accepted the starter's role for the Sugar Kings and was not involved in the decision. Scuffed for four hits and the two deciding runs, Arroyo suffered the loss in relief. A sizable gathering of 21,175 came out in anticipation of a jubilant celebration that was not to be.

Mauch changed his pitching script for Game Six with the hope of pushing the Series to a winner-take-all seventh game. He started right-hander Tracy Stallard, a recently-turned-22-year-old who had compiled a 2–5 record in 16 games, nine of them starting assignments. Stallard was the first non-left-handed starter faced by the Sugar Kings in seven games, stretching back to Game Four of the playoff finals versus the Richmond Virginians. Gómez countered with Mike Cuéllar, who had last started in Game Two, but had been used twice in short relief stints since then. Perhaps the intermediate pitching affected him, for he lost command in the third inning and was sent to an early shower. After he retired the first seven men he faced, four Millers in a row singled, plating one run. Intent on limiting the damage, Gómez yanked his starter with the bases loaded, in favor of Carrillo, who allowed the three inherited runners to score. The Sugar Kings could not recover from the four-run inning, though home runs by González and catcher Jesse Gonder, making his first Series start, chipped away at the deficit. A left-handed hitter, Gonder's insertion in place of the right-handed Izquierdo was a planned counter-measure to Stallard's slants. González collected three hits, giving him eight in 14 at-bats in the six games. On a short leash, Stallard, destined to surrender Roger Maris's historic 61st home run in two short years, was removed in the fifth inning after surrendering his second four-bagger (to González). An intrepid Ted Bowsfield, who had thrown six innings the day before yesterday before being felled by the heat, pitched the last 4⅔ innings for the win. He allowed his only hits (three) in the ninth, which led to the Sugar Kings' last run of the game in the 5–3 final. Offensively, the Millers' Tom Umphlett drove in a pair of runs, while keystone duo John Goryl and Roy Smalley knocked home one each. Smalley, who was also Gene Mauch's brother-in-law, was particularly impressive in the field, making several gold star plays.

The games in Havana had been scheduled for consecutive nights, but rain upset the plans for the showdown finale, postponing it one day until Tuesday, October 6. The 15,012 fans on hand for the sixth game set up Game Seven's gate totals to elevate the Series to the second-biggest drawing JWS on record. The players' winning and losing shares had already been determined, based on the receipts from the first four games. The winning share had been calculated to $888.27 per player, with $592.18 apiece going to those on the not so fortunate side. The owners and leagues split the (hefty) proceeds from the final three contests. Minnesota team executives were eventually handed a check for $38,000 as spoils for the three final games in Havana. Before the final match, Mauch had let it be known that the Sugar Kings pitcher he most feared was Luis Arroyo, even though his team had twice beaten the Puerto Rican left-hander. Mauch selected his top man, Tom Borland, to try to cap the improbable comeback. With a four-day-rested Raúl Sánchez and a three-day-rested Ted Wieand available, Preston Gómez chose to live or die with his winningest pitcher.

Before batting practice had commenced, several time zones away, the Chicago White Sox had staved off elimination in the World Series with a Game Five, 1–0 victory over the Los Angeles Dodgers. For the third consecutive day, more than 92,000 fans filled the Los Angeles Coliseum to witness the action. Though not a football-size arena, Gran Stadium stood up honorably, if not superiorly, to any existing minor league park (and one or two major league ones) as host for the first championship-deciding organized baseball game played outside the U.S. or Canada. Outwardly reinforcing the comparative appraisal, a paid attendance of 24,990, with several thousand more military personnel (including their bearded leader), packed the house that Maduro and Suárez built.

The big crowd had little to cheer for the first seven innings, as Borland stopped cold any aim of scoring by the Sugar Kings, while the throng concurrently endured solo home runs by the Millers' Lou Clinton and Joe Macko. Six outs from having to bitterly swallow a humiliating—from the Sugar Kings' point of view—championship defeat, the islanders rallied in the eighth. Chacón bounced a leadoff hit to center. Borland took care of the next batter, González, presently the only left-handed batter in the Cubans' lineup. With one down, Morejón slashed a ground-rule double that landed in the overflow crowd stationed on the field along the right field foul line. Mauch made a pitching change, bringing in right-hander Murray Wall to pitch to right-hand swinger Ray Shearer. Wall fanned the Sugar Kings' right fielder for the second out. Gómez followed with the strategic move of the game, inserting left-handed-swinging Larry Novak to bat for slugger Borrego Alvarez. Mauch either had no one in the bullpen to counter, or simply decided not to, and let Wall pitch to the pinch-hitter. Down 0–2 in the count, Novak singled to center, scoring Morejón, to tie the score and send the stadium crowd into a frenzy. "Novak hit the same pitch he missed before," Wall would sigh after the game. "I thought I had him."[56] Mauch then pulled Wall. Taking over for the dejected pitcher, Billy Muffett made his third appearance and secured the inning's final out.

Novak was the second Sugar Kings emergency hitter of the game. Cookie Rojas had batted without success in the bottom of the seventh inning for starter Wieand, whose seven-inning pitching line was marred only by the two bases-empty home runs. He gave up two other hits, walked a pair and whiffed five. Novak took over for Alvarez at first base. Pitching in the ninth, reliever Raúl Sánchez duplicated the scoreless inning he had tossed in the eighth. The Sugar Kings took their last licks with a chance to become minor league champions, or at worst, engage the Millers on even footing in extra innings. Muffett broke a cardinal rule by walking his opposite number to start the ninth. Sánchez was sacrificed to second by Davalillo, but Chacón went down swinging for out number two. Playing the percentages, Mauch ordered the dangerous González intentionally passed. That brought Morejón to the plate. The cleanup hitter bounced a base hit to center, plating Sánchez with the championship run. Scoring three runs in their last two at-bats to eke out the one-run victory, the Sugar Kings repeated their modus operandi of two previous late-inning, come-from-behind wins (Games Three and Four).

The rope holding back the fans along the foul lines tore away, as those standing patrons, and thousands more, could not contain their excitement, celebrating the end of what the *Minneapolis Star* called "the most fantastic Junior World Series in history."

"It was a scene of pandemonium, hysteria, delirium and bedlam as the volatile fans exploded onto the field," recorded one newspaper. "They threw pillows, lit bonfires, waved Cuban flags and danced the cha-cha-chá."[57]

Lloyd McGowan, covering the action for the *Montreal Star,* echoed the sentiments of several of his colleagues in his assessment of the Series. "There has been nothing to compare with the games here in spectator enthusiasm in the Junior Series," wrote the veteran reporter. "I say this after covering them for the past 25 years. Until this one, I thought the most exciting Series was back in 1946 when Montreal beat Louisville and Jackie Robinson was carried shoulder high about the field by excited Montreal fans."[58]

The five contests at Gran Stadium attracted 100,260 fans, a figure that naturally delighted the hierarchy of the leagues and teams. The sparse crowds of the first two games left the final attendance figure at 103,808, a figure surpassed only by the 1944 JWS. That series, between the Baltimore Orioles and Louisville Colonels, attracted 129,618, boosted by a first-game turnout of 52,000 (held in a football stadium). Executive heads Shaughnessy and Trautman were unable to soak in final reminiscences, as both were confined to Cuban hospitals for pneumonia (caught in Minnesota). For the visiting players, the Series, needless to say, was one to remember. "No one who was there will ever forget it," said Mauch upon his team's return to the land of 10,000 lakes.[59]

"Despite losing, Minneapolis players agreed that the Junior Series games in Havana were the greatest experiences of their lives," reported *The Sporting News.* "Such items as Premier Castro attending every game, flanked by 35 bodyguards, soldiers, some of them 13-years-old, manning machine guns on the playing field, and live chickens sailing from the stands will remain vivid in the memories of the Millers."[60] (Smacking of animal cruelty under modern-day sensibilities, the chickens—tied at the feet—were considered good-luck rally charms.)

For the still-young Sugar Kings franchise and their fans, lamentably, there were far fewer memories going forward from this climactic day than those already existing in the past.

"Baseball is a religion in Cuba," said one journalist a month after Fidel Castro came to power, "and nobody interferes with it."[61]

"The church is behind Castro," Maduro had said the same week. "And if you have any doubts, this is what we heard from the pulpit Sunday:

The 1959 Junior World Series champions. Back row, left to right: Luis Arroyo, Elio Chacón, Raúl Sánchez, Hank Izquierdo, Leo Cárdenas, Walt Craddock. Middle: Luis Navarro, (trainer), Borrego Alvarez, Danny Morejón, Pedro Carrillo, Carlos Paula, Ted Wieand, Mike Cuéllar, Larry Novak, Bob Moorehead. Seated: Emilio Cueche, Cookie Rojas, Yo-Yo Davalillo, Preston Gómez, manager, Reinaldo Cordiero, coach, Tony González, Jesse Gonder (courtesy Ralph Maya).

'While your heart may tell you this [executions of Batista followers] is wrong, your brain must tell you that it is something that must be done to eliminate a cancer to society.'"[62]

Soon, Castro would kick all priests and nuns out of Cuba and declare his state atheistic.[63]

Six

The End of the Sugar Kings

The Cuban Winter League opened two days after the Sugar Kings became the first non–U.S. Junior World Series champion since 1953, when Montreal defeated the Kansas City Blues in five games. "A history-making Caribbean winter ball venture with plans to televise 26 Cuban Winter League games to major markets in the United States enthusiastically preceded the start of the 1959–1960 campaign," noted one baseball historian. "Nine TV stations, including WOR in New York, WBKB in Chicago and KTTC in Los Angeles, agreed to broadcast the taped action, edited of superfluous proceedings to fit into 90-minute time slots ... the arrangement brokered through the Cuban-American Television Company."[1]

Maduro's involvement, in what had to be considered a promotional coup in exposing Cuban baseball to the North American public during the winter months, was unclear. It would not seem too speculative to think that he did have some hand in it. Maduro's franchise's long-standing motto of *"Un Paso Mas y Llegamos"* ("One More Step and We'll Make It") was a pointed reference to his ultimate goal of breaking into the major leagues. Whoever's brainchild it was, the international television deal had to be viewed as a master stroke for raising awareness and wholesale product branding for Cuba's most prominent sport.

But there was one person whose convictions steered away from advancement for any sector of the general populace that he was not leading. On October 26, Fidel Castro dismissed the 13th anniversary of the opening of Gran Stadium and ordered the scheduled game canceled in order to call a political rally. Attended by tens of thousands outside the Presidential Palace, "Castro dramatically arrived by helicopter with a Belgian automatic rifle in hand."[2] He used the televised event to deliver his strongest anti–American speech to date and to defuse the image-injuring resignation of one of his highest ranking military men. The prior week, Major Huber Matos, military head of Camagüey province and one of Castro's confidant corps commander's during his guerrilla war, had been arrested for treason following his public break with the Maximum Leader.

On November 12, Castro darkened the stadium again to prevent competition in favor of another televised speech focused on more internal damage control. He tried to explain the weeks-old disappearance of co-revolutionary Camilo Cienfuegos. Rumors had abounded over the actual fate of the well-known and popular—too popular to arrest—corps commander, who was lost in an apparent plane crash off the Cuban coast, Castro said. As he had with his October 26 speech, Castro earned page one column space in all major U.S. newspapers. From the *Chicago Tribune*:

> Castro declared the rumors were all part of a "disgraceful intrigue" to discredit the Cuban revolution. Cienfuegos was one of Castro's closest associates from the beginning of the revolution. No trace of him or his plane have been found. He assailed a story in the *Miami News* speculating that the 28-year-old commander had been killed because of differences with the prime minister's leftist brother Raul, who is supreme chief over all Cuban armed forces. Castro switched from this into the anti–American attack.[3]

The annual minor league winter meetings were held in St. Petersburg on December 1. Maduro was present, but more dependent on the kindness of others than perhaps he had ever been in his life. "Fidel Castro was proud of Roberto Maduro when the wealthy young baseball man's Havana Sugar Kings brought the Little World Series crown home to Cuba," explained columnist Bob Broeg. "Castro's gratitude was as short-lived as some of his political enemies. When Maduro attended the winter baseball meetings, he was permitted to take out of Cuba only $80. So the mortified man was forced to accept the charity of the Cincinnati Reds, with whom his club has a working agreement."[4]

The week preceding Maduro's trip, Major Ernesto "Che" Guevara had been named president of Cuba's National Bank, which caused a considerable run of withdrawals from savings accounts in regional banks throughout the island. Meanwhile, Maduro, who had greater considerations to keep in mind, was not yet ready to condemn anyone. He told a longed-acquaintance scribe on the eve of the Florida convention: "Saturday night I took three of my children to a Catholic rally. In all my life I have seen many demonstrations, but never anything like this. It started at 7:30 at night, and there was an outdoor Mass. The papers say there were 400,000 but I say [much more]. It was raining and cold for Cuba. I left at

3:30 in the morning and it was still going strong. Yes, Castro was there. He was there. He is Catholic."[5]

The grand gathering procured widespread northern newspaper coverage, but none mentioned the presence of Castro. In truth, Castro interpreted the large assembly, mobilized by the island's National Catholic Congress, as a threat. The *Orlando Sentinel* captured this perspective: "About half a million Cuban Catholics assembled for a rally last night 24 hours after Prime Minister Fidel Castro accused his foes of trying to use the meeting to turn the church against him. Castro told a meeting of students and other supporters Friday night that 'the privileged class'—whose land holdings are being swallowed up in the agrarian reform program—were trying to turn the congress into a rally against his revolutionary regime."[6] An absolute point of contention for Castro had to be the night's radio transmission from Vatican City. Simultaneously sent to station towers throughout Cuba, Pope John XXIII spoke in Spanish and offered his blessing to his Cuban followers.

Maduro's misstatement about Castro's attendance at the National Catholic Congress convocation appears to be a desire to mold Castro into what he hoped he would be instead of objectively seeing him for what he was becoming. But he was not alone. Castro continued to find enablers, including the very people he had been financially hurting. On December 8, billed as "The Day of the Revolution," Gran Stadium held an all-star game between teams of Cuban and American players, with all proceeds and contributions from the contest earmarked for "social reconstruction" and militaristic funding. "The Cuban Winter League is doing its part to contribute to the Cuban revolutionary government, the agrarian reform and the purchase of planes for the Cuban Air Force," read one pre-announcement of the event. "Everyone will pay his way into the park for the all-star game, including sportswriters and stadium employees."[7]

The International League midwinter meeting usually entailed hammering out schedules to the satisfaction of ownership groups. The January 29, 1960, conclave addressed much more complex issues. Toronto and Buffalo had expressed their desire to join the major league-aspiring Continental League in 1961. Frank Shaughnessy had been firmly negotiating with the involved parties over restitution, setting a $500,000 buyout price for each of the clubs. Montreal also let it be known that it would be willing to join the CL as an alternate candidate, if a currently stalled deal to facilitate the Houston Buffalos' placement into the new league failed. On the front-burner, however, was the matter of what one advance report called "finding a cure for what fast is becoming an international headache."[8]

At a social gathering, possibly in a casino, Maduro quizzically listens to Cuban Sports Director Captain Felipe Guerra Matos (far right), as sportswriters Fausto Miranda (center, dark suit) and Rai García (front, glasses) appear more interested in the camera. Maduro seems to be holding a neck brace, which may explain his necktie-less appearance. The pipe-smoking, unidentified man at left appears to hold one or more playing chips in his fingers (author's collection).

For reasons not given, Maduro did not attend the meeting. GM Paul Miller served as his proxy. (Based on his prior humiliating travel restrictions, it may not be hard to deduce the probable reason for Maduro's absence.) Miller assured everyone that things in Havana were baseball copacetic. He shared the news of the two-day-old signing of Antonio "Tony" Castaño as new manager of the Sugar Kings. (Preston Gómez had decided in December to rejoin the Los Angeles Dodgers organization and take the reins of the Spokane Indians in the Pacific Coast League.) Castaño, 48, had just clinched the CWL pennant as skipper of the Cienfuegos Elephants. Miller advised the interested group that his club was in the process of negotiating a six-figure radio-television contract (which never materialized). He responded to concerns over the winter league's poor attendance by blaming a runaway race by the league's top finisher. Toeing the same line as his boss, Miller avoided the elephant-in-the-room topic of politics.

For his part, Shaughnessy, who was re-elected to a three-year term expiring December 31, 1962, said that he did not like "the anti–American talk in Cuba," but paid a grand compliment to Cuban fans "as the finest ... in the world."[9]

Not everyone, however, was willing to rely on the better angels of a certain Cuban overlord's nature. Rochester Red Wings President Frank Horton introduced a "disaster resolution," which would give the league's chief executive the authority to move any franchise—without requiring consultation or vote from the other owners—in the event of an emergency. It was Horton's team that was on the field during the riotous 26th of July observance last season, and Horton's team that was scheduled to open the 1960 season in Havana in four months. The singularly empowering act was approved by a 6–2 majority. Miller and Toronto GM Danny Menendez cast dissenting votes.

In February, the commissioner of baseball weighed in. In between an agenda of talks with the embryonic Continental League over establishment of territorial rights fees, Ford C. Frick catalogued Havana as "an important member of organized baseball," but said he would not force any American player who was not comfortable playing "under hazardous conditions" in that city to do so. In a reprinted interview appearing in the February 24 edition of *The Sporting News,* by the *New York World-Telegram & Sun's* Dan Daniel, Frick stated that "Bob Maduro had been put on notice" and if things deteriorated "something will have to be done."

Adhering to his position of not mixing sport with affairs of state, Maduro annoyedly responded, as singled out in this wire report out of Havana: "Bobby Maduro, president of the Havana Sugar Kings, said today he will resist any move involving his International League franchise in 'political shenanigans' growing out of U.S.–Cuba relations."[10] Maduro went as far as to send Frick a telegram at his spring training base of Belle Aire, Florida, contesting another of the commissioner's statements. *"I have received no notification as stated in the [TSN] article,"* it partially read, *"but will strongly refuse to permit anyone from playing around with the Havana franchise, which heretofore has abided by all rules and regulations of baseball. I suggest you find better sources of information and by all means let's keep baseball out of politics."*[11]

Maduro's agitation was evident. As if the pressures surrounding him at home were not enough, he now felt, perhaps, that he was being painted into a corner by larger, outside concerns—those he viewed as having no business or say in the matters involving *his* ballclub. "The process through which national and political identity are defined in Cuba is a complex mixture of admiration and rejection of the United States," explained Yale professor and Cuban baseball historian Roberto González Echevarría many years later.[12] Fidel Castro had already begun to villainize the United States and embrace a decades-lasting condemnation of it for what would amount to all of his country's ills—past, current, and future. Maduro's perturbed pronouncements to Frick could be interpreted as not only admonishing but teetering on misplaced nationalistic pride that swept up so many Cubans into falsely believing better times could be in store without a relationship with the United States.

A month away from the start of the season, IL general managers issued a vote of confidence assuredly well received by Maduro and Cuban baseball fans alike. "Their [GMs] willingness to continue with the Havana Sugar Kings as members is based on respect for the club's president and the wild enthusiasm of Cubans for baseball," said the *Miami News*, in a poll conducted of the seven executives. "The big fear is that Castro's bitter tirades against the United States might inspire the man on the street to take it upon himself to harm one of the players."[13] George Sisler, Jr., Rochester's general manager, indicated that he would take an advance trip to Havana prior to his team's April 20 opening date.

But things soured over the last weekend of March, when the Baltimore Orioles canceled a three-day exhibition with the Cincinnati Reds in Havana and rescheduled it to Miami. "Your disregard for Cuban baseball and your irresponsibility in overlooking the material damage you are inflicting upon our club have no justification,"[14] Maduro complained in a cablegram to Orioles president Lee MacPhail, and went as far as to question the Orioles club's fortitude. Player development partner Gabe Paul said the Reds had been looking forward to making the trip and that Baltimore, as the home team, had ultimate choice of venue.

From New York, Commissioner Ford Frick was quick to say that his office was not consulted in the decision. The U.S. State Department also issued a statement of non-involvement, coming from someone who was an obvious follower of the sport: "We would have had no objection [to the trip]. In fact, the department would probably look with some favor on our boys playing there. After all, half the Washington Senators are Cuban."[15] The exaggeration was a reference to the multitude of Cuban players who had suited up for the baseball Senators, including the current crop.

The Cuban sports press took up the mantle of MacPhail-bashing as well. "It is difficult to understand how any big league club could have as president a man whose capabilities are so negative," wrote the president of the Cuban Association of Sports Writers, Fausto Miranda, in an official protest wired to MacPhail. "Your decision against bringing Baltimore here to play is an attack on our baseball that we censure forcefully."[16]

Maduro's better business sense then kicked into gear. In an abrupt halt to the war of words, he retraced to a tactic which had worked well for him in the past. Less than 48 hours after the criticism-provoking cancelation, Maduro adopted a more neighborly approach, using the usual media channels. "Frank Shaughnessy said general managers of all the clubs and sports writers from the league have been invited by the Cuban government to make an all-expense paid trip to Cuba to 'see things for themselves,'" said one such outlet. "What could be fairer than that?" asked the president of the International League."[17]

Maduro astutely masked the invitation as coming from the Cuban government (through the Cuban Tourism Commission), when, in reality, the chances for approval and appropriation of funds in such a short period of time, especially following the perceived Orioles slight, would have been slim to none without some type of financial guarantee from Maduro himself. The hospitality was accepted by seven scribes, a Columbus Jets broadcaster and photographer, and a Buffalo Bisons club secretary. The party of ten spent April 5 through 7 in Havana, with one evening at the famed Tropicana Night Club. The ten left the city wholeheartedly in agreement that there was nothing to worry about.

The Harlem Magicians (a basketball barnstorming knock-off of the more celebrated Globetrotters), an American ballet troupe, and a U.S. auto daredevil show all entertained in Havana during this time without incident, Maduro pointed out from Tampa, Florida, prior to his return to Havana to meet the International League's group of ten. The Sugar Kings owner was in town for a brief get-together with Gabe Paul of the Reds. In an exclusive interview given right at the airport, there was not only detectable frustration and disappointment in his speech but also an underlying sadness in the manner in which he confided to the solitary journalist. "I feel like the child of a divorced couple," Maduro confessed. "I love Cuba and I love the United States. Which way can I turn in this thing? No, I do not wish to discuss politics.

"What I really don't understand is why all this excitement about sending teams to fulfill commitments only 90 miles from your country when you are sending teams in all sports to compete in Russia. Russia is all right. But Cuba is not? Is that the picture?"[18]

A handful of days prior to the scheduled first pitch at Gran Stadium, the *Democrat and Chronicle*, Rochester's biggest daily newspaper, went to press with a story that the Sugar Kings would be moved to Jersey City at the conclusion of their initial 13-game homestand. The story was penned by George Beahon, the same writer who plucked the exclusive conversation with Maduro at Tampa airport. Beahon added a new twist, indicating that the problem now lay *not* in convincing teams to travel to Havana, but "in getting the Sugar Kings out of Cuba for their road games." Beahon did enter into specifics, however.

Reached for comment, Maduro waved off the report as false, with an added idealistic expression of character: "Despite rumors about the shift of the Havana franchise, club owner Bob Maduro insists the franchise will remain here. Maduro said he feels baseball can help ease some of the strain in Cuban-American relations and promote good will at the people to people level."[19]

Opening night finally arrived for the beleaguered owner and his assailed franchise. The Rochester Red Wings arrived in Havana a day before the opener, as did chief of the league Shaughnessy. Red Wings executives and media personnel enjoyed a lunch given for them by the Cuban sports director, Captain Felipe Guerra Matos. Luke Easter, a recognized player not only in Cuba but throughout the Caribbean, appeared on a Cuban TV show that evening.

On the morning of April 20, Cuban baseball fans reveled in the news of a grand major league feat by one of their own. The previous day, in a triumphant first game back with the Chicago White Sox, Minnie Miñoso had clouted two home runs, including a ninth-inning, walk-off dinger, providing the White Sox with a memorable, 10–9 Opening Day victory over the Kansas City Athletics. Miñoso, who also drove in six runs, had been re-obtained by the White Sox via off-season trade. At Gran Stadium later in the evening, two home runs by Red Wings players spoiled the festivities for 12,045 cash customers. The second blast, coming in the top of the tenth inning, off the bat of last night's TV guest, decided the contest, 4–3, in favor of the visitors. Easter redirected a pitch from Luis Arroyo over the left field fence for the game-decider. Earlier, teammate Charlie James had clocked a two-run homer against Sugar Kings starter Mike Cuéllar. Jim Donohue picked up the relief win.

Pre-game ceremonies included a police marching band, flying American, Canadian and Cuban flags, Frank Shaughnessy presenting Maduro with the Governors' Cup, and the gifting of high-end boxes of cigars to each Red Wings player by a Sugar Kings counterpart. The opposing players and their apprehensive owner, Frank Horton, were warmly received with applause during the introductions. The game was delayed 47 minutes for the arrival of Fidel Castro, who threw out the first pitch from the mound to young Cubans catcher José "Joe" Azcúe. Because of the delay, Red Wings starter Bob Keegan warmed up three times in anticipation of his duty.

A second ten-inning encounter developed the next night. Orlando Peña pitched well but tired in the final inning, when the Red Wings pushed across three runs for a 4–1 triumph. Hurling three scoreless innings, Tom Hurd earned Rochester's second victory, after taking the baton from 19-year-old starter Ray Sadecki.

The Havana franchise had faced both uncertainty and adversity in the weeks leading up to the campaign. "Unable to take any money out of the country," wrote a northern reporter, "the Cubans had only ten days of spring training at home and didn't play a single exhibition game against outside competition."[20] The Cubans were able to engage in five intra-squad matches. In comparison, Rochester had played 27 practice games in Florida.

A third loss to Rochester, April 22, may have exposed the defending JWS champions' lack of preparedness. The Red Wings whipped the Sugar Kings, 7–3. Bob Miller opened for the home favorites; he lasted into the seventh inning, allowing four runs and absorbing the loss. Billy Harrell and Ben Mateosky tripled and homered, respectively, as pinch-hitters in Miller's last frame. New third baseman Félix Torres clanged the first Sugar Kings home run of 1960, in the fourth inning with a man on base. Winning pitcher Frank Barnes knocked down the next batter, Borrego Alvarez, with a pitch high and tight. Barnes, who had an intimidating reputation on the mound, hit Alvarez in the helmet with his next delivery. It took players from both sides to keep the incited men apart before play continued. Barely 3,000 fans made their presence known in the two games that followed the opener. A more than three-hour, overlapping Friday night hostile-to-American speech, or "harangue," as many newspapers in the north referred to it, by Fidel Castro may or may not have affected the turnout in the series finale. It was the Red Wings' first sweep in Havana since they began play on the island.

The Sugar Kings' 1960 lineup had undergone some changes. Along with Félix Torres and Joe Azcúe, who beat out Hank Izquierdo as the number one catcher, new faces included outfielders Lou Jackson and Jim Pendleton, who tried to fill the shoes of Tony González, called up by the Cincinnati Reds that spring. Ray Shearer, one of the team's key JWS contributors, was brought back. JWS hero Danny Morejón, whose six seasons donning the Sugar Kings uniform was the most by any position player, was the other returning starter in the pasture. A healthy Cookie Rojas won more infield playing time from Elio Chacón and Yo-Yo Davalillo.

Borrego Alvarez held onto first base, and no one was going to displace the coveted Leo Cárdenas at shortstop. It was Pendleton, a former major leaguer with three different teams, who helped deliver the Sugar Kings' first win, after five unsuccessful tries. In the second game of a doubleheader against the Buffalo Bisons, the outfielder singled home Davalillo with the game-winning run for a 5–4, 14-inning victory. The shortened first act of the twin bill had been lost, 2–1, with hill opponents Ken Lehman and Luis Arroyo both pitching the seven-inning distance.

On April 26, four home runs were hit at Gran Stadium, two by each team, accounting for all the runs in the game. Against Montreal Royals pitcher Babe Birrer, Cárdenas and Alvarez went deep without anyone on base. Joe Altobelli and first-year International League player Alfonso "Chico" Carrasquel each connected with a man on base to pace Birrer's 4–2 win. Cárdenas homered the next night as the Sugar Kings erupted for five runs in the eighth inning against the same team. Félix Torres drove in four runs in the 10–5 decision. The Kings were shut out the following evening, but pulled out a 3–2, getaway game win on April 29. Jim Pendleton whacked a seventh-inning circuit clout to break a 2–2 tie. Arroyo tossed five innings of scoreless relief for the win. Mike Cuéllar started but was removed in the first inning due to arm trouble. Cuban hurler René Valdes suffered the complete-game loss for Montreal.

The Toronto Maple Leafs checked into Havana as the Sugar Kings' last homestand opponent and were held in check by Orlando Peña. A 14-hit attack backed the veteran right-hander's first victory of the year, 7–3, on the last day of April. All the visitors' runs—plated in the ninth inning—were unearned. A Sunday doubleheader the next day was canceled, as were all sporting events and activities, by order of Fidel Castro, in deference to an immense rally planned for International Workers Day. The game was made up as a homestand-closing doubleheader on May 2. The Kings won the abridged opener, 3–2. Borrego Alvarez launched a solo home run in the bottom of the seventh inning to end the game in high-fiving fashion. Arroyo won his third game in relief. The Kings dropped the nightcap, 2–1, to fall to 5–8. Last year's ace, Ted Wieand, made his first start after being sent down to the Sugar Kings by the Reds a few days earlier. Though he was pinned with the loss, the sight of their most valuable pitcher from last season assuredly gladdened the hearts of many of the 3,790 fans at the ballpark.

The Sugar Kings left Havana as the schedule indicated, without any published mention of personal monetary restraint applicable to the players. Mike Cuéllar appeared to have overcome his previous arm issue, as he halted the Montreal Royals, 8–2, in the Cubans' first road game on May 4. Disappointing an Opening Day crowd of 8,725 in Montreal, the left-hander notched his first win, allowing five hits. With five road successes in eight games, the Kings rose out of last place.

With a 5–4 victory over the Columbus Jets, the Cubans reached the .500 mark in their 22nd game, the first back in Havana following their initial road jaunt. The next night, May 17, Bob Miller won his fourth game, 3–2, aided by a five-out save by Luis Arroyo. Miller split two other Gran Stadium starts on the homestand. The loss (May 25) was 1–0, on an unearned run which scored without the benefit of a hit. Miller permitted only one safety, which occurred in the ninth inning and did not figure in the scoring. Following the no-out single, Miller (5–3) flipped his glove in the air, knowing he had lost out on *Bohemia's* $1,000 no-hit prize.

The 24-year-old Miller had debuted in the major leagues seven years earlier, a few weeks shy of his 18th birthday. He would close out his modest big-league career a few years later with the expansion New York Mets. Serving as chairman of the major league players association for retired players (forerunner of the Major League Baseball Players Alumni Association) for 11 years, he says, was his biggest post-baseball playing accomplishment.

> I was signed by Detroit as a bonus baby for $65,000 in 1953. That included three years of salary. So, I didn't get paid again until my fourth year in the league. It wasn't that bad, of course, because at that time the minimum salary was $6,000.
>
> Then Cincinnati acquired me after I came out of the service, and they assigned me to Havana. When you're a winner down there the fans really went crazy. Everybody was friendly. People you met at the supermarket always said hello. We were Americans but not American [Chuckles]. What I mean by that is the warning, or order, had come for Americans to leave Cuba, but it didn't apply to us because we kept on playing. I never felt unsafe. I don't think any of the players did.
>
> I never had any beef [to eat] during my time there [Havana]. Castro moved the cattle, I don't know where—part of his [agrarian] reforms. I lived on chicken and lamb.
>
> The owner [Maduro] was a kind and generous man. He owned different businesses. He invited us to one of his estates. It was 4 o'clock in the afternoon and he served us [players] cocktails. He thought because he was a good guy Castro would not interfere with him. But Castro took everything from him.
>
> I still keep up with the game. Differences? I just remember in my time, with all the minor league teams it seemed like there were 100 pitchers trying to take your job every year. They don't have that now.[21]

While enjoying the home cooking, new manager Tony Castaño's team continued the successful turnaround begun on the road, taking eight of ten decisions against three visiting clubs and securing third place all to themselves.

In late May, Raúl Sanchez became the second Cincinnati Reds pitcher returned to the Sugar Kings. He was tardy in reporting and compounded the issue by squabbling over his new salary; the Sugar Kings suspended the 29-year-old pitcher who had pitched so well for them last season, especially in the playoffs. Disciplinary matters aside, reason for overall optimism existed as the Cubans abandoned their home confines again on May 26, with a record of 18–13. The team's attendance ticked slightly higher than at the same point last season, and all the International League teams had come and gone to the Cuban capital without incident.

By mid–June, however, the club had slipped several games under break-even and into fifth place. On June 16, the Sugar Kings were no-hit for the first and only time in a condensed first game of a doubleheader at Maple Leaf Stadium. Author of the 1–0 gem was Toronto's Frank Funk. Funk, who walked three and struck out one, was aided in the field by two flashy plays by shortstop George "Sparky" Anderson and a "sensational diving catch" by center fielder Jerry Waters. The no-hitter was the first in the IL since the Sugar Kings' Rudy Arias pitched his in August 1958 under similar inning-shortened circumstances. The Kings bounced back in the regulation afterpiece, 6–3. Lou Jackson, an outfielder acquired by the Reds in a December trade for slugger Frank Thomas, homered twice.

Although the team seemed mired in mediocrity, individually speaking, a player whose stock continued to ascend was Leo Cárdenas. The young shortstop was named as a first-team All-Star. Jim Pendleton, among the league leaders in average, home runs and RBI, was the other Sugar Kings representative penciled to start against the Milwaukee Braves in the annual showcase game on June 27.

One day prior to the All-Star clash, a blast at a Havana munitions dump held up the start of a Sunday night doubleheader between the Rochester Red Wings and Sugar Kings. "A deafening explosion at 7:55 p.m. shook Havana and cut off electrical power to Gran Stadium, delaying the opener for an hour and a half. 'About five minutes before game time, there was a terrific explosion,' said George Sisler, Rochester general manager. 'It shook the ballpark, but wasn't close enough to injure anyone at the park.'"[22] One person died and hundreds were injured in what was called an accident. Infielder Félix Torres provided a more rewarding jolt to Gran Stadium fans sometime later, by homering in the bottom of the seventh inning, with a man on base, which held up for a Sugar Kings 6–5 victory. Tied 3–3, the second contest was halted after nine innings due to curfew brought on by the late start of the first game. The Red Wings scored a run in the ninth, denying Raúl Sánchez a 3–2 victory. Afterwards, the Red Wings flew to Miami and the Sugar Kings departed for Buffalo, while Cárdenas and Pendleton detoured to Toronto, site of the All-Star contest. Both clubs, along with the other six, picked up the schedule on June 28, after a one-day "break" for the flashy exhibition game.

Maduro heard about the munitions incident from afar. Attending a special summit in New York, one day ahead of the planned IL owners meeting in Toronto on June 27, Maduro applied for a $20,000 loan with the directors of the league. He cited the plummeting value of the Cuban peso and the need to fulfill key obligations with U.S dollars as necessitating the request. The club owner paid all visiting teams in dollars, and 60 percent of the salaries of all North American players on his payroll in greenbacks, the rest in pesos. Maduro also asked that the Cubans franchise be transferred into his name from the Cuban corporation that owned it. This had to have been particularly painful for the businessman-sportsman. The legal change would facilitate a speedier move of the franchise, if the situation should arise. One might speculate that the change may have been a stipulation of the loan and not initiated by Maduro, as reported. Or that Maduro thought he could better protect the team by placing its full ownership under his personal name.

From Washington, on the day the IL owners met in Toronto, the House Agricultural Committee voted (33–0) to give U.S. President Dwight D. Eisenhower the authority to cut Cuba's sugar quota, in an attempt to prevent payment subsidies from ending up in the coffers of Russian satellite-nations.

> Sugar is the backbone of the Cuban economy. The United States buys a little more than half of Cuba's sugar output at the premium price provided under the U.S. Sugar Act. Some congressmen have protested that Prime Minister Castro is using the U.S. premium price to sell sugar to Soviet bloc countries at less than cost. Castro said American properties in Cuba would be seized in the same proportions of any cuts in the U.S. quota. U.S. officials estimate that Castro has already seized a third of American-owned properties in Cuba.[23]

The same week as the IL All-Star Game, Dan Daniel dedicated a lengthy column to advocating the withdrawal of the International League from Havana on the grounds that the circuit's continuing operations in Cuba "while the communist-spawned Castro regime exists, would not be compatible with our national interest, and the spirit in which we play baseball."[24] Daniel alluded to the undercurrent of internal subterfuge common in totalitarian states that had already manifested itself in Cuba and still exists there today. He quoted Richmond/NY Yankees pitcher Eli Grba in this respect: "If a native talks to you, he first looks around to see if there is an informer in the neighborhood."²⁵ Thinking a mid-season removal would be too messy, the longtime New York sportswriter called for the team's displacement for the 1961 season.

Unbeknownst to Daniel, the countdown had already begun. The end of the Cuban Sugar Kings, and the dramatic alteration of baseball in the Caribbean for the foreseeable future, was at hand. In early July, with the Sugar Kings still on the road, relocation talk intensified in the press. Speculating on different scenarios, a writer who knew Maduro sympathized with the beset man who had been unceasingly pulled in two directions for an extended period of time. "In any event," wrote George Beahon, "Bobby Maduro, who is caught directly in the middle of the situation, would be powerless to resist such an emergency move. Maduro has been good to the league; and good to Cuban baseball; he has been better to the league than the league has been to him. He warrants any and all consideration that has been and may be forthcoming to him."²⁶

During the first few days of July: the U.S. Congress passed the bill allowing President Eisenhower to cut Cuba's sugar quota; asylum-seeking co-pilots of a Cubana Airlines jet flying from Madrid to Havana diverted the plane, carrying 31 passengers, to Miami; the Cuban ambassador-designate to the United Nations, José Miro Cardona, resigned over "ideological differences" with his Prime Minister and sought refuge in the Argentine Embassy; and the "Cuban Cabinet early Wednesday [July 6] authorized the expropriation of all property owned by American companies or U.S. citizens residing in Cuba 'when deemed necessary in the national interest' [and] power to take over of what remains of the nearly one-billion-dollar investment which the United States and its citizens had in Cuba when Castro overthrew Fulgencio Batista 19 months ago."²⁷ The latter move was in retaliation for the U.S. Congressional legislation [July 3] and the suspension of all Cuban sugar imports that followed on July 5 by the Commodity Stabilization Service, until Eisenhower determined the severity of the new legislation.

The soon-to-be nationalized sugar industry comprised a little more than a quarter of all U.S. interests in Cuba, with the vast majority of the economic mainstay not under foreign control. "Taking over the mills probably will mean complete cessation of sugar imports by the United States," collectively pronounced a group of observers. "Cuba would thus be forced to sell exclusively on the world market. Cuban Sugar Union leader Conrado Becquer said Monday that 37 of 161 mills are American-owned with a value of $260 million."²⁸ The revealing data shatters the "justification"

Castro used time and time again for nationalizing Cuban industry, in general, as being all under "Imperialistic control."

On July 6, amid the tumultuous hemispheric reports, U.S. sports pages were rife with pending news of the Sugar Kings' forced move. Finally, the next day, printed confirmation appeared in the same inner sections of those dailies. In Montreal, Frank Shaughnessy advised the press of his decision to relocate the franchise to a soon-to-be-announced city, and then said he would call Bobby Maduro with the news—which he should have done in reverse order. "I don't suppose Maduro is going to like it," Shaughnessy said. "Naturally, we don't like it either. We don't want to leave. But we can't go on down there."[29]

"Maduro was in his office on Amargura Street—'*amargura*' means 'bitterness' in Spanish—when he got the news from Shaughnessy," John Phillips wrote with ironic implication. "Maduro told newsmen that Shaughnessy's concerns about safety were 'ridiculous.'"[30]

Understandably angered, Maduro vowed not to attend the upcoming IL meeting and implied that he would not be a part of his team's future operations, tipping off that he already knew where it was heading. "If they want to take the franchise from us," he said, "Cincinnati will have to operate it alone in Jersey City because I certainly won't."[31]

Maduro denounced Shaughnessy's decision to snatch his ballclub. Making it clear whom he held responsible for the imminent geographic radicalization of his club, Maduro engaged in finger-pointing accusations.

> The International League is making a big mistake. Baseball was a strong link between the Cuban and American peoples, and it should never have been broken. This whole thing has a lot to do with the Continental League. Toronto and Buffalo both want to join the Continental League. They are mad at the International League for setting the value of the franchises too high. They are now using the Cuban situation to torpedo the International League and open the way for their exit into the Continental League.[32]

Truth be known, the Continental League was on life support as a viable entity and was a month away from dissolving completely on its proposed formation as a third major league. Backed into the corner as he was by external forces, Maduro continued to cling to the idealistic notion that sports and domestic policies should not be geopolitically intertwined. He further added that he "found it perfectly incredible to believe that there could be sports competition between the United States and Russia, such as in the Olympic games, but there could not be baseball competition between Cuba and the United States."[33]

A day later, Maduro sounded more adamantly entrenched. "I am not moving the franchise and I am not leaving Cuba," he stated. "If the other teams feel they have not had more than ample demonstrations of friendliness and courteous hospitality of the Cuban people, they can go ahead and do what they want."[34]

But he was powerless. The International League's board of directors approved the transfer of the Cuban Sugar Kings to Jersey City in a special meeting on July 13, and the rebranding of the team as the Jersey City Jerseys. *The Sporting News* lamented that Maduro had not been consulted but supported the relocation as "the only reasonable decision" available. Therefore, the munitions-dump-explosion-delayed-DH at Gran Stadium, June 26, 1960, passed into history as the last relevant baseball games played on Cuban soil by an American baseball team in the 20th century. The Rochester Red Wings and the Sugar Kings, perhaps fittingly, had played to a 3–3 tie in game two because of curfew. Retiring the side without any scoring in the bottom of the ninth inning, 30-year-old Bobby Tiefenauer threw the last International League pitch recorded in Cuba. Behind the plate, 22-year-old Chris Cannizzaro received all of Tiefenauer's throws, as he did for starter Bob Keegan, 39, and reliever Cal Browning, 22, before Tiefenauer came on in the seventh frame. Starting pitcher Raúl Sánchez, who appeared in the most career games by a Sugar Kings pitcher (257), fittingly threw the last pitch by a Sugar Kings hurler in the top of the ninth; Joe Azcúe caught the entire game. Among the six batterymen, only Browning, who came on in the first frame and was later charged with the third Sugar Kings run, and Azcúe, who caught both ends of the DH, survive today.

Immediate fallout from the news came with the resignation of manager Tony Castaño. "When there is trouble, my place is with my wife and daughter," he said, adding that he had something other than baseball to fall back on. "I have a grocery store and can run it."[35] Castaño warned that "five or six" native players would follow his lead—but none did. (Twelve Cuban nationals, at one time or another, were on the Sugar Kings' roster. Trainer Luis Navarro was the only other team member to resign.[36]) Paul Miller continued in his GM capacity and relocated to the States. Maduro stayed in Havana. "If I am going to lose money, I prefer to lose it in my own country,"[37] he said, in a resentful-sounding tone. He explained that the Sugar Kings owed $100,000 in loans to Cuban banks and that there were no reserve funds available to meet the prospect of additional losses incurred in Jersey City.

The official transfer occurred Monday, July 11, following an agreement with the Jersey City Parks Commission to use Roosevelt Stadium as home park for the Jerseys. The rental cost was a flat $7,500, and any profits

Still sporting the blue paint job from the more than $1,000,000 in paint, sod and baseball equipment donated by MLB prior to President Obama and the Tampa Bay Rays' March 2016 visit, Maduro and Suárez's expropriated stadium was hosting part of the 57th Serie Nacional at the time of the author's visit (author's collection).

from the Jersey City operations would "accrue to Bobby Maduro," Shaughnessy said. Gabe Paul inked a deal in New York with station WNTA (Newark) to broadcast the remaining 30-odd home games on radio and television. The station was non-committal over transmitting road contests. The team itself was in Miami; it defeated the Marlins, 3–0, behind a four-hitter by Howie Nunn. Purchased by the erstwhile Sugar Kings from Rochester back in April, Nunn may have spoken for many of his non–Hispanic teammates when he expressed a qualified regret for the team's transfer "because I think we stood a chance at finishing third. There's little doubt, however, the boys have been worried."[38] Some newspapers listed the victory under "Jersey City" in the daily IL standings.

By the next day, the change had been universally adopted in print. The Cuban Sugar Kings were no more. As if showing their disappointment, or discontentment, through their performance, the new Garden State team was defeated by the Marlins, 4–0, scratching out one solitary hit in the game. A second-inning infield single to deep short by Yo-Yo Davalillo kept the Marlins' Herb Moford (two walks) from registering the no-hitter. The day also brought the announcement of a replacement manager. Reggie Otero and Tommy Lasorda had been speculated as candidates, but the club decided to bring back Nap Reyes.

Shut out again the following evening, Jersey City then managed a split in the four-game series by breaking out the heavy lumber on July 14. A seventh-inning, three-run home run by Borrego Alvarez wiped out a 2–0 deficit. Three more runs crossed the plate in the same fashion the following inning, propelled by a Cookie Rojas long ball. Jim Pendleton added a solo shot as Luis Arroyo, with four innings of one-run relief, recorded the first victory for the Jersey City "Jerseys," 7–3. With the win, Jersey City's 41st, against 45 setbacks, the club elbowed into fourth place on the IL leaderboard, one-half game ahead of Rochester and Montreal.

In first place, 57–28, Toronto was far ahead of the pack. Presumably during the series, the team displayed altered uniforms consisting of silk patches reading "Jersey City" sewn over the previous scripted team lettering. Keeping with their color scheme, red caps with the white letter J replaced the white and red-billed ones of the Sugar Kings.

It is unclear who managed the club in Miami. Reyes was said to have planned to join the team in that city, but his first game on the bench came in Jersey City's first home game, Friday, July 15. Reyes had a little more company than usual in the dugout. "Two detectives were assigned today to guard manager Nap Reyes of the Jersey City Jerseys, who was branded a 'traitor' by a Cuban newspaper," a post-game news item explained. "The paper 'Revolucion,' semi-official organ of the Castro government, branded Reyes a 'traitor' for accepting the job of manager of the transplanted Havana Sugar Kings."[39] Reyes responded by saying he was a baseball man and worked where he was sent.

Jersey City officials welcomed their new team (which had arrived in the early morning hours from Miami) with a mid-afternoon motorcade through the city, inclusive of main thoroughfares in predominately black and Hispanic neighborhoods. In the lead car, a white convertible, sat Reyes with Miss Jersey City, Delphine Lisk, two Jersey City commissioners, and players Orlando Peña and Hank Izquierdo, while "the other cars of the motorcade carried the team's players and their wives."[40] At 24,500-seat Roosevelt Stadium, the St. Patrick's Drum and Bugle Corps performed prior to the game. A three-foot-high cake with crossed bats inscribed "Welcome to Jersey City" was wheeled out, prior to Mayor Charles Witkowski's tossing of the ceremonial first pitch. Howie Nunn received the privilege of throwing the first pitch in the Jerseys' new home. Nunn, coming off a fine outing, lasted five innings before being relieved by Peña, who squandered a 3–2 lead. Arroyo took over for Peña and surrendered three additional runs. Emilio Cueche, the last remaining original Sugar

King, also pitched an inning and was nicked for a run. In his seventh season, the Venezuelan right-hander would shortly go down in history as the Sugar Kings' longest-tenured and winningest pitcher (64–59), and the team hurler with the most lifetime innings pitched (1,005), complete games (50) and strikeouts (549). The end result was an 8–3 Columbus Jets victory, spoiling for the 7,155 attending fans an otherwise pleasant and festive return of Triple A baseball to Jersey City for the first time in ten years.

The Jerseys commenced inauspiciously in their new home, getting swept in the weekend series by the Jets. In Sunday's 3–1 defeat, Larry Novak homered for the Jerseys' only run. The outfielder collected two gifts which had been promised to the first home team player to swat one out of the park: a gold watch donated by a local Kiwanis Club and a new suit offered by a Bayonne tailor. Fewer than 3,000 supporters showed up for the Saturday and Sunday games.

After four straight losses, the Jerseys claimed their first win in front of the home crowd. Providing the special victory, Howie Nunn pitched a brilliant 1–0 seven-hitter in 11 innings on July 19. Borrego Alvarez singled home Jim Pendleton with the winning run. Fewer than 2,000 fans paid their way into the park.

A few days later, Gabe Paul sold Luis Arroyo to the New York Yankees, which would lead to a curt but celebrated revitalization of the 33-year-old rescue artist's career. Shortly afterward, Paul called up Leo Cárdenas. The smooth-fielding shortstop played his first game in the majors on July 25 for the Reds—the start of a 16-year big league career.

Back in Cuba, news media did not carry results of the Jersey City team, with International League standings dropped from the government-controlled newspapers. The yanking of their team had given rise to a new wave of nationalism and anti–*Yanqui* sentiment. Echoing the feelings, Fausto Miranda wrote in *Revolución* that Cuba was "without a franchise but without a master."[41] One of Cuba's best-known sportswriters and the older brother of major leaguer Willy, Miranda fled the island the following summer. Cuban fans may have found some reasons to gloat if they had been apprised of the fact that the Jerseys drew an average of only 2,246 fans for their first homestand of 15 games.

Separated from his team, Bobby Maduro also dropped from the radar of international media coverage, left alone to deal with his plight as a man torn between the sport he loved and had given so much to and the rapidly changing country he loved even more.

The Toronto Maple Leafs ran away with the International League race, wrapping up the pennant after 137 games on August 27, the earliest IL clincher in 14 years (Montreal, 135 games in 1946). Four days later, Ford Frick cautioned major league club owners "not to permit any of their non–Cuban players to compete in the Cuban Winter League this year because of the political situation in the island republic."[42] Frick recommended caution in allowing U.S. players to travel to the Dominican Republic because of the political unrest there, but green-lighted participation in the Panamanian, Puerto Rican and Venezuelan leagues. Recent economic sanctions imposed by the U.S. against the Trujillo government would provoke a plaintive response from the state-subsidized Dominican Winter League. League officials vetoed the use of American players for the 1960–1961 season.

The Jerseys played only slightly better than the Sugar Kings, completing the season with a 76–77 record, in fifth place, two games out of playoff contention. In a year-end expenditure examination, *The Sporting News* summarized that the team had avoided an operating loss in large part due to the $35,000 television and radio contract Paul had signed with WNTA. (The station had stopped TV broadcasts during the first homestand and had limited radio transmissions to weekend games by September.) Attendance faltered in New Jersey, coming in at 47,715 for 38 games on 29 dates, compared to roughly 75,000 in 35 home dates in Havana.

It took five games for the Rochester Red Wings to defeat the Richmond Virginians in one of two opening round playoff match-ups. The Maple Leafs swept fourth-place Buffalo and faltered only once in the five-game victory march over the Red Wings that followed.

Having sailed through the post-season, Toronto met their match in the Junior World Series against the Louisville Colonels, losing to the American Association team in six games.

1960 International League Final Standings

	W	L	T	PCT	GB	Manager	Major League Affiliation
Toronto Maple Leafs	100	54	2	.649	—	Mel McGaha	Cleveland Indians
Richmond Virginians	82	70	0	.539	17	Steve Souchock	New York Yankees
Rochester Red Wings	81	73	1	.526	19	Clyde King	St. Louis Cardinals
Buffalo Bisons	78	75	2	.510	21½	Kerby Farrell	Philadelphia Phillies
Cubans/Jersey City	76	77	2	.497	23½	Tony Castaño/ Nap Reyes	Cincinnati Reds

	W	L	T	PCT	GB	Manager	Major League Affiliation
Columbus Jets	69	84	1	.451	30½	Cal Ermer	Pittsburgh Pirates
Miami Marlins	65	88	2	.425	34½	Al Vincent	Baltimore Orioles
Montreal Royals	62	92	2	.403	38	Clay Bryant	Los Angeles Dodgers

Seven

Starting Over as "a Millionaire in Friends"

"Baseball is Dying in Castro's Cuba," headlined a November 1960 special correspondent report in a prominent New York daily. R. Hart Phillips was the reporter identifying the causes of a Cuban Winter League in crisis:

> Baseball, once the favorite sport in the island, is about to become a casualty of the Cuban revolution. For the first time in fifty-three years, there are no United States ball players on the four professional teams in the league.
>
> The poor attendance at the nightly games here is the result of a combination of factors, according to the sports writers. The middle and upper classes, who were always the most ardent baseball fans, have been stripped of their possessions by the Castro regime. There is a lack of good American players. And the continual marching and drilling of the civilian militia composed of workers and students leaves them no time for recreation.[1]

Frank Lane, now the head front office man for the Cleveland Indians, traveled to Cuba in October and took in the first week of games of the moribund CWL. His purpose was to make sure his young rookie infielder, Miguel Angel "Mike" de la Hoz, would be able to leave the island when it came time to report to spring training. Lane told Fred Lieb that he had been assured by Captain Felipe Guerra Matos, the Cuban sports director, that his government would not impede any Cuban professional player from reaching his minor or major league spring camp rendezvous—welcome news for several other major league clubs as well. (Despite the assurance, the Castro regime did not facilitate the egress of its major and minor leaguers after the season. Most had to fly to Mexico to obtain the visa requirement their country had publicly promised but would not grant them to enter the United States.) Lane also conveyed to the long-serving New York sportswriter that he had seen Cuba's most prominent baseball executive: "I had dinner with Bob Maduro at the Hotel National [sic], and it was like dinner in an armed camp. There are ears on every side. We talked baseball and kept away from the personal affairs. [He] has had a difficult time of it. I know he is not the wealthy man he used to be."[2]

After months without publicity in northern newspapers, Maduro's name resurfaced in late November. The written account came from George Beahon:

> Bobby Maduro's closest friends are sweating. Against their advice, and against the wishes of his own associates in Cuba, the owner of the Jersey City (Havana) entry in the IL is remaining in Havana, alone.
> Maduro's dad is living in a New York City hotel. He refuses to return to Cuba. Maduro's wife and seven children now are living in Merion, Pa. Bobby remains in Havana, desperately trying to keep the oceanfront home he built several years ago. If he leaves the country his home will be automatically sealed up by the Castro government.[3]

Jorge Maduro is Bobby and Isolina Maduro's oldest surviving child. A retired health insurance executive, Jorge splits his time between homes in upstate New York and Miami. A once-promising New York Yankees catching prospect derailed by knee and back injuries, he is the father of

Perhaps as a testament to the homestead itself, Salomón Maduro's confiscated residence #302 on the corner of J and 15 streets is maintained, on the exterior, in exceptional condition, as home to the *Alliance Française,* an international organization that teaches and promotes the French language and culture worldwide. The other once-stately homes on the same leafy Vedado street have not fared nearly as well (author's collection).

four children, sons Jorge, Jr., and Jon, daughters Jessica and Jennifer, and five grandchildren. The University of Miami baseball Hall of Fame inductee has been married to Joanne for 46 years.

I'll be 70 in July. My brother Robert was five years older and mostly into cars. Felipe loved baseball.

The construction of the stadium was before my time, I cannot remember. But I would go to the stadium quite often, especially Saturday and Sunday to see Cuban Winter League games. I would sit in my father's box. I remember the Sunday doubleheaders most. Cienfuegos and Marianao would play the early game, followed by Habana and Almendares. My dad would meet with the manager after every game. I remember having to go to the Stadium Club and wait for him.

Every December 31 my dad would take my mother to the stadium and bring in the new year there. Take a bottle of champagne. No kids. Only he and my mother—in a romantic setting.

Growing up, I had a pony "Pinto" and a boxer named "Rexie." We got him as a pup. My mother would feed him from a bottle. Really spoiled him. One day I put him in the yard outside the kitchen and he disappeared. My mother had told me to bring him inside, too. We had a poodle later in Jacksonville and Miami.

We had a Cuban chauffeur named Julio, he would take us to school. At my grandfather's house there was a Spanish lady named "Concha" and another Spaniard, José, who acted as our butler, and a cook named Ovilio. He was Cuban. We had tutors for English and French—and I didn't learn either language because I always wanted to be outside playing baseball. We lived at J and 15 Streets [grandfather's house] except for the last year or two when we moved to the house my dad built next to the Havana Biltmore. We had our own back entrance into the country club beside its bowling alley, which stood right next to our house.

With the Sugar Kings, I was a batboy for many games. I was at the Frank Verdi game with the Red Wings [in the stands]. I remember the Little World Series, Castro came to all the games, with all the guns. I only saw a couple of games in Jersey City. What sticks out, because it shocked me, was the name Jersey City pasted over the same Cubans' uniform.

I remember most of all my father as being a very dedicated, almost fanatically so, person who really cared about the game of baseball, with a mission to help Cuban kids to be able to develop a better life and proudly represent the country he loved so much. His most dedicated mission was trying to get his team into the major leagues. My grandfather had an insurance company. At the end of the business day, kids would throw balls against the big wall of his building. One day they put up a sign prohibiting ball playing. My father got mad and made them take down the sign. He loved seeing kids playing baseball.

My father was well known and people respected him. Remember, when you talk about the Sugar Kings, you had the academies all the way down to los Cubanitos. He was always upbeat. You would never see in him qualities of a man who was super down. He had to leave his whole fortune in Cuba. Walter O'Malley helped him in the beginning, here. My father had helped O'Malley's Dodgers team in player development, with Sandy Amorós and Chico Fernández, and had hired Al Campanis as manager of Cienfuegos. He had a great relationship with Gabe Paul, from Cincinnati to Jacksonville, and then when Paul went to Cleveland.

The only thing I remember about leaving Cuba is that my parents told me, "Hey, we're going to the United States." It was a surprise. Roberto was already in the States, staying with my grandfather. I came with my mother. My father was not with us. We stayed in Philadelphia with our uncles, Max Borges and Jorge Echarte. I went to eighth grade in Philadelphia. I then did four years of high school in Jacksonville.

I signed with the Yankees in 1969 out of the University of Miami. I reached Triple A Syracuse. The reason was I was promoted was to take the place of Thurman Munson, who had reserve duty for a couple of weeks. I was set to see some action in the Mayor's Trophy Game, but the team doctor saw my bad knee and did not let me play. I made the all-star team after being sent back to Double A.

None of my family has returned to Cuba. My son George is slowly convincing me. I never thought about going back until recently.[4]

Beatríz McDaniel is the oldest surviving Maduro daughter. An administrative assistant for a national healthcare company in Miami, Betty, recently widowed, is the mother of four children—daughters Betty, Lisa, Ellie and son Robert, nicknamed GM—and nine grandchildren.

I don't have a good recollection of my past. I've told my brothers this, I don't know why that is, I'm probably the worst of everyone trying to recall things.

I went first to escuela Margot Párraga, an all-girl private school. It might have been for kindergarten because then I went to Las Esclavas del Sagrado de Corazón. We lived with my grandfather. Then a couple of years before we left Cuba, my parents built a home, it was right beside the Biltmore Yacht & Country Club. The bowling alley of the Biltmore was next door to our house. There was a fence that divided the properties.

My childhood ... we went to the Havana Yacht Club. We danced ballet with Alicia Alonso [world-renowned ballet instructor]. Robert, my brother, had a poodle Linda. I was tutored in English. We had a nanny, Alvarina. I'm sure I went to the stadium but memories of it I don't have.

For no particular reason, I remember the dress I was wearing the day we left Cuba. I know I left with my two sisters, Adela and Rosi. My youngest sister Isabel did not go. I would think it was my father who brought us [to the U.S.], but I'm not sure. When my mother arrived later with Isabel, Alvarina came with her. She lived with us for a couple of years in the U.S. Then she went back to Spain.

I would cry a lot in the beginning, here. Fanny, my mother's youngest sister, who lived with us, would go and wait to pick me up from school every day.

My mother was very loving and dedicated to the family. She was like so many other Cuban women of that era. She adored my father. She was a very good mother. She was very religious. She lost a son and that's the worst thing that can happen to a mother.

My father traveled a lot and did a lot for ballplayers, I know. All of the children respected him. Grandmother died when mother was pregnant with Jorge. Grandfather eventually remarried a French woman named Suzanne. Adela passed away 13 years ago, and Roberto 11 years back. My father's sister, Adrianna, passed away about six or seven years ago, or probably longer ... she lived a long life. She left Cuba for Curacao.[5]

The Maduros' youngest son, Al, is Senior Vice President of Licensing for Perry Ellis International, a Miami-based, publicly-traded clothing company. Four years old when he left Cuba, he is the proud parent of two teenagers—Max and Ava—with wife Carmen Cecilia aka CC.

> *I consider myself very Cuban. My family laughs at that because I'm the most Americanized and worst dancer of the group. I fly to Latin America a lot on business and when I fly over Cuba, even though I've never been back, I get very emotional every time. When we moved to Miami Beach, I was in fifth grade. I felt goose bumps when the Cuban national anthem played at school.*
>
> *I remember three things from Cuba: A street guy, a hobo-type named "el caballero de París" ["the gentleman of Paris."]. Dressed in a black cloak with long white hair and a long white beard, he would give out pencils, looking for donations. He would hang in front of our house, waiting for us to get home. I was deathly scared of the guy. He's stuck in my memory.*
>
> *I used to drive through the state years ago as a sales rep. Whenever I used to pass through Belle Glade, Clewiston, the aroma of sugar in the air reminded me of our farm. We had a farm in sugar country, and that smell brought me back to my childhood, to the Cuban countryside. The third thing is a little difficult to describe but it's being at my father's ballpark—no scenes—just the sounds of the game, of the balls hitting the mitts and the bats striking the ball.*
>
> *We originally went to Philadelphia and lived there for about a year and half. The reason we found our way to Philadelphia was because of our uncle Max Borges. He was a famous, big-time architect in Cuba. He was an architect for Chase Manhattan. Max told my dad to open a bank account in the States. Max settled in Philadelphia so his two boys could attend prep school there.*
>
> *We had 17 people living in the house at one time. My uncle had signed a lease limiting the number of people who could stay there. When the landlord would come by to collect the rent check, all the kids had to go down to the basement—we thought it was fun. We would lay down and they would put blankets and boxes on top of us and the landlord would come down and look around. He had been told that in the mornings a school bus stopped in front of his place and a whole bunch of little kids came out.*
>
> *Well, the grandfather made a lot of money, and the son blew a lot of money. The thing about building the stadium, which was financed, and the hope of getting a major league team was that my dad understood he was going to lose money at first. I admire people who are community minded. Sure, part of it had to be ego, wanting to own a major league baseball team. But on the other hand, my dad was extremely proud of being Cuban and bringing a team to Cuba would make Cuba a big-time place, and for that he was willing to sacrifice. I'm sure my grandfather was beside himself—what kind of business is this? My grandfather owned an apartment in a hotel in New York called the Biltmore [New York Biltmore Hotel]. It used to be next to the Roosevelt Hotel. The Roosevelt is still there.*
>
> *When I interviewed here, the founder of Perry Ellis, George Feldenkreis, who was a poor Jewish guy in Cuba, said to me "Your grandfather was one of the smartest Jews Cuba ever produced. He helped out financially and did more for the Cuban Jewish community after he converted [to Catholicism]."*
>
> *My mom was one of five kids. She was the oldest. When she was 13, her dad died. He was a pharmacist. My maternal grandmother, whose name was Narcisa, did a tremendous job of marrying off her three oldest daughters to successful families. One of her daughters married Max Borges. He did the design of our last house in Cuba,*

Seven—Starting Over as "a Millionaire in Friends" 155

which was a modern style house. The third daughter married George Echarte, a successful engineer and builder. My uncle George was the engineer that built Gran Stadium, and my uncle Max was the architect that designed Gran Stadium. My uncle George also served on the Board of Directors for the stadium. Aunt Mignon married the architect. The aunt I was closest to was Maricusa, who married George. The third and youngest daughter—there was a boy in between—never married. She was Francisca, called Fanny. My mom's brother worked the concessions in Jacksonville.

When you're the sixth of seven children in a new country, with all the issues, yeah, I probably wasn't under my parents' thumb that much. But they were strict enough. I had curfews. I never popped off to my dad. I was scared of him to a certain extent. I was considered a pretty good high school player. Everyone knew who I was because of my last name and in the '70s we were a lot closer to that time than now. My father was kind of tough on me on the baseball side. I would go two-for-four and he would point out that one of the hits was a bloop. But my mom, I would go 0-for-four, and she would say, "but son, you hit three line drives." She knew how to say things when it came to baseball. She knew baseball. Tommy Lasorda said my mom was one of the prettiest woman in Havana.

Speaking of Lasorda—here at Doral, many years ago, at a tournament for Miami Dade North, Tommy was the guest of honor. After I registered, they made an announcement: "Al Maduro, you've dropped your scorecard, can you come and get it." At the registration desk, the woman tells me, "That man over there picked it up." I look and there's Tommy Lasorda, and he had a whole bunch of people around him. I went up to him, "Oh, Mr. Lasorda, I believe you have my scorecard." In front of a whole group of people, he says mockingly, "Ohhh, Miss-ter La-sorda—come here you little shit," and he gave me a kiss on the cheek. He says to everyone, "Guys, I had this guy on my lap in Cuba and he comes to me here and says, "Ohhh, Miss-ter La-sorda … come over here," and starts kissing me on the cheek, and his friends are just blown away.

When Lasorda was managing the Dodgers, my brother George would go to the game with his sons George, Jr. and Jon, and Lasorda would let them on the field. This was at the football stadium against the Marlins. Lasorda said to George Jr., who wanted to be a baseball player, "Honor your grandfather by always hustling on the field."

It wasn't just Lasorda. I saw Juan Marichal at the Admiral's Lounge of American Airlines. My friends tried to get me to go over. Finally, someone goes over to him and says, "Hey, that's Al Maduro." He comes over to me. "I haven't seen you since you were this big," and gave me a big hug. Another time at the airport, I introduced myself to Rod Carew. "Rod, I'm Al Maduro." "Geez," he says, "Your dad suspended me." The story behind that was he left winter ball early one year and received a sanction when my father was working in the commissioner's office. That ambassador's job my dad had was much more. This was before the prevalence of agents. He [dad] heard the grievances and meted out the punishment for players in the winter leagues.

We used to have a Cuban Old Timer's Game in Miami. The committee in charge called my dad one year. We need someone to throw out the first pitch. My dad asked who they wanted? They said Joe DiMaggio. He lived in San Francisco. My dad called Joe, and Joe said he'd do it. Give me a round trip ticket, $100 and a driver. So guess what? I was that driver. He did it two years in a row. DiMaggio was very gracious.

I was at FIU [Florida International University], on summer vacation with two of *my midwestern friends, and we drove to their farms in Kentucky and Illinois. One day we were driving, and boom there's Wrigley Field. And there's a game today. I had never been to Wrigley Field. But we have no money. So I called my father, it was pay phones then, and I called collect. Dad, I'm in Chicago and I want to go to the Cubs game. Well son, when do you want to go? Well, today and the game starts in 12 minutes. He says, God, talk about not being organized. How many tickets do you want? He says call me back in ten minutes. I call him back in ten minutes. He says go to gate one. A tall guy is going to come and call your name out. And it was Dallas Green. And my friends were blown away. The general manager of the Cubs coming to give us tickets. Al, where do you want to sit? he asked. In the press box with us or in the stands? Can we do both? We saw half the game in the stands and half from the press box.*

My best summation of my father.... I admired his strength and fortitude against the odds, and never giving up and always trying to be a man of his word. The pressure he was under with seven kids in a new country with mounting debt.... He owed a lot of money and vowed to pay everyone off, and he pretty much did by the time he died. And he always helped a lot of people, exiles, who needed help.

I don't think there has ever been a group of immigrants that have done so quickly what Cubans have done in acclimating and becoming successful at the national level. There are eight Cuban Americans in Congress, and we're six-tenths of one percent of the population.[6]

Rosario "Rosi" Chica has worked for 44 years for a branch of the Federal Reserve System in Miami and is looking forward to retirement in the near future. Married to Manuel for over four decades, she and her husband have three children, Christina, Manny III, and Diana, and three grandchildren.

All of us were born in J and 15 street [grandparents' house]. I went to school at Las Esclavas del Sagrado de Corazón *in Havana. I remember little about the house I was born in, which was in Vedado. We lived there with my grandfather until we moved to a new house built on the beach next to the Biltmore country club. It was a beautiful modern style house right on the water. I remember the fisherman in little boats selling us fresh fish. There was a retaining wall. We had an inlet that served as a natural pool. We would go swimming. We had a pet poodle named Linda.*

We had a house in Cunagua, where the sugar mill plantation was. Grandfather's sugar farm was called Los Cocos. *We'd go out there on weekends. At the farm there was a boxer [dog] that was kind of crazy. I believe our sugar farm was later used as a place to quarantine AIDS patients. That's what Cuba used to do with them.*

What I remember about the stadium was not baseball-related. I remember special events other than baseball there—the car races and daredevil shows they used to put on. In between doubleheaders they would have clown routines with the umpires. I remember more about the Jacksonville Stadium.

I remember when we left Cuba, what I was wearing, the doll I was carrying. I remember we stopped over at the Miami Airport. It had to be September 1960 because school had just started in Philadelphia. I was seven years old and started second grade at St. Margaret's Catholic School. It was my sister Adela, Betty and I. My dad brought us, or my mom, one of the two. The boys came later with my mother and my younger sister Isabel. We stayed with my Uncle Max in a rented a house.

Seven—Starting Over as "a Millionaire in Friends" 157

Some of my cousins, some of my dad's friends came also. Our landlady used to keep a close watch on the house. On the way home from school, we would send a couple of kids ahead to scout, make sure she wasn't around. It was a very cold winter that 1960.

It was difficult on my mom, with her background of having help in Cuba, then coming to Philadelphia with no help.

I always remember thinking how beautiful my mom was and how she made everything seem so simple. Having three kids of my own, I can't imagine what it was like to have seven kids in a new country and managing to keep us all happy. And making sure we went to good schools and got a good education, and making it seem relatively easy. She did a wonderful job keeping the family together and not letting us feel that we were being deprived of anything compared to our life in Cuba. She nurtured a happy environment.

My mom spoke English. I remember having an English tutor coming to the house in Cuba. All the kids down to me were tutored in English. Albert and Isabel were too young. Adela and Robert had studied in the States. Adela went to the Asheville School for Girls [today, the Asheville Academy for Girls]. Robert attended the same Asheville prep school as dad. I never suffered because of the language, here. I was always able to communicate. I remember the kids in school in Philadelphia being surprised when I spoke Spanish in recess and wondering why I had pierced ears. I guess pierced ears for children my age wasn't the norm here in the States back then.

I remember going to pick my father up at the airport with my mom. It wasn't like today where you can pick passengers up at the curb. I remember my father getting up in the mornings and putting on Cuban records to listen to Cuban songs and music. I remember family meals, especially when he was home. My father would get the steak and the kids would get the picadillo *[chopped beef].*

My parents' greatest legacy is that all of their children have led nice lives and have nice families with beautiful kids of their own as a tribute to how they raised us.[7]

On January 3, 1961, President Eisenhower severed diplomatic relations with Cuba, joining six other hemispheric countries that had previously done the same (Dominican Republic, Guatemala, Haiti, Nicaragua, Paraguay and Peru). "There is a limit to what the United States in self-respect can endure," read part of the president's announcement. "Our friendship to the Cuban people is not affected. It is my hope and my conviction that in the not too distant future it will be possible for the historic friendship between us once again to find its reflections in normal relations of every sort. Meanwhile our sympathies go out to the Cuban people now suffering under the yoke of a dictator."[8]

The 8:30 p.m. "last straw" declaration came after the Cuban government had ordered, shortly after 1:00 a.m. the same day, U.S. Embassy staff in Havana cut to 11 from 87, reduced from 120 six months earlier. Fidel Castro said the embassy harbored "spies directing counterrevolutionary activities," and he had previously accused the United States of planning an imminent attack against Cuba prior to January 20, the day of President-elect John F. Kennedy's swearing-in as new U.S. commander-in-chief.

On the sports side, the rupture temporarily threw into doubt the future involvement of Cuban players abroad. "Washington's official attitude about issuing baseball visas still is not known," discerned a printed advisory nine days after Eisenhower's executive decision. "In the past Cubans entered the United States under special permits renewable annually."[9] The team for which the Cuban player performed made visa requests on their behalf through the U.S. State Department, which the Cuban government, in the past, rubber stamped.

Despite the collapse of the world he knew occurring around him, an obstinate Maduro stuck to the tenet of keeping state and sport separate. "I know personally our boys are proud of their contribution to American baseball and are anxious to return there to further their careers," he said from Havana on the visa issue. "This is not a political matter. Baseball is an international sport and should be kept apart of any other considerations not related to its development."[10]

Less than a month later, on February 8, 1961, the second-oldest professional baseball league in the world played its final game. (Only the National League was older than the Cuban Winter League.) The largest crowd of the year showed up, nearly 20,000, including the country's tyrant-in-the-making. Almost assuredly Bobby Maduro was on hand, too. As it happened, the game on tap between Maduro's original team, Cienfuegos, and Almendares would decide the CWL pennant, with both clubs (34–31) in a dead heat on the season's last day. Managed by Tony Castaño, Cienfuegos stomped the Scorpions, 8–2, behind league MVP Pedro Ramos (16–7). In registering the complete-game, championship victory, Ramos threw the last pitch of the last professional baseball game played in Cuba in the 20th century. "On February 23, 1961, the government created the National Institute of Sports, Physical Education and Recreation (INDER) under the direction of José Llanusa Gogel," traces Cuban blogger Dimas Castellanos. "A month later the INDER issued National Decree Number 936, which prohibited professional sports."[11]

Ramos and his Washington Senators teammate Camilo Pascual, along with Minnie Miñoso, were among the best-known Cuban players who had to enter the United States early that spring through a third country. Not-so-established players found a more direct lane with a pricey proviso attached. "If Chico Fernandez asks for a raise the first day in camp, the Tigers shouldn't be surprised," wrote the *New York Mirror's* Harold Weissman. "When he leaves Cuba, Chico must pay the Castro people $50 for his visa. And then they'll let him take only $6 with him!"[12]

As the first week of the 1961 major league season neared completion,

Castro's intelligence proved valid. The foreign attack, with its disastrous (for the U.S.) outcome, was launched by the new American president. Roberto Maduro appeared to have decided luckily to leave the island right before the CIA-backed paramilitary assault by Cuban exiles on the southern coast of Cuba. "My dad was on the last flight out of Cuba before the Bay of Pigs invasion,"[13] says Jorge Maduro.

All Maduro had left in the spring of 1961 was his family and his deposed ball team. Thanks to his background, the 44-year-old Cuban refugee needed little time for acclimation or transition to his new environs. By mid–June, he saw no future in Jersey City and, at an IL directors meeting in Buffalo, he pushed to relocate his team to the vacated terrain of what had been the International League's most southern continental city. A neighboring city's newspaper, the *Fort Lauderdale News*, revealed the proposal, including a contingency measure:

> Plagued by poor attendance and live major league television, Jersey City owner Roberto Maduro has requested that he be allowed to move his team to Miami. Another plan, which would move the Jerseys into Jacksonville and touch off a full scale minor league war between the International League and Southern Association will be discussed.
>
> Lucrative radio agreement with a Spanish-speaking Miami station and a low, flat rental fee for Miami Stadium are the keys to Miami's return to the league. Maduro wants to pay Miami five per cent of the gross profit for use of the 11,000 seat Miami Stadium.
>
> Miami was an IL member for five years but the ties were severed last September when owner Bill MacDonald moved the Marlins to San Juan, Puerto Rico, and then to Charleston, W. Va. under pressure of a league mandate.[14]

The Miami bid was compromised when it was revealed that new International League president Tommy Richardson had secretly met with a Miami City Commissioner, indicating that the ballclub transfer would require a $50,000 "gift" from Miami. The money, Richardson said, would buy nothing "other than the satisfaction of bringing baseball back to Miami."[15]

The IL owners voted not to make any changes, with the expectation that the bleeding Jersey City franchise could be saved. "We hope now that we are telling people that we are staying there," said Richardson, who had replaced the retired Frank Shaughnessy, "that they will come out and support the club. It isn't as if it was a bad team. The club is in third place and is one of the soundest in the league."[16]

The competitive Jersey City squad was averaging about 1,000 patrons per game, not much better than Havana during its worst times. Maduro figured he needed 3,000 fans per game to make the franchise viable, not a far reach by any stretch with a population of 1,000,000 living within a five-mile radius of Jersey City. Detrimentally, though, interest in the club seemed to be lacking from all quarters. In July, Maduro attempted to renegotiate a new lease for Roosevelt Stadium for 1962. A drastic reduction request in the $15,000 annual rental fee was met with a cold shoulder by new Jersey City Mayor Thomas Gangemi. The mayor rebuffed Maduro's overtures, stating that he would not cancel the contract made by the previous administration.

On July 21, Maduro traveled to Jacksonville, Florida. Pressed for comment, Maduro confirmed the obvious. "Provided everything broke just right from the standpoint of territorial rights," he said, "the main thing I would have to be assured of would be that we were wanted in Jacksonville. By that I mean full cooperation from city administration, service clubs and, above all, the fans themselves."[17] Montreal had also been bandied about as a possible transfer site for the Jerseys. The Los Angeles Dodgers had severed their affiliation with their celebrated Royals subsidiary, and the team had moved to Syracuse this season. But, in a telltale sign, Maduro never visited Montreal.

Instead, by September, he had already tipped his hand. "Bobby Maduro is so sure that his Jersey City club will be transferred to Jacksonville," reported one International League newspaper, "that he already has bought a home in that Florida city and is sending his children to Jacksonville schools."[18]

On September 26, the Houston Sports Association, parent of the National League's expansion-ticketed Houston Colt .45s, agreed to relinquish their Single-A minor league territory in Jacksonville to Jersey City in exchange for just under $11,000 and the contract of the Jerseys' Jim Pendleton. (The outfielder would play in over 100 games for the Houston Colt .45s in 1962.) As part of the agreement, the existing South Atlantic League team, the last-place Jacksonville Jets, would move to Savannah, Georgia. To lessen travel burdens, the IL's vagabond Charleston Marlins shifted to Atlanta, its third home in two years.

From New York, a day prior to the World Series opening game between the New York Yankees and Cincinnati Reds, the International League owners voted their approval for Jacksonville as its second-ever Florida member. Spearheaded by local baseball man and industrialist Sam W. Wolfson, Jacksonville kicked off a two-week ticket drive with a goal of 100,000 game tickets to be pre-sold. Successfully reaching the mark with more than 2,000 ducats to spare a fortnight later conveyed a rousing sign of civic enthusiasm for the higher-level brand of baseball, pronouncedly

Seven—Starting Over as "a Millionaire in Friends"

so, since the Single-A Jets had drawn fewer than 35,000 for the entire 1961 season.

Two days after the Maris-Mantle-Ford-Arroyo Yankees disposed of the Reds to win the first of two Fall Classic titles in the decade, Maduro signed Ben Geraghty to a three-year managerial deal to direct his new Jacksonville team. Geraghty, a former minor league Manager of the Year, had skippered the Louisville Colonels in the recently concluded Junior World Series, but had been knocked off by the IL's Buffalo Bisons. Shortly thereafter, Maduro signed a working agreement with the Cleveland Indians, whose front office boss now happened to be old pal Gabe Paul.

On December 7, the day before his 60th birthday, Paul Miller suffered a heart attack and died. The sudden death of the former treasurer of the Cuban Winter League and general manager of the Cuban Sugar Kings patently came as staggering news to Maduro as he prepared for his first Christmas in exile. Miller, who ran the Jerseys until Maduro's arrival, had been named Jacksonville's assistant GM. (Maduro had placed himself as the club's general manager, perhaps as a means to draw additional income. Sam W. Wolfson, who was instrumental in helping Maduro land in Jacksonville, assumed the presidency of the club. It's likely Wolfson, along with others, also took a stake in the franchise, as Maduro gave up 49 percent ownership of the team during the transition.) Miller left behind a wife and two sons.

During the holiday season, a well-known New York writer uncovered benevolent actions on behalf of Maduro by someone who had drawn what would evolve into the life-long ire of many greater New York baseball fans. "Roberto Maduro is a name that probably doesn't mean much to you, but to baseball people he is a symbol of class and courage," wrote Dick Young.

> Not long ago, Maduro was a multimillionaire. Then came Castro.... By June there wasn't enough money in the Jersey City box office to support his family. One day the phone rang, jarring Maduro out of his worry. It was Walter O'Malley. "You're on the Dodger payroll," said O'Malley. "One thousand a month. Just sit tight. I'll think of something for you to do."
>
> Each month a check for $1,000 has arrived to keep the Maduros going. As yet, O'Malley hasn't thought of anything for Maduro to do. Maduro will pay O'Malley back, every cent; you may be certain of that. Old Brooklyn Dodgers fans should know of O'Malley's part in it. Nobody is wrong all the time.[19]

Maduro confirmed O'Malley's help in a January 1962 interview, in which he bared the details of his family's lost fortune and a little of his soul. "My dad lost close to $6 million, including a sugar plantation, the largest insurance company in Cuba and a $150,000 home," he told a syndicated newspaperman. "I lost close to $2 million, a small cattle business, a bus line, controlling interest in Gran Stadium and my $150,000 home. What little I had I lost in Jersey City. Fortunately, I found out there are more important things than money. It's having friends. I have no money but I am a millionaire in friends."[20]

The same month, Maduro announced the exhibition schedule for the Jacksonville Suns. Thirteen pre-season games were slated against Triple- and Double-A competition, seven of the games to be played in the Suns' spring home of Kissimmee, 160 miles south of Jacksonville. Report date for the players was March 25.

In early February, Maduro was in Washington making arrangements with Voice of America, the U.S. government-sponsored broadcasting institute, to transmit to Cuba a 15-minute recap in Spanish after every Suns game. Highlights of every game were to be phoned in to VOA headquarters. Maduro recorded the opening segment to the program. He believed that though now the majority of his team's players were not Cubans, or Hispanic, the Cuban people would always remember the Sugar Kings and "will always have a place in their hearts" for the team.

During the last week of the month, Maduro addressed the Kissimmee Lions, Kiwanis and Rotary clubs, expressing his keenness for the upcoming spring camp and the integration of the International League into the area. "Since I have been here we haven't missed a thing," Maduro said, obviously playing to his audience. "We have found a second home in Jacksonville. That city is excited about AAA baseball."[21] Under the circumstances, he sounded more than a bit naïve when he continued to stress that "baseball played an important part in creating friendly relations between the United States and nations in Latin America" and that "for two years Castroites have talked against the U. S., but the Cuban people like America; the Communists have not succeeded [in turning the people]. That's what baseball has done."[22]

In what can only be seen as a desire to praise the game and raise its international importance, Maduro once again elevated Fidel Castro as a greater champion of the sport than he was. He blatantly exaggerated the dictator's role in keeping the Sugar Kings in Cuba in 1959, telling the audience that he had asked for and received a $100,000 contribution from Castro following their meeting in New York, after threatening to move his team to the United States because of poor attendance. As documented in a prior chapter, the lifeline Maduro received was less than half that amount—and did not come from Castro. In actuality, Maduro gave Castro much more than Castro ever gave him, i.e., the packed-house receipts of the July 24, 1959, *Barbudos* agrarian reform game and the December 8, 1959, winter league all-star contest for declared military build-up and upgrades. More than likely, the miscalculated, false claim provided a topical story to tell an inquisitive audience about a man who had dominated hemispheric events over the past few years. In retrospect, it seems difficult to conceive that Maduro would have moved his team, especially considering that it ultimately required an externally-imposed prying of the franchise from its Cuban roots. (Curiously, the author never found an early instance in which the apolitical Maduro publicly criticized the man most responsible for his financial ruin. Perhaps that was because like so many Cubans at that time, Maduro believed the existing situation in Cuba would not last long, or because the era called for behavioral stoicism.)

On March 10, Maduro and his family were dealt a severe blow with the passing of the family patriarch. Salomón Maduro died of a chronic liver ailment in Jacksonville. He was survived by wife Suzanne, his two children and nine grandchildren. One can wonder what his last few months were like, ailing, forcibly expatriated and knowing he had the 2018 monetary equivalent of $50,300,000 stolen from him.

Spring training commenced as scheduled, and Maduro and manager Ben Geraghty were given the key to Kissimmee by the chamber of commerce at a party at the Tropical Hotel, April 2. Both men's wives were present.

Displaying a touch of Bill Veeck–type showmanship, Maduro installed two unique components at Jacksonville Baseball Park, the home of the Suns, as part of an extensive facelift that included new club office space and renovations to the home, visitors and umpires' clubhouses. "A huge, $60,000 sunburst scoreboard in left-center field approximately 50 feet in diameter is shaped like a big sunflower," described one written promo. "The top towers 60 feet above the field. A second feature, located atop the right-center field fence, is 'Dancing Waters.' It is a combination of rising and falling waters with colored lights, playing to music. The club has shelled out $12,000 to rent this for the season."[23] Add the eye-pleasing sway of Florida palm trees that encircled the park, and it is easy to visualize an idyllic setting for baseball.

So that fans could fully appreciate these park dynamics, the Suns played all night games at home. Here's how son Al Maduro remembers it:

> I was starting elementary school and remember going to the ballpark a lot because [brother] George was the bullpen catcher. He was 15 and he was the bullpen catcher for a AAA team. We'd go in the morning at 11:00 o'clock and stayed there until after the games and it was time to go home. My dad put in these water fountains,

when a guy hit a home run they would go off. He put in the Jacksonville Sun scoreboard, the sun would light up when the Suns scored.[24]

There was just enough "lighting up" of the scoreboard on opening night, April 25, for the Suns to nose out the visiting Syracuse Chiefs, 4–3. Former New York Giants hurler and World Series champion Rubén Gómez threw 7⅓ innings for the win, indubitably putting a smile on the face of his owner and the majority of the 8,500 fans attending (7,414 paid).

One and a half years removed from Jersey City, the exiled Maduro addresses the Jacksonville Suns crowd on opening night, April 25, 1962. Suns manager Ben Geraghty is in the background (author's collection).

Seven—Starting Over as "a Millionaire in Friends" 165

Gómez won his first eight decisions and was called up by the Cleveland Indians. The Suns did not miss him, as the first-year team won the International League pennant with a record of 94–60. Maduro received a telegram of congratulations from Florida governor Farris Bryant upon clinching the title.

Cleveland may have "taketh" by way of pitcher Gómez, but they also allocated to the Suns a "pennant-drive boost," personnel-wise, the same month as Gómez's June recall. Four months earlier, infielder Mike de la Hoz had copped the winter league batting title in Puerto Rico with a .354 average. De la Hoz, 23, was in his third year with the Cleveland Indians. But as he tells it, he saw the majority of his playing time with Jacksonville in 1962.

> Monchy de Arcos signed me in 1957. He was part owner of Almendares and later a scout with Cleveland here in the States. I was playing amateur ball and had intended on attending the University of Havana. I was the first Cuban "bonus baby." I got $10,000. That was a lot of money back then! I was assigned to the Minot Mallards [Class C] in 1958, my first year in professional baseball. I was 19. I made it to Cleveland in 1960. In 1961, a group of us [players] got visas for Mexico. I'm talking about major leaguers. Our teams here [U.S.] arranged it. The major league representatives met us at the airport in Mexico and took us to a hotel, where we spent the night. The next day, we went to the U.S. embassy and got the paperwork to enter the country.
>
> The next year, 1962, Gabe Paul asked me to go down to Jacksonville. *Listen Mike, the Jacksonville team is fighting for the pennant and you're not really playing much here. I'll give you an extra $2,000 to go.* So, I went. I played third base and we won the pennant. I still have my championship ring.
>
> Bobby Maduro was a helluva a nice guy. He loved baseball.[25]

The Suns drew 229,479 fans in 61 home dates, a tremendous achievement, especially placed next to the measly 33,131 sold tickets from one year ago in the same venue and considering that Jacksonville was the smallest International League city in population. Yet because of an initial hefty "buy-in" and only a one-third radio broadcast purchase of the scheduled Suns games, the team lost an estimated $50,000. Though Maduro expected to make much of it up in the post-season, the third-place Atlanta Crackers partially ruined the plan by upsetting the Suns in the Shaughnessy playoff finals, four games to three. Down in the series, the Crackers beat the Suns in games six and seven at Suns Stadium. Atlanta went on to capture the Junior World Series over the Louisville Colonels.

The International League underwent a divisional realignment in 1963, with ten teams splitting into North and South divisions. The league had originally proposed incorporating six teams from the disbanding, historic American Association. To try and smooth the expected rocky transition,

National Association President George M. Trautman appointed a five-man committee to handle the execution. Maduro was one of three minor league team leaders, along with major league representatives Joe Johnson of the New York Yankees and the Los Angeles Dodgers' Buzzy Bavasi, who made up the council. In the end, only Indianapolis was absorbed into the IL, joining Jacksonville, Columbus, Atlanta and Arkansas in the South division. The Arkansas Travelers were a new club, a re-emergence of the defunct Southern Association's Little Rock Travelers.

During that same 1962–1963 winter, more logistical planning was needed for the Junior World Series, which was envisioned to include, for the first time, perhaps the strongest of all minor leagues—the Pacific Coast League. A three-man IL brain trust of Maduro, Rochester's George Sisler, Jr., and Max Schumacher, representing Indianapolis, were appointed to iron out the arrangement. The JWS could not be hashed out between the leagues and was not played again until 1970 (following the reorganization of the American Association).

When he was not occupied with special committees, Maduro spent time on the banquet circuit. In early February, he was invited to speak at the annual Athlete of the Year dinner of the Fraternal Order of Eagles in Milwaukee. Los Angeles Dodgers stolen base king Maury Wills was the honoree.

In April, the Cuban transplant flew to Puerto Rico to convince Rubén Gómez to return to the Suns. Gómez had announced his retirement following a falling out with Cleveland manager Mel McGaha and an eventual trade to the Minnesota Twins. Gómez returned and became the Suns' winningest pitcher with a 13–12 mark in 30 appearances, 26 starts. Perhaps Gómez's greatest contribution occurred on the sidelines. The rubber-arm pitcher taught Mike Cuéllar, in his first season with Jacksonville, how to throw the screwball. The deviant pitch was not quickly mastered by Cuéllar, who went 6–7 in 16 starts and ten relief outings. Eventually, the 25-year-old Cuéllar would perfect the pitch, which would help carry him to his four 20-game-winning seasons in the major leagues.

Gómez won four more games than the next winningest pitcher on the team, and no other hurler notched more than six victories. The numbers added up to a striking collapse in the standings by the 56–91 Suns, all the way to last place. Incidentally, the Suns had several notable pitchers on their squad. Apart from Cuéllar, Sonny Siebert, Tommy John and Sam McDowell were all mound components of the poorly performing team. All finished with sub-.500 records.

Maduro's club was also dealt two tragic blows during the campaign.

Manager Ben Geraghty died following a heart attack in his Jacksonville home on June 18. The well-respected manager was a month and a day shy of his 51st birthday. His wife Mary and five children were among immediate family survivors. Geraghty's death came as "a great shock to me," Maduro said upon hearing the news. "We still planned to make a fight for the pennant and last night we discussed players we might still obtain."[26] Player coach Casey Wise was named acting manager. On August 16, the Suns chairman of the board and president, Sam W. Wolfson, succumbed to an ongoing illness. A civic leader and philanthropist, Wolfson had been an influential force in bringing the Suns to Jacksonville. The married father of three was only 54.

The terrible 1963 season, on several counts, hit particularly hard at the Suns' box office and, residually, the organization's bottom line. Last-place Jacksonville drew a tad over 100,000, compared to the 230,000 of the inaugural season. "My dad put a lot of money into the ballpark," says Al Maduro. "He owed money, he got into debt in 1962, '63. An attorney advised him to declare bankruptcy. *That's how it works in this country. With your connections, you'll find a job with any major league team.* 'No, I'm going to pay everyone back,' my dad insisted."[27] Maduro suffered a combined six-figure loss in his first two seasons with Jacksonville.

Weeks after the dismal campaign, Maduro's debt reduction plan became public. The majority Suns owner offered to sell his controlling shares to the people, following the lead of other IL community-owned ballclubs in Columbus, Rochester, Buffalo, Indianapolis and Little Rock. The initial stock sale price was set at $10 per share, its full completion to bring in $200,000, netting Maduro $135,000 and leaving $65,000 for the team's operations in 1964. The six-week-long sales drive reached $180,000, with a group of local businessmen underwriting the outstanding $20,000 in order to meet the goal. (As last season was winding down, Maduro had traveled to Montreal to gauge the city's desire for a return to the IL through a possible "sweetheart deal" for his club. Nothing obviously came of it.) Following the successful conversion that made it clear Jacksonville was intent on remaining part of the International League, Baseball Amusements, Inc., the corporation that owned the Jacksonville Suns, transferred ownership to the new Community Owned Baseball of Jacksonville, Inc. and its 4,300 shareholder members—and Roberto Maduro, for the first time in 14 years, was not in principal command of a professional baseball team.

On January 6, 1964, Maduro was hired in his previous dual role of Suns general manager. A month later, Maduro hired Harry "The Hat"

Walker away from the Atlanta Crackers to pilot the Suns. Walker had been named by the writers the IL's outstanding manager for the job he did with last year's Governors' Cup finalist.

As the International League prepared for its 81st season, Maduro decided to cut season ticket packages by $25, to $100 and $75, respectively. Maduro also severed business ties with longtime friend and associate Gabe Paul. The Suns' new major league working agreement embraced the St. Louis Cardinals. The reason behind the change appears to involve the former Cardinal Harry Walker and his hiring. The Cardinals switched their previous working agreement from Atlanta.

After a 13–7 exhibition record, Walker's Suns took a promising first step in the new campaign with a 3–2, ten-inning win over the Rochester Red Wings on April 22. The opening night victory was attended by 6,839, presumably many of whom were part-owners. Future Boston Red Sox manager Joe Morgan scored the winning run on a single by Ron Cox.

Jacksonville players responded to Walker and his tactics throughout the season, to the tune of an 89–62 record, good enough to capture a second International League pennant in three years. Walker, who registered his third pennant in nine managerial campaigns, did a fine job guiding a team whose winningest pitcher, Dick LeMay, registered a 12–7 mark and that had only one other hurler win as many as ten games. But fourth-place Rochester (82–72) defeated the Suns in four straight opening round games. Damage to the Suns ballpark from Hurricane Dora forced the team to play the first three playoff games on the road.

On September 3, Dr. Roy Baker, president of Community Owned Baseball of Jacksonville, Inc. announced that GM Bobby Maduro had been rehired for 1965. No salary was given, but it was expectedly higher than the $15,000 Maduro received for 1964. The decision to bring Maduro back was unanimously made by the 14-member board of directors, Baker said, who were also pleased with the upswing in attendance to 177,164 in 64 home dates.

During the last month of the 1964 season, Mexican slugger Héctor Espino had joined the Suns. The way was paved by Maduro directly with Anuar Canavati, the owner of Espino's Monterrey Double-A team in the Mexican League. Espino was with the Suns in spring training in Tucson but had trouble culturally adapting. Chalked up to homesickness, he returned to the Sultans, where he racked up a Triple Crown season (.372/46/117) in his third year in the league. At the close of the Mexican campaign, Maduro beckoned Espino again, this time bringing with him two teammates, Nicaraguan Rigoberto Mena and Cuban native Evelio

Hernández. Hispanic players were a scarce commodity on the Suns, mostly due to the Cardinals' control over the roster. (The Cardinals would seek to change this shortly.) José "Coco" Laboy had not started the season with the club, but the lower-level Puerto Rican infielder had been promoted late in the year, and thus played sparingly with the Suns. The team's only other Hispanic player, Mike Cuéllar, had been "lifted" by the Cardinals after a 6–1 start. Espino, playing first base, hit an even .300 in an even 100 at-bats, with three homers and 15 RBI.

Walker won another IL writers' Manager of the Year Award, and Maduro was named General Manager of the Year. Joe Morgan was voted the league's outstanding player and Richmond's Mel Stottlemyre the top hurler.

Los Cubanitos Reborn

On January 28, 1965, Los Cubanitos were reorganized in Miami by Emilio Cabrera, according to one of the Little League's earliest members and current blogger Evelio Pérez. Cabrera's "goal was not only to have the youngsters play baseball and keep them off the streets but also have them learn some basic Cuban history."[28] Los Cubanitos charted the same strict rules of academia and personal conduct in order to play in the Miami leagues as the original Little League organization had in Cuba.

A former winter league player and manager, Cabrera received help in the endeavor from his better half. "My dad and mom put their hearts and souls in it to see those kids grow up right," says Barbra Cabrera, Emilio and Doris Cabrera's daughter. "There are many great stories. Fredi González was one of the young Cubanitos, for one. There were many, many young men who did not make it to the big leagues, but became what Emilio wanted ... fine upstanding citizens."[29]

As Los Cubanitos were reforming, Maduro was scouting for talent in Puerto Rico, while at the same time trying to organize an all-star game for the upcoming season between Triple-A U.S. players and Latin American minor leaguers.

During the first week of October 1964, Maduro and Walker were summoned to St. Louis by Cardinals GM Bob Howsam, for "organization meetings," as the Cardinals were preparing for a hopeful World Series berth in the waning days of the major league season—inspired by the recent monumental collapse of the Philadelphia Phillies. Seven days after the Cardinals completed their unexpected Fall Classic win over the New

York Yankees, the *St. Louis Post-Dispatch* disclosed an expanded role for its baseball team's top minor league deal maker (explaining his talent-seeking Caribbean journey): "Bob Maduro, who had 11 of his prospects in the major leagues last season, has been appointed Latin American representative of the Cardinals, general manager Bob Howsam announced today. Maduro will travel extensively in Central and South America and the Caribbean area on travel hunts."[30]

Before his Puerto Rican trip, Maduro took part in negotiations to iron out the details of the purchase of the Atlanta Crackers by the Milwaukee Braves. As part of a special committee, Maduro and four others (including IL president Richardson), came to terms with the Braves for territorial indemnification for the other IL clubs, stemming from the Braves' intended move to the Crackers' home base in 1966. Milwaukee paid $285,000 for the Crackers and another $250,000 in territorial rights fees.

Meanwhile, Harry Walker parlayed his sterling minor league resume to earn a major league dugout post with the Pittsburgh Pirates in 1965. Maduro replaced Walker with Grover Resinger, the Cardinals' successful Double A manager at Tulsa last year. Resinger experienced rougher sledding with Jacksonville. The roller coaster-like Suns, who had finished first, last and then first again the past three seasons, fell to sixth place in 1965. The 71–76 team was staggered by the Cardinals' mid–June trade of 9–1 Mike Cuéllar to the Houston Astros.

Six weeks after the season, Maduro decided to part ways with Jacksonville, resigning from his post. On December 8, 1965, he accepted the "newly-created position of Director of Inter-American Relations" under new baseball commissioner William Eckert. A retired Air Force general with no previous involvement in baseball, Eckert appears to have anticipated the globalization of the game, while reiterating a long-held Maduro belief. "I can visualize within the foreseeable future the spread of major league baseball on an international scale to include Japan, Canada and several Latin American countries," he said, not long after his November 1965 appointment by the owners. "I see major league baseball as a means of contributing to international friendship."[31]

In his new capacity, Maduro's role as the coordinator between organized baseball and the Latin American winter leagues was historically unique. In addition to facilitating broader communications channels between Hispanic players and the commissioner's office, Maduro was also to serve as minor league ball's liaison to three Mexican summer and winter leagues, as well as to promote the continued growth of baseball at the

Latin American amateur level. The appointment was hailed at every quarter.

"In Latin America, they are playing baseball more than ever," Maduro said in June 1966. He did not waver on his pro-baseball/pro–American link, saying he noticed in travels through Barranquilla and Cartagena, Columbia, where baseball was played, that people liked Americans. "But in Bogota, where it is not played, there is more anti–Yankee feeling."[32] Maduro hoped to persuade the U.S. State Department and U.S. sporting goods manufacturers to donate equipment to the poorer areas of countries of the Americas where the game was flourishing. There were 50 Latin Americans on major league rosters this season, a record, Maduro noted, with 26 from Cuba, 11 with Dominican roots, six Puerto Ricans, three Venezuelan nationals and two natives each from Mexico and Panama.

In his first year on the job, Maduro helped resolve a "raiding" situation between Caribbean basin leagues and promoted a "goodwill exhibition tour" through Central and South America. The winter circuits of Venezuela and Puerto Rico were accused of pilfering players from the Dominican Republic. Based on Maduro's information, Eckert decided in favor of the sovereignty of the Dominican circuit, ruling that the other leagues had violated established organized baseball agreements with their actions. The goodwill tour, a ten-game exhibition through Brazil, Nicaragua and Venezuela, took place over 17 days of the following off-season, organized by Billy Herman and Maduro. Herman, the ex–Cienfuegos and more recently former manager of the Boston Red Sox, directed a team which included big leaguers Frank Howard, Rusty Staub, Tommy Helms and Jackie Moore. José Cardenal and pitcher Marcelino López were two Hispanics named to the squad. Future Hall of Fame executive Pat Gillick served as the traveling secretary. An all-star team from Panama was part of the competition. The games in soccer-dominant Brazil were played on converted fútbol fields.

In December 1966, salary improprieties in one winter loop, exposed by one Dominican League executive, pointed Maduro toward a Venezuelan League club that was illicitly paying North American imports. OB had capped a $1,000-a-month salary limit, plus a flat $350 in expenses, for all U.S. players playing in the tropics. However, because no penalties had been established for such suspected improprieties and no "paper trail" existed (the under-the-table payout(s) were in cash), Maduro was not able to bring swift justice, and many feared that the illegal practice would continue. Johnny Naranjo, the executive who brought the original accusation, suggested the reestablishment of the Caribbean Confederation, which had been formed in Havana in 1948 but disbanded following Cuba's withdrawal from Caribbean Series participation. Incidentally, Maduro and National Association president Phil Piton were the only two executives presently active in the sport from that pivotal time in the late 1940s, in which much of Latin American baseball entered the orbit of organized baseball.

Two months afterward, a February 1967 *Sporting News* editorial advocated expanding the special coordinator's power. "We think Maduro could be even more successful if his post carried wider authority," the international sports weekly proposed.

> He is limited largely to an advisory capacity.... Maduro probably could eliminate much bickering and resentment if he were empowered to negotiate for all U.S. players intending to compete in Latin winter leagues.
> Baseball's destiny is international. Maduro is capable of reducing ill will and cementing Inter-American friendships on the sports front. He needs a few more tools to do the job. Baseball should see that he gets them.[33]

Later in the year, Roberto Maduro became a naturalized citizen of the United States. His completed August 2, 1967, United States of America Petition For Naturalization certificate, Clerk of Court No. 37, 171, states Maduro's residence as 1830 Meridian Avenue, Miami Beach, Florida, and that he was "lawfully admitted to the United States for permanent residence on November 14, 1961," which dims some of the drama previously mentioned with respect to his escape from Cuba. (The Bay of Pigs invasion occurred on April 17, 1961.) Messrs. Sy Chadroff and William Castrillo, both of Miami, signed the document as required witnesses knowing Maduro for at least five years.

Several months afterward, Maduro had a chance to immerse himself briefly in his parental roots. Representing the commissioner's office, Maduro attended a five-game baseball series held at Willemstad, Curaçao. The November 1967 series pitted a team from Holland and an all-star team composed of players from the Netherland Antilles. (It's quite probable that Maduro had visited the island territory during his youth.)

In 1968, his third year on the job, Maduro and Mexican League president Antonio Ramírez delved into starting summer leagues in some Latin American countries (only Mexico had a summer league), with the purpose of establishing a championship series among the competing countries. This appears to have been an attempt at reviving a type of Caribbean Series. It did not meet with much success. But on August 29, Maduro surely became pleased with the appointment of Preston Gómez as the first Hispanic hired to manage a major league ball club. The former Sugar Kings dugout leader signed on to guide the expansion San Diego Padres.

Seven—Starting Over as "a Millionaire in Friends"

The following year, under newly elected (February 4, 1969), baseball commissioner Bowie Kuhn, Maduro worked on getting better draft compensation packages from major league teams for Mexican prospects and presided over two winter league disputes (1969–1970 season). Taking a prideful pause first, the Caribbean consul was doubtlessly delighted following the major league draft, where son Jorge became the fourth-round pick of the New York Yankees.

"I went with George when he signed with the Yankees," remembers brother Al. "We went to Fort Lauderdale Stadium, just me and him, to sign his contract."[34]

The signing took place within two weeks of the June 5 draft. "This is a great organization," the older Maduro boy said. "Where I was drafted doesn't matter now. I just thought it would be a thrill for my father if I'd gone in the first or second round."[35] Jorge was assigned to the Class A Yankees in Fort Lauderdale, a short commute from his home.

A bit of disconcerting news did intrude its way into Maduro's summer. In July, Gabe Paul was relieved of his duties as general manager of the Cleveland Indians. Paul had lent his good friend a hand during the Maduro family's initial phase of resettlement. "My wife and I had seven dollars between us when Gabe took us in," Maduro commented following the Paul firing. "He made it possible for us to regain our dignity. I'll never be able to repay him for what he did for my family."[36] (Paul would go on to bigger and better things in his career.)

The first winter league issue involved the Puerto Rican loop, which granted the Santurce Crabbers' request to activate manager Frank Robinson for the playoffs. Maduro decreed Robinson, who not played all season, ineligible, because of the rule prohibiting major leaguers with more than four years experience from playing winter ball. In the Venezuelan League, Maduro recommended the lifting of a heavy-handed, three-year suspension given to three North American players for wishing to leave the country after their team did not make the playoffs. It was customary in all winter leagues to reinforce post-season squads with top players from second-tier teams. The players, however, were not interested in post-season play. The trio's contracts were with a specific team for the season and did not obligate them to another, Maduro contended.

In both cases, Kuhn, having the ultimate say, backed his Latin American attaché.

Eight

Cuban Sugar Kings Foundation

In May 1971, taking an apparent page from the Maduro sports-political doctrine, Preston Gómez initiated a plan to take a group of major leaguers, including Cubans, to Havana in October. "I am not a political person and baseball is not a political game," defended the San Diego Padres manager. "I'm not suggesting that this [trip] is a counterpart of Peking's Ping Pong diplomacy or that it will necessarily improve relations between the Cuban and American governments. But I am saying, most emphatically, that it won't hurt and might help, especially the people involved."[1]

Gómez argued, on a humanitarian front, that there were Cuban players, such as José Cardenal, interested in going because they had not seen their parents in more than ten years. Gómez himself had successfully traveled to Cuba in 1969 "to bring out his mother and ease the confinement of a brother who is a political prisoner."[2]

But Maduro, after a decade in exile, now displayed a radical change of heart and was "strongly opposed to the junket." He stated that he was sure his boss would not give permission for the excursion. He used, as part of his stance, a selected passage from a letter written to Padres president Buzzie Bavasi by a Miami exile leader which, in its criticism, casually rekindled the alleged affinity between the sport and the island's absolute ruler: "Just because Castro likes baseball, we must not pass over his crimes and the evil he has done and is doing to this hemisphere."[3]

"I sympathize with Bobby's views and his losses," Gómez responded, "but I insist I am thinking mostly of the Cuban people, those playing ball here and those left behind. Beside what would be wrong with professional or amateur baseball players going to Cuba when I understand the U.S. volleyball team is going there."[4]

Bowie Kuhn sided with his Ibero-American baseball envoy and forbade the proposed trip.

Maduro continued dutifully in his office for the next several years, his name slipping more and more from the sports pages even as more and more Hispanics were breaking into the sport's highest levels. In 1972, he coordinated the Venezuelan end of a spring visit to Caracas by the Cincinnati Reds and Pittsburgh Pirates. In January 1973, representing the commissioner's office along with Monte Irvin, who had been named special assistant to the commissioner, Maduro attended the funeral services of Roberto Clemente in San Juan. The ecumenical service took place at Hiram Bithorn Stadium, with 5,000 mourners on hand, a few days after an 11-day search by the U.S. Navy and Coast Guard, including many volunteer divers, failed to find the body of the superstar, lost in a New Year's Eve plane crash off the San Juan coastline.

The following year, in September, Maduro lost his wife of 34 years, Isolina. "Everybody's mom is a saint," Al Maduro recalls fondly.

> Mine was no different. My mom got cancer of the liver when I was in the sixth or seventh grade, and she died when I got right out of high school. I probably didn't realize it as much at the time but she was often bedridden. She went from being a pampered woman in Cuba—to cooking and sewing dresses for my sisters, and mowing the lawn with me. Not with a power mower, a push reel mower. I got a paper route when I was kid in Miami Beach. It was an afternoon paper but on Sunday they had a morning edition. She'd get up early every Sunday and help me fold the papers. Bowie Kuhn came down for her funeral. It was one of two times I saw my Dad cry.[5]

Approximately three years later, in 1977, Maduro found marital companionship once more with Marta Jackson. "He and Marta had first met back in Havana in 1952, when she was 22 years old,"[6] specified a Maduro internet profile. It was her second marriage as well.

That same year, a new administration in Washington explored bettering relations with Havana. As a first step, newly elected president Jimmy Carter had indicated a receptiveness to loosening travel restrictions for Cuba. As a result, boxing promoter Don King trumpeted Havana as a viable site for Muhammad Ali's next world heavyweight title defense. A professional soccer team, the New York Cosmos, with world-renowned star Pelé, received an invitation to play in the Cuban capital. And, in an about-face to a previous decree, Bowie Kuhn, targeting the spring of 1978, had come out with a plan to send a major league all-star team, including Cuban players, to the suddenly "en vogue" communist island.

"If any Cuban players go," said Maduro from the bastion of anti–Castro sentiment, "their lives may be in danger. Here in Miami the Cuban people are bitterly opposed to the trip. I would never send a Latin player, much less a Cuban. I've let the Commissioner's office know that."[7]

New York Times columnist Dave Anderson, who had reached out to Maduro for comment on Kuhn's intentions, also spoke with others in the local community to get their points of view. "[What about] those who lost everything," asked one unremitting émigré, "who had big jobs in Cuba and then had to work in hotels or cafeterias or gas stations when they fled to here?"[8]

"Cuba uses its baseball team as one of its biggest propaganda weapons," said another opposed to the contemplated trip. "That's why Castro won't risk losing any of his players. He wants them to keep playing for Cuba."[9]

In the end, the trip did not come off, and MLB would have to wait another two decades before officially setting foot in Cuba again.

However, not unlike the back-channel dealings that led to rapprochement between the two nations in 2014, the Carter White House and the Cuban government began secret talks in February 1978, the result of which was the creation of de facto embassies, known as "Special Interest Sections," in each other's capitals. The United States' hope for establishing diplomatic relations was dependent on Cuba agreeing to stop supporting and exporting leftist foreign policies around the globe. A worthwhile endeavor but perhaps with naïve expectations on Carter's part. Cuba had already begun flexing its military muscle in Angola and Ethiopia, countries into which Fidel Castro would commit five percent of the Cuban population, in troops and civilian personnel, from the late 1970s into the 1990s.

In April, Carter released an official statement with detectable traces of exasperation: "There is no possibility that we would see any substantial improvement in our relationship with Cuba as long as Castro is committed to this military intrusion policy in the internal affairs of African people."[10] But thinking he could still gain something, Carter kept the dialogue open, clandestinely so.

Bernardo Benes was a lawyer who had defected from Cuba a year before his friend Bobby Maduro. Benes was a Cienfuegos fan in his younger days and became Maduro's attorney in the States. "He was the closest Cuban exile to the Carter administration, after Alfredo Durán, the Florida Democratic Party chair,"[11] said *Secret Missions to Cuba* author Robert M. Levine. Benes also, for reasons not altogether clear, had the confidence of Cuban intelligence agents. Benes turned into the principal negotiator of Jimmy Carter's secret Cuba talks, making, in 1978, his first return trip to the imprisoned island in 18 years. He met directly with Fidel

Castro and led the first talks between Cuban exiles and Castro's totalitarian government. In various segments of the Cuban exile community, he was vilified. But the 43-year-old lawyer-turned-banker and later civic leader achieved a humanitarian victory for Carter and many Cuban exiles torn from their families. Castro agreed to release 3,600 political prisoners and to permit exiles to travel to Cuba for the first time under family reunification programs.

In conjunction with the first prisoner liberations that October, Benes, who was seldom accompanied by more than one person on his covert trips to Havana, petitioned the Cuban government to allow an entourage of six. In the party was Bobby Maduro. On the evening of October 20, 1978, Maduro boarded a charter aircraft and returned to his treasured country. Author Levine detailed the nature of the short visit:

> Perhaps the most touching event during the committee's visit was Bobby Maduro's visit to *Cementerio de Colón* to take flowers, provided by the Cuban government, to the tomb of his late son [Felipe]. Benes knew that Maduro longed to visit his son's cemetery, and was the main reason Benes invited him to be a member of the exile commission. To be able to put flowers on the grave, Benes said later, Maduro swallowed his hatred for the Castro regime for twenty-four hours.[12]

Around the time of his bittersweet return to Cuba, Maduro catapulted into the sports headlines as one of the key figures involved in a startup baseball league geared to foreign players. "A longtime dream of Bob Maduro to bring Latin America and the United States closer together through the game of baseball has been realized through the formation of the Inter American League," proclaimed the official announcement.[13]

The league, which was financially backed by two well-to-do Washington businessmen, Alex Lankler and George Orhstron, would set up operations as a Triple A circuit with six teams in five countries: U.S., Panama, Venezuela, Puerto Rico and the Dominican Republic. Venezuela would have two franchises, in Caracas and Maracaibo. A 130-game schedule was planned, with no infringement upon any applicable country's winter league play.

Maduro viewed the venture as providing the ultimate stepping-stone to the major leagues for Hispanic players, who he felt did not always receive fair evaluation in comparison to other ethnic players. "I have dreamt about extending the scope of Latin American baseball and bringing people closer together," he happily said. "It will be wonderful for human relations. My dream is fully realized."[14]

Major League Baseball and the National Association sanctioned the new league, but would not be providing any players. The international circuit would operate independently, with no major league affiliations. Both conditions would ultimately loom as inhibiting the success of the league. Ending 13 full years of service, Maduro resigned from his commissioner's office post, effective December 31, 1978, to assume the presidency of the Inter-American League.

"My dad always had different irons in the fires," Al Maduro wistfully recalls. "He had a dog track project in Curaçao, a Jai-Alai Casino in Aruba. He was always swinging for home runs, instead of maybe swinging for singles or doubles."[15]

The U.S. entry of the IAL made its home in Maduro's adopted hometown. The Miami Amigos were to share Miami Stadium with the Class A Miami Orioles club. Former Baltimore Orioles all-star Davey Johnson was hired as manager. On April 11, 1979, the Amigos opened the season in Panama City in front of 10,000 fans at Arosemena Stadium. The Panama Banqueros (Bankers) eked out a 6–5 win. The successful start was the exception and not the rule for what evolved into an unsuccessful turn of events that doomed the ambitious undertaking. One bad luck omen devel-

Three years before starting the Inter-American League in 1979, a 60-year-old Maduro peruses the cover of the latest issue of *The Sporting News* (courtesy *History Miami*).

oped just before the season. The Amigos had their brand-new uniforms stolen from Miami Stadium. The team was forced to use old Miami Marlins suits until theirs could be replaced.

Throughout the first months of the campaign, inter-continental travel hampered many players who had invalid papers or visas, causing outright cancellation of games. Travel costs and erratic plane scheduling became a constant drain on team coffers and players' constitutions. Rain plagued much of the early season, postponing an inordinate number of games (70), especially in the Dominican Republic. A fundamental lack of organizational know-how confronting day-to-day problems set back several of the novice franchises.

Though the league was sprinkled with recent major league players, or those eyeing a comeback, the new venture never could gain sufficient footing with the fans. Bobby Tolan, Mike Cuéllar, César Tovar, Tito Fuentes, Chico Salmón, Hal Breeden, Dave May, Cito Gaston, Wayne Granger and George Mitterwald were some of the league's names recognizable to big league baseball followers. One Miami Amigos player, Porfirio Altamirano, went on to play in the major leagues. The Nicaraguan pitcher appeared with the Philadelphia Phillies and Chicago Cubs in parts of three seasons, 1982–1984. Two months in, one team's operating budget (San Juan) ran dry; they were removed from competition in mid–June. Facing other mounting concerns, Maduro was forced to call a cessation of operations on June 30.

Ever the optimist, the 63-year-old Maduro indicated reboot plans for 1981, acknowledging late marketing efforts and inadequate radio and television sponsorship as reasons for weighing down the crumbled league from the start. He was in Cincinnati for the Reds' traditional "early" opener in 1980, trying to revive interest in the circuit. In a *Cincinnati Enquirer* article titled "Foreign Players Have Big Roles in American Baseball"—which appeared on April 9, the day the Reds and Atlanta Braves jumped off ahead of the rest of the big league clubs—reporter Lonnie Wheeler featured Maduro in his lead: "Bobby Maduro holds that two truths would be self-evident today, were it not for Fidel Castro. One—there would be major league baseball in Cuba; and two—Bobby Maduro would be a rich man. 'Havana would be in the major leagues if not for Castro,' Maduro says flatly."[16]

Maduro did not find the support he had hoped in Cincinnati—or elsewhere. The experimental Inter-American League was Roberto Maduro's last hurrah in the sport he so loved and to which he dedicated his entire adult life.

"In 1986, my dad had a car accident close to his house," recounts Al Maduro.

> He blacked out while driving. It turned out he had an aneurysm, and they found a brain tumor. We gave the go-ahead for a biopsy. The tumor was cancerous. The procedure left him partially paralyzed on one side. He talked out of the side of his mouth afterward and did not sound coherent sometimes. He ended up at Jackson Hospital. It was weird because from his room, which faced northeast, he had a view of Miami Stadium. It was a talking point for everybody who visited. He lasted for eight or nine months [after the accident].[17]

Roberto Maduro died on October 16, 1986; he was 70 years of age. The opening sentence of his *Sporting News* obituary referred to him as "the principal figure in the development of professional baseball in Cuba" and, later in the death notice, as spending his final years "organizing an amateur baseball league in Miami whose members were primarily of Latin American extraction.... Always interested in baseball, the younger Maduro always found time to establish a system of youth baseball leagues in and around Havana, which was without baseball of any sort at the time. Maduro supplied much of the equipment, money and often the ground for playing fields."[18]

In his later years, he had also been part of the Cuban Baseball Hall of Fame committee in Miami, officially known as the Federation of Cuban Professional Players in Exile, which maintained the tradition begun in 1939 in Cuba of eternally honoring winter league era players. Maduro himself was (tardily) elected to the Hall in 1985, along with Gran Stadium partner Miguelito Suárez.

Five months after his death, Miami city commissioners approved a renaming of Miami Stadium in honor of their fallen baseball man. Letters from the general managers of the Los Angeles Dodgers, Texas Rangers and San Francisco Giants helped put through the vote. Built in 1949, the stadium on NW 10 Avenue and 23 Street went back almost as far as Maduro did with his long-lost Havana baseball edifice. Apart from minor league baseball, the stadium had been the main training facility and home exhibition park for the Baltimore Orioles since 1959.

"He knew what his life's accomplishments had been," said his 57-year-old widow, Marta. "He knew at his death people would remember him."[19]

The formal dedication occurred March 8, 1987, prior to the first Orioles spring game versus the New York Yankees, who trained in nearby Fort Lauderdale. "Billy Martin was there and George Steinbrenner," recollects Al Maduro. "Billy and George especially went out of their way to congratulate the family."[20]

"I remember being proud of dad," Rosi Chica says of the more than three-decades-old event. "But the stadium was kind of run down at that time. Even though it was an honor that people thought enough to name the stadium after my dad, it wasn't like a 'wow' thing."[21]

Author Sam Zygner explored some of the reasons behind Maduro's daughter's lack of enthusiasm in his *The Forgotten Marlins, A Tribute to the 1956–1960 Original Miami Marlins*:

> Some of the future troubles of Miami Stadium could be attributed to the slow deterioration of the surrounding neighborhood that brought with it a perception of being a crime-ridden area. The development of Interstate 95, which circumvented traffic and hurt accessibility to the park, didn't help. Almost as an omen to impending doom, the newly christened Bobby Maduro Stadium was painted in large letters across cheap plywood and bolted unceremoniously to the facade. By 1990, the Orioles skipped town for better digs farther north.[22]

The major league Orioles' desertion led to the stadium's ultimate end. Abandoned by the city of Miami to the ravages of weather and wear and tear from years of neglect and neighborhood vandalism, the stadium became a dilapidated eyesore. The 13-acre ballpark lot was rezoned for habitational use in 1998, with the structure razed in 2001. In its place, the Miami Stadium Apartments were eventually built.

In November 2011, months prior to the opening of Marlins Park, the major league Miami Marlins resurrected the Maduro name by naming one of the four streets surrounding their state-of-the-art baseball facility *Bobby Maduro Drive*. Also grandly honored with a street naming was Marlins Ford Frick Award-winning announcer Felo Ramírez.

Shortly after the Sugar Kings' displacement, Neil MacCarl of the *Toronto Star* opined: "I am truly sorry to see the passing of Havana from the International League but I believe under the circumstances President Frank Shaughnessy had no alternative. The Sugar Kings were a colorful asset to the league for most of the six and one-half seasons, climaxed by the tremendous spectacle of their Junior World Series triumph over Minneapolis last October.... Havana is gone but not forgotten."[23]

More than half a century after their demise, a third generation of Maduros is making sure that the Sugar Kings are not forgotten. Jorge Maduro, Jr., runs the Cuban Sugar Kings Foundation in Miami. A residential and commercial realtor, George established the non-profit entity in 2015. Drafted out of Monsignor Pace High School by the Tampa Bay Devil Rays, George played for two other big league organizations, Seattle and Kansas City. Like his father, he was a catcher, but shoulder surgery ended his career at the Triple-A level. He is the father of a young son, Mason.

In front: sons Jorge, left, and Al Maduro hold up a sign commemorating the naming of the street around Marlins Park after their father in November 2011. In the background, the late broadcaster Felo Ramírez and Marlins president David Samson display the other designated thoroughfares ringing the state-of-the-art stadium (courtesy *El Nuevo Herald*).

When I was with the Rays, Frank Howard [coach] talked to me about my grandfather. The baseball gene went down one line—with my dad and me. My dad always envisioned a foundation in my father's name. I took the mantle from him, you might say, in bringing it about. Its purpose is to foster goodwill and cultural exchange through baseball-related initiatives. One of the initiatives is this league with the Rec ball atmosphere, with five teams, very family-involved. It's all about providing the kids with the experience. Not everyone is going to play in the major leagues or even high school, but we can give them an experience to remember. We are detail-oriented. We play the national anthem and introduce the kids, like in the majors. Details, I think, that are often overlooked.

Rec ball leagues are dying out because the competitiveness is gone. The stronger kids want to play into Travel Ball. Travel Ball is killing high school teams because it's so serious; there's no chance for inclusion for kids that are not as athletic. I wanted to create something that blended both: I'm a true believer in fundamentals and competitive baseball. But I also believe in the attributes that the game teaches that you can take into all walks of life. In our league, we have developed a system in which we grade each kid, and then assign them, spreading the talent throughout the clubs. We don't leave any kid out. Another thing we are doing are clinics in the inner cities. Every Sunday at Gibson Park. And we are sending equipment to Cuba.

The Foundation's baseball exchange recently expanded to cultural exchange with Cuban painter Tamayo.[24] We want to build a bridge. ESPN made a sports documentary on the Sugar Kings. I was in it. My grandfather was in it, of course. A similar *documentary was made and shown on Cuban television as part of a baseball series hosted by Yasel Porto, a well-known baseball commentator there.*

For the longest time among my friends, I was known as "el nieto de Bobby Maduro" ("Bobby Maduro's grandson"). I have two memories of my grandfather when I was young. I remember the ribbon-cutting, the renaming ceremony at Miami Stadium. All the family went. And I remember him when he was sick in a wheelchair. He had a home out near Metrozoo. I would hit balls out in front of his house—hitting the ball over the house and that always brought a smile to my grandfather's face.

I want to say the whole experience with the Sugar Kings team and the finish over there, and Cuba in general, is almost like a post-traumatic stress type of situation with us. My dad mostly talked about his childhood when it came to his dog and pony. To this day, my dad still talks about those two things to his grandkids. I guess the things that were most significant were not talked about as much in our family. But the love of baseball always came through. Even my aunts don't realize the significance of it all. I think now with my pursuit, everyone in the family is starting to better understand the magnitude of it, even though it's only a memory now.

There are rewards associated with owning a major league-type of franchise, but the hard part is, since there is nothing left, there's nothing tangible to point to with pride.[25]

In Havana, however, Gran Stadium (though its name has long been changed) still stands as an enduring tribute to the two men who erected it. Thanks to the efforts of the descendants of one of those men, Bobby Maduro, his legacy carries on.

Epilogue
Special Latin American Committee and International Hall of Fame Wing

The National Baseball Hall of Fame recognized Negro Leagues baseball nearly five decades ago with the establishment of its first Special Committee. That committee, and a subsequent one decades apart, magnanimously endorsed black Hispanic players for Cooperstown enshrinement. Yet the Hall has never convened a special committee for the game's biggest ethnic minority. It is now high time.

It is inexcusable that the 2015 Golden Era Committee failed to elect a single person in December 2014. Minnie Miñoso, the player with a higher lifetime OBP than Mays, Aaron and Clemente, could not gain enough support. He has since died, taking his longtime desire with him to the grave. As of 2017, the small committees have failed to elect a *living* ex-player since Bill Mazeroski in 2001.

There was only one Hispanic (Rod Carew) among the 16 Golden Era Committee voters. There were four African Americans on the panel. That stark cultural imbalance strongly requires the establishment of a special Latin American Committee.

The National Baseball Hall of Fame should not only create a special committee dedicated solely to Hispanic players and executives, but also consider one for the establishment of a new International Hall of Fame wing. This would be an all-inclusive way to pay tribute to the globalization of the sport. I can think of at least one slam dunk electee in Sadaharu Oh. The international wing would certainly beckon such baseball lifers as Adolfo Luque and Mike González, whose winter league accomplishments as players and managers, combined with their major league resumes, would astound most baseball fans. I also think of Felipe Alou, who bravely overcame not only his skin color but a language barrier during harshly intolerant times, and yet managed to accomplish an impressive baseball career as a player and then dugout chief.

Has there been a Bobby Maduro in Mexico or Canada or Japan or Korea? Wouldn't baseball fans around the globe want to find out?

Chapter Notes

Introduction

1. Dimas Castellanos. "Separating Baseball from Politics." Diariodecuba.com, April 13, 2017.
2. Nora Gámez Torres. "Decades After Losing It All in Cuba, U.S. Seller Wants $1,500 for Wedding Album." *The Miami Herald*, May 6, 2018.

Prologue

1. According to Franklin W. Wright's *A Case Study of Cuba, 1750–1900*, the 1820 "compensation agreement," in which Spain received 20 million pounds from Great Britain to cease slave trading did not immediately eliminate the abhorrent activity. "After that date, the slave trade was technically illegal," part of the study reads. "Nevertheless, by 1833 another 126,000 Africans were brought to the island. Altogether, more than 600,000 Africans arrived in Cuba during the nineteenth century, accentuating the consciousness of Africa.... Africans not only revitalized Cuban culture but were instrumental in transforming its agriculture." 13.
2. Rory Costello. "Bobby Maduro," bioproject.sabr.org. S.E.L. Maduro was Salomon Elias Levy Maduro.
3. *Ibid.* Costello adds: "The Jews that came to Cuba from Curaçao spoke Papiamentu, the Creole lingua franca of the Dutch Antilles. Ladino, the Hebrew-influenced tongue that is to Spanish what Yiddish is to German, had been one of the many influences that filtered into Papiamentu. It helped them adjust to life in Cuba more easily. The Jewish community was the first group to actually speak this language on a daily basis."
4. Alan Fredric Benjamin, *Jews of the Dutch Caribbean: Exploring Ethnic Identity on Curacao*. (New York: Routledge, 2002), 58. The oil reference is to a future economic revitalization of Curaçao, due to its 40-mile geographic proximity to the northern coast of petroleum-rich Venezuela.
5. Rory Costello, "Bobby Maduro," at bioproject.sabr.org.
6. Phone conversation with Mercedes de Marchena, October 17, 2016. Later travel documents consistently show Maduro's full name as Roberto Maduro de Lima, the third name being his mother's father's surname.
7. Phone conversation with Mercedes de Marchena, October 17, 2016.
8. Interview with Al Maduro, March 6, 2017.
9. Louisiana Sugar Planters' Association, et al., *The Louisiana Planter and Sugar Manufacturer, Volume 47*, Reprinted Palala Press, 2016. Costello cites the American Sugar Refining Company, the name behind the Domino Sugar brand, as having operations in Central Cunagua. Incidentally, a *Central* refers to a sugar mill with combined planting, cultivating and refining capacities. Its operations were usually named for the closest town.

Chapter One

1. George Beahon. "In This Corner..." *Rochester Democrat and Chronicle*, De-

cember 3, 1953. A classmate of Maduro's at Cornell was Jerome "Brud" Holland, the university's first African American football player, who later became an accomplished academic and U.S. ambassador.
  2. Phone conversation with Lourdes Reguera, January 24, 2017.
  3. Fausto Miranda. Untitled column, *El Miami Herald*, March 28, 1977.
  4. Interview with Jorge Maduro, January 28, 2017.
  5. Suárez was forced out of Cuba in 1960. In the United States, he dedicated himself to a career in sales advertising, with notable magazines such as *Bohemia, Vanidades, Reader's Digest* and the Spanish newspaper daily *Diario las Américas*. He died December 30, 1999, of a stroke at the age of 81. His brother Roberto founded the Spanish-language sister newspaper of *The Miami Herald—El Nuevo Herald* (originally called *El Miami Herald*).
  6. César Brioso, *Havana Hardball: Spring Training Jackie Robinson, and The Cuban League* (Gainesville: University of Florida Press, 2015), 9.
  7. J.G. Taylor Spink, "Game Booming in Cuba Despite Some U.S. Slaps." *The Sporting News*, January 22, 1947, 6. According to César Brioso, the day before the league's inaugural, Cuba's bishop of Havana, Monsignor Alfredo Muller, blessed the steel and concrete structure in front of more than 2,000 people. Maduro and Suárez were no doubt present for the occasion. An exhibition game took place on October 2, and probably others were held prior to the October 26 Cuban Winter League grand opening.
  8. Lou Hernández, *The Rise of the Latin American Baseball Leagues, 1947–1961* (Jefferson, NC: McFarland, 2011), 94.
  9. The Dodgers' strategy in training in Havana may have been well-intentioned, but it sadly failed Robinson off the field. Brooklyn's coaches and players stayed at the prestigious Hotel Nacional. The Montreal players were billeted at the Havana Military Academy, where the team trained while in Havana. Robinson and black teammates Roy Campanella, Don Newcombe and Roy Paltrow were forced to reside at segregated, much less hospitable accommodations within the city.
  10. Wendell Smith, "Robinson May Need a Minor Operation," *Pittsburgh Courier*, March 22, 1947.
  11. César Brioso, *Havana Hardball: Spring Training Jackie Robinson, and the Cuban League* (Gainesville: University of Florida Press, 2015), 222.
  12. Lou Hernández, *The Rise of the Latin American Baseball Leagues, 1947–1961* (Jefferson, NC: McFarland, 2011), 101.
  13. Roberto González Echevarría, *The Pride of Havana: A History of Cuban Baseball* (New York: Oxford University Press, 1999), 71–72.
  14. Lou Hernández, *The Rise of the Latin American Baseball Leagues, 1947–1961*. (Jefferson, NC: McFarland, 2011), 235.

Chapter Two

  1. "Snead Takes Havana Meet," *Decatur Herald* (IL), December 16, 1948.
  2. Interview with Jorge Maduro, January 28, 2017.
  3. Cy Kritzer, "Maduro, One of Cuba's Best Golfers, Paired With Snead," *The Sporting News*, June 29, 1955, 13.
  4. As an indication of Emilio de Armas' standing in Cuban baseball, when the Caribbean Professional Baseball Federation was formed on April 12, 1948, de Armas was one of the original signing members of the pact. It can be conjectured that de Armas served as an early and valuable mentor for Bobby Maduro. De Armas, according to Roberto González Echevarría, also helped the Maduro-Suárez team in "selling" the concept of the new stadium, presumably to the civic financiers and the general public.
  5. Jorge S. Figueredo, *Beisbol Cubano: A un Paso de las Grandes Ligas, 1878–1961* (Jefferson, NC: McFarland, 2005), 283.
  6. Roberto González Echevarría, *The Pride of Havana: A History of Cuban Baseball* (New York: Oxford University Press, 1999), 301.
  7. Rory Costello, "Bobby Maduro," at bioproject.sabr.org. A hotbed of Cuban baseball talent over the years, Matanzas is a coastal city about an hour's drive east of Havana.
  8. Carroll Rines, "Skillin to Umpire Pro Ball," *Portland Sunday Telegram*, October 15, 1950.
  9. Jorge S. Figueredo, *Beisbol Cubano:*

A un Paso de las Grandes Ligas, 1878–1961 (Jefferson, NC: McFarland, 2005), 291. Per Figueredo, October 24, 1950, was the first TV transmission date in Havana.

10. Interview with Felo Ramírez, September 24, 2016. That evening Felo called the Marlins' game as usual. Although he did not pitch, it was José Fernández's last game. The young, energetic, charismatic, extremely talented hurler lost his life in a devastating boating accident early the next morning. The nonagenarian Ramírez passed away during this writing as well.

11. J.G. Taylor Spink, "U.S. Players Get Polish; Gonzalez Gold in Havana," *The Sporting News*, January 10, 1951, 2.

12. J.G. Taylor Spink, "Looping the Loops," *The Sporting News*, May 2, 1951, 4.

13. Lou Hernández, *The Rise of the Latin American Baseball Leagues, 1947–1961* (Jefferson, NC: McFarland, 2011), 124.

14. "Bucs Due to Train in Havana in '53," *Pittsburgh Press*, April 20, 1952.

15. Edgar Munzel, "Maduro Stresses Cuba's Aid to O.B," *The Sporting News*, September 17, 1952, 8. The four Cubans were Miñoso and pitchers Luis Aloma, Mike Fornieles and Sandy Consuegra.

16. Ibid.

17. Lou Hernández, *The Rise*, 129.

18. Les Biederman, "The Scoreboard," *Pittsburgh Press*, March 3, 1953. The Pirates brought their meal preparer from the Forbes Field pressroom, a Mrs. Marie Piper, to keep the food in line with their players' cultural liking.

19. "Ralph Kiner Cause of Cuban Concern," *Cincinnati Enquirer*, March 2, 1953.

20. Jack Hernon, "Bucs Not Worth Current They Use," *Pittsburgh Post-Gazette*, March 27, 1953.

21. Les Biederman, "Bucs Train for Free, Cubans Pay $50,000 Tab," *Pittsburgh Press*, April 3, 1953.

22. "Maduro Quits Game 'Temporarily.'" *The Sporting News*, March 11, 1953, 19.

23. Dick Meyer, "Lions Take F-I Lead to Cuba," *Fort Lauderdale News*, June 8, 1953.

24. "Maduro Promises FIL Improved Cuban Team," *News Tribune* (NJ), May 5, 1953.

25. Rory Costello, "Bobby Maduro" at bioproject.sabr.org.

26. Tony Pérez, speaking at The Legends of Cuban Baseball Luncheon, Miami, Florida, September 24, 2016.

27. Les Biederman, "The Scoreboard," *Pittsburgh Press*, September 12, 1953.

28. Lou Hernández, *The Rise*, 133.

29. John Phillips, *The Story of the Havana Sugar Kings* (Kathleen, GA: Capital, 2003), 8.

Chapter Three

1. "Havana Seeks League Spot," *Baltimore Sun*, November 8, 1953.

2. "Richmond and Havana May be Added to International League," *Perkasie (PA) News-Herald*, November 14, 1953.

3. "Package Deal Would Include Richmond, Va," *Pittsburgh Press*, November 16, 1953.

4. Ibid.

5. Gayle Talbot. "Best Thing Since...," *Asbury Park (NJ) Press*, January 10, 1954.

6. Ibid.

7. "Havana Joins IL," *Kansas City (MO) Times*, January 13, 1954.

8. "It's 'Sugar Kings' Now for IL," *Palm Beach Post*, January 11, 1954.

9. George Beahon, "Maduro Sees 30,000 Minimum," *Rochester (NY) Democrat and Chronicle*, January 20, 1954. Beahon noted that Maduro was questioned about whether Havana citizens were really interested in baseball. *Are they?* replied Maduro, who went on to tell of a time when the country's strong-arm leader Fulgencio Batista had scheduled a speech to the nation that conflicted with an Almendares-Habana game. The speech was postponed until after the game, Maduro said.

10. Frank Eck, "Gigantic Fight Seen for Maduro in Establishing Cuban Ball Team," *Asbury Park (NJ) Press*, February 7, 1954.

11. Ibid.

12. Irving Vaughan, "Minoso Says No to New Sox Bid," *Chicago Tribune*, February 10, 1954. Maduro also eased the way for the White Sox to sign Venezuelan Chico Carrasquel, per SABR BioProject editor Rory Costello.

13. It's probable that the Japanese played a Cuban all-star team and not the actual Sugar Kings in the games played March 4–6. Raúl Sánchez handled the Nippon squad, 4–1, on seven hits, in the opener. Behind Takumi Otomo's three-hitter, Yomiuri then

blanked the Cuban opposition, 5–0. Julio Moreno stopped the Giants cold, yielding six hits, in the one-sided, 11–0 third game.

14. "Havana Triumphs Over Maple Leafs in Home Debut," *Hartford Courant*, April 21, 1954.

15. This cap style appears to be the most widely used by the team. The Cincinnati Reds also wore white caps with red bills from the late 1950s through the mid–1960s.

16. Phone interview with Billy DeMars, April 11, 2017.

17. "Havana Sugar Kings Miss Noise-Happy Fans on the Road," *Kansas City* (MO) *Times*, June 2, 1954.

18. Bob Mellor, "Errors Help Cubans Take Series' 3rd Game," *Ottawa* (ONT) *Journal*, May 21, 1954.

19. "Havana Sugar Kings Miss Noise-Happy Fans on the Road," *Kansas City* (MO) *Times*, June 2, 1954.

20. Phone interview with Jim Melton, March 23, 2017.

21. George Beahon, "Sugar Kings Topple Red Wings, 5 to 4, On Late-Inning Pitching Wildness," *Rochester Democrat and Chronicle*, July 7, 1954.

22. Interview with Jorge Maduro, January 28, 2017.

23. Phone interview with Jim Melton, March 23, 2017.

24. George Beahon, "In This Corner…," *Rochester Democrat and Chronicle*, April 29, 1954.

25. John Phillips, *The Story of the Havana Sugar Kings* (Kathleen, GA: Capital, 2003), 8.

26. "Maduro for Florida Shift," *Kansas City* (MO) *Times*, December 11, 1954.

27. "Minnie Minoso Named Top Cuban Athlete," *Bridgeport* (CT) *Telegram*, February 2, 1955.

28. Phone interview with Jim Melton, March 23, 2017.

29. Pedro Galiana, "Maduro Scours All of Cuba with His Own Scout Staff," *The Sporting News*, March 16, 1955, 26.

30. "Cuba Spruces Up to Greet Summer Vacation Travelers," *Hartford Courant*, May 22, 1955.

Chapter Four

1. "Miami Switch Approved by IL," *Morning News* (DE), January 4, 1956.

2. Sam Zygner, *The Forgotten Marlins: A Tribute to the 1956–1960 Original Miami Marlins* (Latham, MD: Scarecrow, 2013), 86. Funds for Miami Stadium's construction were tied to money stolen by alleged corrupt Cuban cabinet minister José Alemán, Sr., who died of a leukemia-related illness in 1950 at age 44. Much of his holdings, including Miami Stadium, went to his teenage son José Jr.

3. "Miami Opener Slated April 18," *Palm Beach Post*, January 4, 1956.

4. Frank Eck, "Boys Have to Go to School to Play Baseball in Cuba," *Oneonta* (NY) *Star*, April 11, 1956.

5. George Beahon, "Red Wings Beat Sugar Kings, 8–6," *Rochester Democrat and Chronicle*, June 16, 1956.

6. Rory Costello, "Bobby Maduro," at bioproject.sabr.org.

7. George Beahon, "Wings Drop Opener on Ninth Inning Homer," *Rochester Democrat and Chronicle*, April 19, 1956.

8. Email correspondence with Reggie Smith, March 20, 2017.

9. Phone interview with Fred Kipp, April 25, 2017.

10. "Satchel Wins Aching Bones Battle," *Fort Lauderdale News*, July 12, 1956.

11. "Redlegs' Cuban Rookie Began Organized Baseball in 1952," *Wilmington* (OH) *News-Journal*, November 22, 1956.

12. "Tuning In," *The Sporting News*, August 29, 1956, 38.

13. The other four-home-run sluggers were: High Pockets Kelly (6/24/19), Buzz Arlett twice (6/1/1932, 7/4/1932), and Bob Seeds (5/6,1938).

14. In 1941, the International League's New Jersey Giants sold over 55,000 tickets for their home opener. Continuing an annual occurrence begun in the late 1930s, the oversold ticket sales were driven as an annual pet project by Jersey City Mayor Frank Hague and his political machine. More than half the tickets sold were purchased by Hague constituents and could not be used for a stadium with a capacity of 25,000.

15. "Arms Cache Spotted in Cuba," *Cincinnati Enquirer*, March 16, 1957.

16. Máximo Sánchez, "Colorful Pre-Game Show Marked Havana Inaugural," *The Sporting News*, April 24, 1957, 28.

17. George Beahon, "Cuban Manager 'Upgrades' Club," *Rochester Democrat and*

Chronicle, May 11, 1957. The TV pact, including doubleheaders, beamed four games on any given week into Cuban living rooms.

18. Paul Pinckney, "In the Pink," *Rochester Democrat and Chronicle*, June 20, 1957.

19. Kenny Van Sickle, "Sport Tower," *Ithaca (NY) Journal*, June 12, 1957.

20. John Phillips, *The Story of the Havana Sugar Kings* (Kathleen, GA: Capital, 2003), 28.

21. "Atlanta Crackers May Advance to IL Next Season," *Wilmington (DE) Morning News*, July 17, 1957.

22. *Ibid.*

23. *Ibid.*

24. "Montreal Players 'Protest' Flight to Havana After Anonymous Threats," *Hartford Courant*, July 27, 1957.

25. George Beahon, "What Is the Real Situation in Cuba?" *Rochester Democrat and Chronicle*, August 11, 1957.

26. Phone interview with José Santiago, April 10, 2017.

Chapter Five

1. latinamericanstudies.org/us-cuba/gardner-smith.htm. The quote is from the transcript of Smith's testimony before a U.S. Senate Subcommittee to Investigate the Administration of the Internal Social Act and Other International Laws, under the heading COMMUNIST THREAT TO THE UNITED STATES THROUGH THE CARIBBEAN, 86th Congress, August 30, 1960. The thriving business environment in Cuba was criminally undermined by a systemic kleptocracy.

2. Milton Richman, "Havana and Miami Not Interested in Moving Teams to Jersey City," *Ottawa (ONT) Journal*, October 18, 1957.

3. *Ibid.*

4. "Cuban Rights Eased Except in Rebel Zone," *New York Times*, January 26, 1958.

5. Joe Reichler, "Rookie Bob Shaw Tabbed as 'Can't Miss' Hurler," *Hagerstown (MD) Daily Mail*, January 23, 1958.

6. "Havana Baseball Club Faced with Franchise Move," *Hampton (VA) Daily Press*, January 27, 1958.

7. Maduro later revealed that Batista had denied his request for a $60,000 government subsidy. The former army sergeant, who in 1952 led a military coup to assume control of Cuba, did accede to one concession proposed by Maduro for the new season. Instead of posting weapons-bearing government troops inside Gran Stadium, he agreed to relegate the detail to a sidearm-carrying force outside the park, along with some secret police.

8. "Jersey City's Bid for IL Club Fails," *Somerville (NJ) Courier-News*, February 6, 1958.

9. "Denies Cuban Violence Will Affect Baseball," *Terre Haute (IN) Star*, March 29, 1958.

10. *Ibid.*

11. "Cubans May Defy Rebels," *Lincoln (NE) Evening Journal*, April 4, 1958.

12. "Cuban Unrest Has IL Heads Worried," *Jackson (MS) Clarion-Ledger*, April 6, 1958.

13. "Baseball Will Keep Going in Cuba, but No Shooting Will be Allowed," *Nyack (NY) Journal News*, April 7, 1958.

14. "Havana Nine Confident of Playing in Home Ballpark," *Wilmington (DE) Morning News*, April 12, 1958.

15. "Buffalo Says 'No' to Cuba Tilt," *Elmira (NY) Star-Gazette*, April 14, 1958.

16. *Ibid.*

17. "Buffalo Balks as League Orders Play in Havana," *Tallahassee Democrat*, April 14, 1958.

18. "Peace Breaks Out in International League," *News Journal (DE)*, April 15, 1958. Although he helped pacify Shaughnessy at this time, Smith, in private, held deep misgivings over the current political and social situation in Cuba. A few months before his "If children play in the streets" acquittal, at a U.S. State Department press conference, January 16, 1958, Smith predicted that "the United States will never be able to do business with Fidel Castro and he will not honor his international obligations and will not be able to maintain law and order."

19. Phone interview with Rosi Chica, March 8, 2017.

20. Lou Hernández, *The Rise of the Latin American Baseball Leagues, 1947–1961* (Jefferson, NC: McFarland, 2011), 164.

21. George Beahon, "Havana Shuts Out Red Wings, 5 to 0," *Rochester Democrat and Chronicle*, May 25, 1958.

22. "Cubans Owner Knows Value of Publicity," *The Sporting News*, November

26, 1958, 35. Today, there is one national daily newspaper in Cuba, the state-run *Granma*.

23. "Nap Reyes Gets Axe," *Fort Lauderdale News*, July 24, 1958.

24. In his August 30, 1960, Congressional testimony, Ambassador Smith stated, "The Batista government was overthrown because of the corruption, disintegrating from within, and because of the various agencies of the United States who directly and indirectly aided the overthrow of the Batista government and brought into power Fidel Castro." The ambassador pointed to three key elements which, in his learned opinion, facilitated the dramatic shift of events: "Three front-page articles in *The New York Times* in early 1957, written by editorialist Herbert Matthews, served to inflate Castro to world stature and world recognition. Until that time, Castro had been just another bandit in the Oriente Mountains in Cuba, with a handful of followers.... When we [U.S.] refused to sell arms to the Cuban government [in March 1958] and persuaded other friendly governments not to sell arms to Cuba. These actions had a moral, psychological effect upon the Cuban armed forces which was demoralizing to the nth degree.... The reverse, it built up the morale of the revolutionary forces. Obviously when we refused to sell arms to a friendly government, the existing government, the people of Cuba and the armed forces knew that the United States no longer would support Batista's government." Fulgencio Batista initially fled Cuba in the early morning hours of January 1, 1959, for the Dominican Republic. He died in exile in Spain in August 1973.

25. "Havana Owner Thinks Club Can Stay in IL," *Lincoln* (NE) *Star*, January 30, 1959.

26. "Fidel Castro to Toss Out First Pitch," *Monroe* (LA) *Morning World*, December 31, 1959. The Numbers Game was a tolerated and thriving subculture in Cuban society. Betting on games at the ballpark may have occurred, but the author found no blatant evidence of its reported existence or of any U.S. organized crime influence therein.

27. Jim Schlemmer, "Majors Expected to Ignore Lewis," *Akron* (OH) *Beacon Journal*, January 31, 1959.

28. Cy Kritzer, "Int Ball on Sounder Basis Than Ever in Cuba, Maduro Says," *The Sporting News*, February 11, 1959, 23.

29. George Beahon, "League OKs '59 Baseball in Havana," *Rochester Democrat and Chronicle*, January 31, 1959.

30. John W. Fox, "Milwaukee, Yawkey Make Talkie-Talkie," *Binghamton* (NY) *Press and Sun-Bulletin*, February 1, 1959.

31. Frank Eck, "Castro to Give International Loop 'Shot in Arm' with Added Interest," *Hampton* (VA) *Daily Press*, April 12, 1959.

32. John Phillips, *The Story of the Havana Sugar Kings* (Kathleen, GA: Capital, 2003) 44.

33. George Beahon, "League OKs '59 Baseball in Havana," *Rochester Democrat and Chronicle*, January 31, 1959.

34. Frank Eck, "Castro to Give International Loop 'Shot in Arm' with Added Interest," Hampton (VA) *Daily Press*, April 12, 1959.

35. Phone interview with Fred Kipp, April 25, 2017.

36. Frank Finch, "Dodgers Nose Out Cincinnati, 4–3," *Los Angeles Times*, March 22, 1959.

37. Jim Murray, "Between You 'n' Me," *Indiana Gazette*, March 26, 1959.

38. "Will Castro Give Help to Mired Ball Club?" *Tallahassee* (FL) *Democrat*, April 22, 1959.

39. "Donating $20,000 to Baseball Team," *Simpson's Leader Times* (PA), April 29, 1959.

40. John Phillips, *The Story of the Havana Sugar Kings* (Kathleen, GA: Capital, 2003), 52.

41. Luther Evans, "Maduro Ready to Sell, Castro Offers New Aid," *Miami Herald*, July 19, 1959.

42. "Castro Pledges Backing for Slumping Ball Club," *Fort Lauderdale News*, July 21, 1959.

43. "Fidel Castro Makes Debut in Baseball," *Chicago Tribune*, July 25, 1959. The Agrarian Reform Laws prevented foreign ownership of agricultural land and redistributed confiscated farm property, in lots, to Cuban *campesinos*. Under the guise of land ownership for the poor, the *campesinos*, or peasant farmers, would work the gifted land for the benefit of the state.

44. On July 26, 1953, anti–Batista rebels, including Fidel Castro, assaulted the Mon-

cada military barracks in Santiago de Cuba. The attack was repelled. Castro, and his brother Raúl, were eventually captured, tried and sent to prison. In 1955, the Castro brothers were pardoned by Batista and exiled themselves to Mexico, before returning to Cuba as guerrilla warfare combatants in late 1956. Today, July 26 has become Cuba's National Rebellion Day, a national holiday.

45. "Bullets Cause International Incident," *Pittsburgh Press*, July 27, 1959.
46. Cy Kritzer, "Volunteer Fireman Wieand Snuffs Out Blazes for Cubans," *The Sporting News*, August 19, 1959, 31.
47. "Arroyo Stars for Havana," *St. Louis Post-Dispatch*, September 23, 1959.
48. John Phillips, *The Story of the Havana Sugar Kings* (Kathleen, GA: Capital, 2003), 82.
49. Dwayne Netland, "Baseball Way of Life in Cuba," *Minneapolis Star Tribune*, September 28, 1959.
50. Bob Beebe, "Junior Series Moved to Havana Because of Weather," *Minneapolis Star Tribune*, September 29, 1959.
51. Ibid.
52. Bob Beebe, "Millers Shrug Off Cubans Home Edge," *Minneapolis Star Tribune*, September 30, 1959.
53. Ibid.
54. "Havanans Roll Out Clamorous Carpet," *Minneapolis Star Tribune*, October 1, 1959.
55. Bob Beebe, "When 'Fee-Dell' Pitches, There's Something on It," *Minneapolis Star Tribune*, October 2, 1959.
56. Bob Beebe, "One Pitch Kills Millers in Cuba," *Minneapolis Star Tribune*, October 7, 1959.
57. "24,990 See Havana Nab Series, 3–2," *Fort Lauderdale News*, October 7, 1959.
58. John Phillips, *The Story of the Havana Sugar Kings* (Kathleen, GA: Capital, 2003), 100.
59. Bob Beebe, "Junior Series a Huge Success," *Minneapolis Star Tribune*, October 8, 1959.
60. "Junior Series Nets Cubans $888 Each, $592 to Millers," *The Sporting News*, October 21, 1959, 16.
61. Jim Schlemmer, "Majors Expected to Ignore Lewis," *Akron (OH) Beacon Journal*, January 31, 1959.
62. George Beahon, "League OKs '59 Baseball in Havana," *Rochester Democrat and Chronicle*, January 31, 1959.
63. From the weekly publication of the Diocese of Miami: "More than half of Cuba's 732 priests and approximately 2,000 nuns were told to 'start packing their bags' by Castro in his warning that they would be expelled soon. It was becoming increasingly difficult, if not impossible, for people to receive any of the sacraments.... Churches either were closed or under guard of militiamen. Hundreds of priests were already in prison or under house arrest. All Church schools were in the process of being nationalized (a total of 339 throughout the island, with 173 and 36,000 students in the Havana Archdiocese alone)."—"Reds Smash at Church, Schools to Drive Religion Out of Cuba." *The Voice*, May 5, 1961.

Chapter Six

1. Lou Hernández, *The Rise of the Latin American Baseball Leagues, 1947–1961* (Jefferson, NC: McFarland, 2011), 170.
2. "Angriest Castro Yet Scores U.S.," *Pittsburgh Post-Gazette*, October 27, 1959.
3. "Castro's New U.S. Blast," *Chicago Tribune*, November 13, 1959.
4. Bob Broeg, "Sports Comment," *St. Louis Post-Dispatch*, December 18, 1959.
5. George Beahon, "In This Corner," *Rochester Democrat Chronicle*, December 1, 1959. Castro and his brother Raúl received a Jesuit education through high school.
6. "Half-Million Cuban Catholics Assemble for Rally in Havana," *Orlando Sentinel*, November 29, 1959.
7. Máximo Sánchez, "Cuban All-Star Game Slated, Funds to Castro Government," *The Sporting News*, November 18, 1959, 20.
8. "International Loop Ponders Problems," *Troy (NY) Times Record*, January 27, 1960.
9. "Wings to Open in Havana," *Ithaca (NY) Journal*, January 28, 1960.
10. "Maduro Opposes Political Moves," *Pensacola (FL) News*, February 24, 1960.
11. Ibid.
12. Roberto González Echevarría, *The Pride of Havana: A History of Cuban Base-*

ball (New York: Oxford University Press, 1999), 353.
13. "Managers Back Play in Havana," *Bridgeport* (CT) *Post*, March 20, 1960.
14. "Wary Havana Sugar Kings Ready To Defend Laurels," *Bridgeport* (CT) *Post*, April 17, 1960.
15. "Exhibition Shift Jars Cuba Relations," *Nashville Tennessean*, March 29, 1960.
16. *Ibid.*
17. "Minor League Moguls Deny Havana Franchise Switch," *Fort Lauderdale News*, March 30, 1960.
18. George Beahon, "Maduro Sees No Reason Why IL Should Quit Cuba," *Rochester Democrat and Chronicle*, April 5, 1960.
19. "Havana Club May Switch to Jersey," *Monroe* (LA) *Morning World*, April 17, 1960.
20. "Eyes of Baseball World Centered on Havana Opener," *Hartford Courant*, April 17, 1960.
21. Phone interview with Bob Miller, May 31, 2017.
22. "Red Wings Lose First Game, Tie in 2nd," *Rochester Democrat and Chronicle*, June 27, 1960.
23. "Sugar Bill Quota Stirs Cuban Blast," *St. Cloud* (MN) *Times*, June 28, 1960. The United States bought sugar from Cuba at two cents above world price.
24. Dan Daniel, "Cuba's Political Climate Is Not Healthy for O.B.," *The Sporting News*, July 6, 1960, 10.
25. *Ibid.*
26. George Beahon, "In This Corner," *Rochester Democrat and Chronicle*, July 3, 1960.
27. "Cabinet Gives Castro Power to Order Grab," *Chicago Tribune*, July 6, 1960.
28. "Cuba to Seize U.S. Sugar Mills," *Brownsville* (TX) *Herald*, July 6, 1960.
29. "IL Pulls Havana Team Out of Cuba," *Philadelphia Daily News*, July 8, 1960.
30. John Phillips, *The Story of the Havana Sugar Kings* (Kathleen, GA: Capital, 2003), 112. The office building address was Calle Amargura #203. The expropriated building today houses *El Instituto Cubano de Antropología*, the Cuban Anthropological Institute.
31. "IL Pulls Havana Team Out of Cuba," *Philadelphia Daily News*, July 8, 1960.
32. John Phillips, *The Story*, 112.

33. "IL Pulls Havana Team Out of Cuba," *Philadelphia Daily News*, July 8, 1960.
34. Sid Moody, "Sport Angles," *Asbury Park* (NJ) *Press*, July 9, 1960.
35. "Move to Jersey City Greeted with Regret," *Jackson* (MS) *Clarion-Ledger*, July 14, 1960. Before ultimately defecting to the United States, Castaño tried managing in the first year of Cuban amateur baseball in 1962, guiding a team ironically called Azucareros. He went on to manage many years in Mexico afterward.
36. A primary roster force of nine Cubans played for the Sugar Kings/Jerseys in 1960: Borrego Alvarez, Andrés Ayón, Joe Azcúe, Mike Cuéllar, Hank Izquierdo, Danny Morejón, Orlando Peña, Cookie Rojas and Raúl Sánchez. Three others, Enrique Marota, Elio Toboso and Mario Zambrano, each played fewer than ten games. Also forming part of the team's Latin American DNA were Venezuelans Elio Chacón, Emilio Cueche, and Yo-Yo Davalillo, along with Puerto Ricans Luis Arroyo and Félix Torres.
37. "Havana Franchise Ordered to Jersey," *Palm Beach Post*, July 9, 1960.
38. "Move to Jersey City Greeted with Regret," *Jackson* (MS) *Clarion-Ledger*, July 14, 1960.
39. "Traitor Reyes Gets Protection," *Fort Lauderdale News*, July 16, 1960.
40. Joseph O. Haff, "Ex-Sugar Kings Get a Noisy Welcome in New Home," *New York Times*, July 16, 1960.
41. Roberto González Echevarría, *The Pride of Havana: A History of Cuban Baseball* (New York: Oxford University Press, 1999), 345. González Echevarría points out that the phrase is a play on the title of a poetic verse by José Martí, Cuba's father of colonial independence, *No Country, No Master*: *"I want, when I die/With no country, but no master/To have on my tomb a bouquet/Of flowers—and a flag!"*
42. "Cuban Baseball Curbed by Frick," *Baltimore Sun*, September 1, 1960.

Chapter Seven

1. "R. Hart Phillips, Baseball Is Dying in Cuba," *New York Times*, November 11, 1960.
2. Fred. G Lieb, "Castro Chief Prom-

ises Hands Off Cubans in U.S. Ball," *The Sporting News*, November 2, 1960, 2.

3. George Beahon, "In This Corner," *Rochester Democrat and Chronicle*, November 26, 1960.

4. Interview with Jorge Maduro, January 28, 2017; telephone interview with Jorge Maduro, March 9, 2017.

5. Phone interview with Betty McDaniel, March 7, 2017.

6. Interview with Al Maduro, March 6, 2017. Max Borges, Jr. (July 24, 1918–January 18, 2009) has a Wikipedia profile. It highlights, as some of his best-known works, the remodeling of the Tropicana Night Club (1951) and Club Náutico (1953). His *Washington Post* obituary stated that he and his brother Enrique were responsible for designing and building "many residential and commercial buildings in the Washington, D.C., metropolitan area." The exiled architect received the Cintas Foundation Lifetime Achievement Award in 2006. His wife Mignón preceded him in death in 2007. The eight Cuban Americans in Congress in 2017 are: Senators Ted Cruz (R-Texas), Robert Menéndez (D-New Jersey) and Marco Rubio (R-Florida), Congressmen Carlos Curbelo (R-Florida), Mario Diaz-Balart (R-Florida), Alex Mooney (R-West Virginia), and Albio Sires (D-New Jersey), and Congresswoman Ileana Ros-Lehtinen (R-Florida).

7. Phone interview with Rosi Chica, March 8, 2017.

8. "Ike Breaks Off Ties with Castro Regime," *Pittsburgh Post-Gazette*, January 4, 1961.

9. "Cuban Baseballers Await U.S. Ruling," *Fort Lauderdale News*, January 12, 1961.

10. Ibid.

11. Dimas Castellanos, "Separating Baseball from Politics," diariodecuba.com, April 13, 2017. The Spanish acronym of INDER stands for *Instituto Nacional de Deportes y Recreación*. The decree proves that the United States, nor organized baseball, abandoned baseball in Cuba.

12. Ray Gillespie, "Diamond Facts and Facets," *The Sporting News*, March 1, 1961, 8.

13. Interview with Jorge Maduro, January 28, 2017.

14. "Move or No Move? That's IL Puzzler," *Fort Lauderdale News*, June 15, 1961.

15. "Proposed Shift to Miami Blasted," *The News Journal* (DE), June 6, 1961.

16. "Jerseys Hope for Support from Fans," *Asbury Park* (NJ) *Press*, June 16, 1961.

17. "AAA Club Eyed for Jacksonville," *Orlando Sentinel*, July 22, 1961.

18. Bill Ready, "Keeping Posted," *Post-Standard* (NY), September 19, 1961.

19. Dick Young, "Running the Bases," *Salt Lake* (UT) *Tribune*, December 3, 1961.

20. Franck Eck, "Castro Refugee Will Run Jacksonville Club," *Mason City* (IA) *Globe-Gazette*, January 13, 1962.

21. "Baseball Erases 'Yanqui No' Signs," *Orlando Sentinel*, February 23, 1961.

22. Ibid.

23. "Dancing Waters, Sun Board Add Sparkle to Suns' Park," *The Sporting News*, May 9, 1962, 33. The following year, Maduro installed electric fans in the Suns' dugout. The visitors were not afforded the same amenity.

24. Interview with Al Maduro, March 6, 2017.

25. Conversation with Mike de la Hoz, June 3, 2017.

26. "Ben Geraghty, Minor League Manager, Dies," *Bridgeport* (CT) *Telegram*, June 19, 1963.

27. Interview with Al Maduro, March 6, 2017.

28. loscubanitos1.blogspot.com/

29. Email correspondence with Barbra Cabrera, July 29, 2017.

30. "Maduro Seeks Latins For Birds," *St. Louis Post-Dispatch*, October 23, 1964.

31. Brian McKenna, "William Eckert," at bioproject.sabr.org.

32. "Baseball Ambassador Sees It Helping U.S.," *Asbury Park* (NJ) *Press*, June 5, 1966.

33. "Bobby Maduro—Baseball Diplomat," *The Sporting News*, February 18, 1967, 14.

34. Interview with Al Maduro, March 6, 2017.

35. "Maduro Signs; Yanks Canceled," *Fort Lauderdale News*, June 15, 1969.

36. Regis McAuley, "Seven Managers Used," *Tucson Daily Citizen*, July 11, 1969.

Chapter Eight

1. Bob Broeg, "Padres' Gomez Seeks Cuban Baseball Mission," *St Louis Post-Dispatch*, May 25, 1971.
2. *Ibid.*
3. "Cuban Exiles Hot Foes of Gómez' Junket Plan," *The Sporting News*, May 29, 1971, 35.
4. Bob Broeg, "Padres' Gomez Seeks Cuban Baseball Mission," *St Louis Post-Dispatch*, May 25, 1971.
5. Interview with Al Maduro, March 6, 2017. "The other time I saw my dad cry—I walked into my parents' bedroom in Miami Beach; he was in bed, crying. I said, 'Mom, what's the matter?' 'Al, we have to come up with $18,000 or we're going to get evicted.' How do you get out of bed and figure out, how am I going to get that kind of money? I was in grade school. It was early in the morning before school. I always believed everything he told us. 'We're going to make it,' he said … but it was a struggle for him."
6. Rory Costello, "Bobby Maduro," at bioproject.sabr.org. Marta Jackson-Maduro, an accomplished classical ballet instructor and operator of her own school of dance, passed away September 23, 2014, age 84.
7. Dave Anderson, "Baseball in Cuba," *Cincinnati Enquirer*, April 6, 1977.
8. *Ibid.*
9. *Ibid.*
10. Robert M. Levine, *Secret Missions to Cuba Fidel Castro Bernardo Benes and Cuban Miami* (New York: Palgrave Macmillan, 2001), 9.
11. *Ibid.*, 5.
12. *Ibid.*, 118.
13. "Sanction Granted for Inter-American," *Tennessean*, December 10, 1978.
14. *Ibid.*
15. Interview with Al Maduro, March 6, 2017.
16. Lonnie Wheeler, "Foreign Players have Big Roles in Baseball," *Cincinnati Enquirer*, April 9, 1980.
17. Interview with Al Maduro, March 6, 2017.
18. "Roberto Maduro," Obituaries, *The Sporting News*, January 12, 1987, 48.
19. David Hancock, "Maduro's Widow Tells of Her Life Since His Death," *Miami Herald*, March 10, 1988.
20. Interview with Al Maduro, March 6, 2017.
21. Phone interview with Rosi Chica, March 8, 2017.
22. Sam Zygner, *The Forgotten Marlins: A Tribute to the 1956–1960 Original Miami Marlins* (Latham, MD: Scarecrow Press, 2013), 325.
23. Harold Rosenthal, "Cheering Jersey Fans Hail O.B. Return," *The Sporting News*, July 27, 1960, 13.
24. Reynerio Tamayo is a Cuban artist specializing in baseball caricatures. He like other Cuban painters and better-known artists, including in the music industry, such as Gente de Zona, are permitted to come to the United States, earn money, and freely go back to Cuba, under the broadened "cultural exchange" parameters initiated by the Obama administration and maintained under President Trump. However, Cuban exile painters and musical artists, such as Willy Chirino, are not permitted by the Cuban government to display their works or perform their songs in Cuba in the decidedly "one-way" exchange.
25. Interview with Jorge Maduro, Jr., January 28, 2017.

Bibliography

Books

Benjamin, Alan F. *Jews of the Dutch Caribbean: Exploring Ethnic Identity on Curacao.* New York: Routledge, 2002.
Brioso, César. *Havana Hardball: Spring Training Jackie Robinson, and the Cuban League.* Gainesville: University Press of Florida, 2015.
Figueredo, Jorge S. *Beisbol Cubano A un Paso de las Grandes Ligas, 1878–1961.* Jefferson, NC: McFarland, 2005.
_____. *Cuban Baseball: A Statistical History, 1878–1961.* Jefferson, NC: McFarland, 2003.
_____. *Who's Who in Cuban Baseball, 1878–1961.* Jefferson, NC: McFarland, 2003.
Fitts, Robert K. *Wally Yonamine: The Man Who Changed Japanese Baseball.* Lincoln: University of Nebraska Press, 2008.
González Echevarría, Roberto. *The Pride of Havana: A History of Cuban Baseball*, New York: Oxford University Press, 1999.
Hernández, Lou. *The Rise of the Latin American Baseball Leagues, 1947–1961.* Jefferson, NC: McFarland, 2011.
Levine, Robert M. *Secret Missions to Cuba: Fidel Castro, Bernardo Benes, and Cuban Miami.* New York: Palgrave Macmillan, 2001.
Louisiana Sugar Planters' Association, et al. *The Louisiana Planter and Sugar Manufacturer, Volume 47.* Reprinted Palala Press, 2016.
Phillips, John. *The Story of the Havana Sugar Kings.* Kathleen, GA: Capital, 2003.
_____. *A Short History of the Florida International League.* Kathleen, GA: Capital, 2003.
Smith, Earl E.T. *The Fourth Floor: An Account of the Castro Communist Revolution.* New York: Random House, 1962.
Zygner, Sam. *The Forgotten Marlins: A Tribute to the 1956–1960 Original Miami Marlins.* Lanham, Maryland: Scarecrow, 2013.

Articles

"The 1979 Miami Amigos." Fun While It Lasted (website). Accessed November 24, 2017, http://www.funwhileitlasted.net/2011/12/08/62-miami-amigos/.Beahon, George; "League OKs '59 Baseball in Havana." *Rochester Democrat and Chronicle*, January 31, 1959.
Arthur Gardner on the Communist Threat to the United States Through the Caribbean. Testimony Before the Subcommittee to Investigate the Administration of the Internal Security Act and Other Internal Security Laws, August 27, 1960. Latin American Studies, accessed at http://www.latinamericanstudies.org/us-cuba/gardner-smith.htm.

Bibliography

Bevis, Charlie. "Frank Shaughnessy." SABR BioProject, https://sabr.org/bioproj/person/022eb7.

Campbell, Monica. "The Cuban History Lying Behind an Old Door in Mexico City." Public Radio International, November 28, 2016, accessed November 24, 2017, http://www.pri.org/stories/2016-11-28/cuban-history-lying-behind-old-door-mexico-city. http://www.diariodecuba.com/deportes/1492082012_30361.html

Castellanos, Dimas. "Separating Baseball from Politics." *Diario de Cuba*, April 13, 2017, accessed November 24, 2017, http://www.diariodecuba.com/deportes/1492082012_30361.html.

Corbett, Warren. "Harry Walker." SABR BioProject, http://sabr.org/bioproj/person/3bbe3106.

Costello, Rory, and José Ramírez. "Tony González." SABR BioProject, https://sabr.org/bioproj/person/859e2b7d.

Costello, Rory. "Bobby Maduro." SABR BioProject, https://sabr.org/bioproj/person/c34ce106.

———. "Fausto Miranda." SABR BioProject, https://sabr.org/bioproj/person/74d350f9.

Fisaro, Joe. "New Name, but Deep-Rooted Tradition in Miami." MLB.com, November 10, 2011, accessed November 24, 2017, http://www.m.mlb.com/news/article/25948494//.

Gerard, Joseph. "Lázaro Salazar." SABR BioProject, https://sabr.org/bioproj/person/f2fa0932.

Gómez Masjuán, Miguel Ernesto. "De nuestro béisbol: Gigantes japoneses en La Habana." C. Deportes.com, July 13, 2013, accessed November 24, 2017, http://www.cronodeportesonline.com/de-nuestro-beisbol-gigantes-japoneses-en-la-habana/.

Knight, Franklin W. "Migration and Culture: A Case Study of Cuba, 1750–1900." Paper presented at the Historical Society's 2008 Conference on Migration, Diaspora, Ethnicity, & Nationalism in History, June 5–7, 2008. Johns Hopkins University. Accessed at http://www.bu.edu/historic/conference08/Knight.pdf.

Markusen, Bruce. "The Short Wild Life of the Inter-American League." Harballtimes.com, July 8, 2014, accessed November 24, 2017, https://www.fangraphs.com/tht/the-short-wild-life-of-the-inter-american-league/.

Miroff, Nick. "New Fidel Castro Memoir Recalls Rebel's Life in Mexico." Public Radio International, February 24, 2016, accessed November 24, 2017, http://pri.org/stories/2012-02-24/new-fidel-castro-memoir-recalls-rebel-s-life-mexi.

Reichard, Kevin. "Remembering the Inter-American League." Ballpark Digest.com, July 8, 2014, accessed November 24, 2017, http://www.ballparkdigest.com/201407087467/minor-league-baseball/news/remembering-the-inter-american-league.

Rivera-Lyles, Jeannette. "Fallece Un Destacado Empresario Cubano." *El Nuevo Herald (Miami)*, December 30, 1999.

"Roberto (Bobby) Maduro." Juan F. Pérez (personal site), last edited April 21, 2015, http://www.juanperez.com/baseball/maduro.html.

Robinson, Eric. "The Miami Amigos." In *The National Pastime*, edited by Cecilia M. Tan. Society for American Baseball Research, Phoenix Arizona, 2016.

Sargent, Jim. "Joe Brovia." SABR BioProject, https://sabr.org/bioproj/person/62c4fa4d.

Snyder, Matt. "Veterans Committee Doesn't Elect Anyone to the Hall of Fame." CBS Sports.com, December 8, 2017, accessed November 24, 2017, https://www.cbssports.com/mlb/news/veterans-committee-doesnt-elect-anyone-to-hall-of-fame/.

Spencer, Clark. "Florida Marlins' Ballpark Boundary Streets Given Names." *Miami Herald*, November 2, 2011.

"Sugar Kings." ESPN.com, March 20, 2016, http://www.espn.com/video/clip?id=15023991.

Vines, Alex. "Why Fidel Castro's Greatest Legacy in Africa is in Angola." Newsweek.com, November 30, 2016, https://www.newsweek.com/fidel-castro-greatest-legacy-africa-angola-526321. November 30, 2016.

Wancho, Joseph. "Billy Herman." SABR BioProject, https://sabr.org/bioproj/person/d6297ffd.

Weaver, Jay. "Bobby Maduro Baseball Stadium Rezoned as Site for Public Housing." *South

Florida Sun Sentinel, June 28, 1998, http://www.articles.sun-sentinel.com / 1998–06–28/news/9806270090_1_baseball-stadium-13-acre-housing.
Weber, Bruce. "Roberto Suarez, Founder of El Nuevo Herald, Dies at 82." *New York Times*, July 12, 2010.
Wild, Chris. "1959 Fidel Castro and His American Admirers." TorontoForumonCuba.com, December 17, 2014, accessed November 24, 2017, http://www.torontoforumoncuba.com/history/1959-fidel-castro-and-his-american-admirers.

Newspapers

Akron (OH) *Daily Press*
Asbury Park (NJ) *Press*
Baltimore Sun
Beacon Journal Press and Sun-Bulletin (NY)
Bridgeport (CT) *Post*
Bridgeport (CT) *Telegram*
Brownsville (TX) *Herald*
Chicago Tribune
Cincinnati Enquirer Jackson (MS)
Clarion-Ledger (MS)
Daily Mail (MD)
Daily Press (VA)
Decatur Herald (IL)
El Miami Herald
El Nuevo Herald (Miami)
Fort Lauderdale News
Hartford Courant
Indiana Gazette
Ithaca (NY) *Journal*
Journal Morning News (DE)
Kansas City (MO) *Times*
Lincoln (NE) *Evening*
Lincoln (NE) *Star*
Mason City (IA) *Globe-Gazette*
Miami Herald
Minneapolis Star
Minneapolis Star Tribune
Monroe (LA) *Morning World*
Nashville Tennessean
New York Times
News Journal
News Tribune (NJ)
Oneonta (NY) *Star*
Orlando Sentinel
Ottawa (ONT) *Journal*
Palm Beach Post
Pensacola (FL) *News*
Philadelphia Daily News
Pittsburgh Courier
Pittsburgh Post-Gazette
Pittsburgh Press
Portland Sunday Telegram News
Rochester Democrat and Chronicle
Salt Lake (UT) *Tribune*
Simpson's Leader Times (PA)
St. Cloud (MN) *Times*
St. Louis Post-Dispatch
Star-Gazette (NY)
Syracuse (NY) *Post-Standard*
Tallahassee (FL) *Democrat*
Times (NY) *Record*
Tucson Daily Citizen
Wilmington (DE) *Morning News*
Wilmington (OH) *News-Journal.*

Interviews

Broadcaster: Felo Ramírez
Players: Billy DeMars; Fred Kipp; Jim Melton; Bob Miller; Jose "Pantalones" Santiago
Maduro family: Rosi Chica; Al Maduro; Jorge Maduro; Jorge Maduro, Jr.; Mercedes de Marchena; Betty McDaniel

Websites

Ancestry.com
Baseball-Reference.com
Los Cubanitos (blog), http://www.loscubanitos1.blogspot.com/
Newspaper.com
PaperofRecord.org
Retrosheet.org
Sabr.org
Walteromalley.com

Index

Numbers in **_bold italics_** indicate pages with illustrations

Aaron, Hank 184
Alacranes (club) 16
Alemán, José, Jr. 54, 66
Ali, Muhammed 175
Almendares Alacranes (Scorpions) 11, 13, 17–18, 21, 23–24, 28, 80, 152, 158, 165
Alou, Felipe 184
Alston, Walt 105
Altamirano, Porfirio 179
Altobelli, Joe 138
Alvarez, Rogelio "Borrego" 94–95, 97, 99–100, 105, 108–110, 112–113, 115–116, 121, 126, **_128_**, 137-138, 146
Alvarez, Ultus 67, 72, 73–74, 77, 80, 86
Amando Llano, Florence 56
Amaro, Santos 16
American Association 4, 54, 82, 86, 120–121, 148, 165
American Baseball Cap Company 81
American League 35, 89, 118
American Society of Newspaper Editors 107
Amor, Vicente 63, 67–68, 70, 76–77, 86, 95, 106, 109, 115
Amorós, Edmundo "Sandy" 41, 152
Anderson, Dave 176
Anderson, George "Sparky" 140
Antillano, Otto 17
Appling, Luke 52, 64
Arcos, Julio "Monchy" de 165
Arias, Rodolfo "Rudy" 93, 98–100, 140
Arkansas Travelers 166
Armas, Emilio de 20, **_24_**, 30, 32–33
Arosemena Stadium 178
Arroyo, Luis "Tite" 84, 106, 109, 111, 113, 115–118, 121, 124, **_128_**, 138–139, 146–147, 161
Arthurs, Stanley 18
Asheville Academy for Girls 157
Asheville Country Club 24
Asheville School 9
Asheville Tourists 71
Asociación Cubana de Béisbol Internacional 53
Atlanta Braves 179
Atlanta Crackers 81–82, 165, 168, 170
Atlético de Cuba (club) 20
Azcúe, José "Joe" 137, 144
Azorbe, Luis **_24_**

Babe, Loren 40
Bacallao, Miguel "Coco" 51
Baer, George 46
Baker, Dr. Roy 168
Baltimore Orioles (American League) 35, 72, 76–77, 120, 134–135, 149, 180
Baltimore Orioles (International League) 47
Barnes, Frank 137
Baró, Asdrúbal 57, 60, 62
Baseball Amusements, Inc. 167
Baseball Guide 53
Batista, Fulgencio 76, 89–90, 101–102, 128, 142
Bavasi, Emil "Buzzy" 104
Beahon, George 136, 142, 151
Bécquer, Conrado 142
Bécquer, Julio 40–41, 44
Bell, Les 52
Benes, Bernardo 176–177
Benjamin, Alan F. 7
Bernard, Pablo 67, 77, 86

201

Berry, Bernard J. 90
Betzel, Bruno 75
Bevan, Hal 70, 74
Biederman, Les 33
Big State League 50
Biltmore Yacht & Country Club 11, 153, 156
Birrer, Babe 95, 106, 138
Bisher, Furman 81–82
Black, Joe 25–28
Blackburn, Ken 29
Blake, Eddie 63
Blanco Herrera, Julio 10, 13
Blaylock, Bob 70, 83
Bohemia magazine 26, 99, 139
Borges, Max 153–156
Borges, Mignon 155
Borland, Tom 123, 125–126
Bosch, José 37
Boston Braves 13, 36
Boston Red Sox 33, 122, 124, 168, 171
Boudreau, Lou 84
Bowsfield, Ted 121, 123–125
Bracho, José "Carrao" 59–63, 69
Bragan, Bobby 38
Bragaña, Ramón 16
Breeden, Hal 179
Breithaupt, Louis 43
Brickell, Fritz 117
Brioso, César 11, 15
Broeg, Bob 130
Brooklyn Dodgers 13–15, 23, 25–28, 33, 47, 52, 54, 64, 66, 72, 74–75, 85–86, 161
Brovia, Joe 59
Browning, Cal 144
Bryant, Clay 99, 101, 120, 149
Bryant, Farris 165
Buffalo Bisons 43, 46, 48, 52, 57–58, 60, 64, 70, 75, 77, 79, 82, 84, 86, 92–96, 101, 108, 113, 115, 117, 120, 135, 138, 148, 161
Bunning, Jim 60, 89
Burns, Jimmy 21, 54
Buvasi, Emil "Buzzy" 166, 174

Cabrera, Barbra 169
Cabrera, Doris 169
Cabrera, Emilio 56, 169
Caffie, Joe 86, 108–109
Caguas Criollos 21, 38, 89
Calderone, Sam 93
Calloway, Cab 74–75
Cambria, Joe *31*, 32
Campanis, Al 33, 152
Canavati, Anuar 168
Cannizzaro, Chris 144

Cardenal, José 171, 174
Cárdenas, Leo 106, 108, 112–115, 118, 121, *128*, 138, 140–141, 147
Cardwell, Don 69, 71, 73–74
Carew, Rod 155, 184
Caribbean Baseball Federation (aka Caribbean Confederation) 17, 21, 33, 171
Caribbean Series I (1949) 17–18
Caribbean Series II (1950) 21
Caribbean Series III (1951) 24
Caribbean Series IV (1952) 26
Caribbean Series V (1953) 28
Caribbean Series VI (1954) 38
Caribbean Series IX (1957) 78
Caribbean Series X (1958) 89
Carnevale, Danny 64
Carrasquel, Alejandro "Alex" 11
Carrasquel, Alfonso "Chico" 138
Carrillo, Pedro 108, 115–116, 118, 124, *128*
Carta Vieja Yankees 21
Carter, Jimmy 175–177
Castaño, Tony 56, 132, 139, 144, 148, 158
Castellanos, Dimas 158
Castrillo, William 172
Castro, Fidel 1–2, 84, 92, 101–104, 106–108, 110–111, *111*, 118, 122–123, 127–131, 134, 136–138, 141, 150–151, 158–159, 161–162, 174, 176–177, 179
Cavarretta, Phil 75, 86, 93, 101
Cementerio de Cristóbal Colón 11, 177
Central Cunagua 8
Central Hershey 11
Cervecería Caracas "Brewers" 17–18
Chacón, Elio 94, 98, 100, 108, 115, 118, 124, 126, *128*, 137
Chadroff, Sy 172
Chandler, A.B. "Happy" 12, 15, 25
Charleston Marlins 160
Chevalier, Maurice 67
Chica, Christina 156
Chica, Diana 156
Chica, Manny III 156
Chica, Manuel 156
Chica (Maduro), Rosario "Rosi" 32, 93, 153, 156, 181
Chicago Cubs 23, 74, 179
Chicago White Sox 21, 27, 38, 41, 55, 71, 99, 125, 136
Chittum, Nelson 122
Cicotte, Al 148
Cienfuegos, Camilo 110, 130
Cienfuegos Elefantes (Elephants) 4, 20–26, 28–31, 33–35, 37, 72, 132, 152, 158, 176

Index

Cienfuegos Petroleros (Oilers) 11, 20
Cincinnati Reds 28, 42, 47–48, 64, 70–71, 74–76, 86, 98, 101, 104–106, 108–109, 111, 116, 120, 130, 134–135, 137, 140, 147–148, 160–161, 175, 179
Clark, Gilberto 115
Clemente, Roberto 47, 175, 184
Cleveland Indians 40, 65, 148, 150, 161, 165–166, 173
Clinton, Lou 121, 126
Club Náutico de Marianao 29
CMBZ-Radio Sala 11
Colegio De la Salle 48
Coleman, Ray 40, 45
Coles, Chuck 106
Collum, Jackie 106
Colombian Winter League 98
Columbia Reds 72
Columbus Jets 60–61, 64, 73, 75, 78–79, 81, 85–86, 98, 100–101, 108, 110, 114–117, 120, 135, 139, 147–148
Columbus Red Birds 54
Comelles, Jorge 11
Commodity Stabilization Service 142
Compañía Operadora de Stadiums 11
Connolly, Theresa "Tess" 46
Consuegra, Sandalio "Sandy" 72
Continental League 107, 131, 133, 143
Cordeiro, Reinaldo *39*, 56, 72, 108, *128*
Córdova Díaz, Jorge Luis 17
Cornell University 9
Costello, Rory 6–7
Cox, Glenn 49
Cox, Ron 168
Craddock, Walt 106, 109, 113, 116–118, 124, *128*
Crimian, Jack 43, 63
Crosley, Powel, Jr. 75
Cruz, John 75
Cruz, Tomás "Tommy" de la 16
Cuba (club) 16
Cuban-American Television Company 129
Cuban Association of Sports Writers 134
Cuban Sugar Kings [1954–55] 22, 37–64
Cuban Sugar Kings [1956–57] 65–87
Cuban Sugar Kings [1958–59] 88–128
Cuban Sugar Kings [1960–61] 4, 5, 129–145, 161–162, 181–183
Cuban Sugar Kings Foundation 181
Cuban Sugar Stabilization Institute 107
Cuban Sugar Union 142
Cuban Tourism Commission 110, 135
Cuban Winter League 4, 10–11, 15, 17, 22, 28–30, 33–35, 37, 40, 43, 46, 71, 78, 89, 101, 106, 131–132, 148, 152, 158

Cueche, Emilio 38–39, 40, 42–46, 48, *49*, 51–52, 57, 59–62, 73, 77, 100, 108, 109, 115, 118, 123, *128*, 146
Cuéllar, Miguel Angel "Mike" 61, 77, 79–80, *80*, 84–86, 94, 96, 99–100, 108, 113, 115–118, 121, 123–124, *128*, 136, 138, 166, 169–170, 179
Cueto, Mario del *24*
Cullop, Nick 64, 75

Dallas Eagles 50
Dandridge, Ray 16
Daniel, Dan 133, 141–142
Daniels, Jack 94, 96
Davalillo, Pompeyo "Yo-Yo" 61, 84, 93–95, 112, 117, 123, 126, *128*, 137–138, 145
Davalillo, Vic 93
Deal, Ellis "Cot" 61, 67–68, 86, 101, 112, 120
Delís, Juan 40, 70
Delorimier Stadium 47, 80, 85, 99
DeMars, Billy 40–41
DeMars, Catherine 41
Denver Bears 86
Detroit Tigers 52, 60, 64, 86, 89, 139
Devine, Vaughan "Bing" 37, 51
Diemer, Bill 71
DiMaggio, Joe 38, 155
Dios Castrello, Juana de (aka Diosa Costello) 97
Doherty, Ed 122
Dolan, Bobby 71
Dominican Winter League 148, 171
Donohue, Jim 136
Dotterer, Dutch 67
Drysdale, Don 60
Durán, Alfredo 176

Easter, Luke 74, 84, 86, 95, 136
Echarte, Jorge 153, 155
Echarte, Maricusa 155
Eck, Frank 37, 104
Eckert, William 5, 170–171
Eisenhower, Dwight D. 141–142, 157, 158
Erickson, Hal 57
Ermer, Cal 116–117, 120, 148
Escalera, Saturnino "Nino" 61–62, 67, 69, 71, 74, 77, 79, 86, 94–95, 98–99
escuela Margot Párraga 153
Espino, Héctor 168–169
Essegian, Chuck 98
Evans, Luther 110

Farrell, Kerby 100–101, 120, 148
Faszholz, Jack 50, 52

Federation of Cuban Professional Players in Exile 5, 180
Feldenkreis, George 154
Feller, Bob 84
Fernándes, Walter 37
Fernándes Morell, Andrés *24*
Fernández, Humberto "Chico" 152, 158
Fernández, Rafael 33
Fields, Wilmer 18
Figueredo, Jorge S. 20
Finch, Frank 105
Finch, Robert L. 17
Fine, Tommy 21
Finlay, Carlos J. 2
Finol, Dalmiro 18
Fisher, Maury 44
Florida International League 4, 13, 15, 21, 25, 31, 33–34
Florida International University 40, 155
Florida Marlins 155
Florida State League 104
Ford, Whitey 161
Formental, Pedro 46–48, 50, 52, 58–59, 62
Fornieles, José Miguel "Mike" 28, 62–63
Fort Lauderdale Lions 32, 34
Fort Lauderdale Stadium 173
Fort Worth Cats 121
Frick, Ford 25, 33, 133–134, 148, 181
Friend, Owen 70, 74
Fuentes, Rigoberto "Tito" 179
Funk, Frank 140

Galiana, Pedro 55
Gangemi, Thomas 160
García, Edward Miguel "Mike" 84
García, Luis "Camaleón" 40–41, *49*, 57, 62
García, Ofelia 61
García, Rai *132*
García, Silvio 24, 40
García Ledo, Gladys 61
Gardella, Danny 16
Gardner, Arthur 39
Gaston, Clarence "Cito" 179
Gentile, Jim 77
Geraghty, Ben 161, 163, *164*, 167
Geraghty, Mary 167
Gettel, Al 28
Gibbon, Joe 116
Gillick, Pat 171
Goliat, Mike 40, 109
Gómez, Pedro "Preston" 104, 106, 109, 114–118, 123–126, *128*, 132, 172, 174
Gómez, Rubén 164–166
Gómez, Vernon "Lefty" 23, 81
Gonder, Jesse 110, 124, *128*

González, Andrés Antonio "Tony" 95, 97, 106, 110, 113, 115–118, 122–126, *128*, 137
González, Efren 122
González, Fredi 169
González, Miguel Angel "Mike" 12, 15, 22, *24*, 25, 184
González Echevarría, Roberto 18, 20, 134
Goryl, John 125
Graham, Stamford 17
Gran Stadium (del Cerro de la Habana) 11, 13–17, 22, 24–25, 29–30, 32, 36, 38–39, 42, 44, 47–49, 53, 56–58, 60–61, 64, 68, 70, 73, 77–78, 81–83, 85, 88, 99, 101, 105, 107–109, 111–113, 119, 125, 127, 129, 131, 135–136, 138–140, 144, 162, 180, 183
Granger, Wayne 179
Grba, Eli 142
Green, Dallas 156
Green, Gene 84
Griffith, Clark 21, 31
Grob, Connie 77
Guerra, Fermín 18, 21, 41, 43
Guerra Matos, Felipe 102, *132*, 136, 150
Guevara, Ernesto "Che" 130
Guzzetta, Frank 72, 112

Haas, Bert 26
Habana Leones (Lions) 12, 20–24, 26, 28, 152
Habana Yacht Club 11
Hahn, Fred 40
Handy, George 40
Haney, Fred 28–29
Harlem Magicians 135
Harrell, Billy 112, 137
Harris, Charles "Bubba" 46, 51, 58, 62
Hartung, Clint 40–42, 44, 47, 52, 59
Hatten, Joe 72–74
Hausemann, George 16
Havana Country Club 19
Havana Cubans 4, 13, 15, 25, 31, 35, 37, 53–54, 65, 98
Havana Hilton Hotel 88
Havana Sugar Kings *see* Cuban Sugar Kings
Heard, Jehosie 73
Helms, Tommy 171
Herbert, Ray 85
Herman, Billy 22–23, 25–26, 28, 33, 171
Hernández, Angela 61
Hernández, Evelio 169
Hernández, Salvador "Chico" 22
Herrera, Francisco "Pancho" 117
Hetki, Johnny 63

Index

Hiram Bithorn Stadium 175
Hitchcock, Billy 52
Holmes, Tommy 86
Horton, Frank 90, 133
Hotel Capri 88
Hotel Chateau 44
Hotel Nacional 41, 71, 83
Hotel Riviera 88
Houston Astros 170
Houston Buffalos 131
Houston Colt .45s 160
Houston Sports Association 160
Howard, Elston 40, 42
Howard, Frank 171, 182
Howsam, Bob 169–170
Hoz, Miguel Angel "Mike" de la 150, 155
Hurd, Tom 137
Hurricane Dora 168
Hurricane San Felipe 84

Ibáñez, Amado 67
Inclán, Rafael 17, *24*, 25
Indianapolis Indians 86
Inter-American League 177–179
International League 35, 37, 46, 52–53, 65, 66, 69, 76, 78–79, 82–83, 85, 88, 90, 96–98, 101–102, 107, 114, 131, 135, 138, 140, 144, 146–148, 151, 159–160, 165, 167–168, 181
Iott, Clarence "Hooks" 44
Irvin, Monte 175
Izquierdo, Enrique "Hank" 77, 95, 99, 118, *128*, 146

Jackson, Al 117
Jackson, Lou 116, 137
Jacksonville Baseball Park (Suns Stadium) 163, 165
Jacksonville Jets 160
Jacksonville Suns 162–170
James, Charlie 136
James, Johnny 117–118
Jersey City Jerseys 144–148, 151–152, 159
Jersey City Parks Commission 144
Jet magazine 32
Jethroe, Sam 40
Jets Stadium 73, 116
John, Tommy 166
Johnson, Davey 178
Johnson, Deron 117–118
Johnson, Ken 46
Johnson, Joe 166
Jones, Fred 81
Junior World Series (1944) 47
Junior World Series (1953) 129
Junior World Series (1954) 51
Junior World Series (1955) 64
Junior World Series (1956) 75
Junior World Series (1957) 86
Junior World Series (1958) 100
Junior World Series (1959) 4, 120–128, 181
Junior World Series (1960) 148
Junior World Series (1962) 165

Kahn, Lou 64, 120
Kansas City Athletics 54, 64, 75, 84, 86, 101, 136
Kansas City Blues 129
Kansas City Royals 181
Keegan, Bob 112, 137, 144
Kennedy, John F. 157
Kiner, Ralph 29, 30, 81
King, Clyde 101, 148
King, Don 175
Kipp, Fred 70–71, 105
Klein, Lou 12, 16
Koufax, Sandy 85
Kretlow, Lou 85
Kritzer, Cy 19
Kryhoski, Dick 61
Kuhn, Bowie 5, 173, 175–176
Kuzava, Bob 79

Laboy, José "Coco" 169
Ladera, Julián 57, 60
Lakeland Pilots 15, 21
Lane, Frank 21, 27–28, 38, 73, 150–151
Lane, Jerry 73–74, 79
Lanier, Max 12–13, 16
Lankler, Alex 177
Lansdowne Park 44
Las Esclavas del Sagrado de Corazón 153, 156
Lasorda, Tommy 5, 47, 60, 94, 99, 106, 109, 114, 145, 155
Lehman, Ken 48, 52, 58, 62, 138
LeMay, Dick 168
Lemon, Bob 84
Leones (club) 16
Levine, Robert M. 2, 176–177
Lieb, Fred 150
LiPetri, Angelo 72
Lisk, Delphine 146
Little Rock Travelers 166
Llanusa Gogel, José 158
Lopat, Eddie 75, 86, 101
López, Marcelino 171
Los Angeles Coliseum 125
Los Angeles Dodgers 91, 101, 104–105, 120, 125, 132, 149, 160, 166, 180
Los Cubanitos 67, 70, 81, 152, 169
Louis, Joe 14

Louisiana Planter and Sugar Manufacturer Company 8
Louisville Colonels 51, 127, 148, 161, 165
Lovenguth, Lynn 73, 85
Luque, Adolfo 12, 16, 25, 184

MacArthur Stadium 51
MacCarl, Neil 181
MacDonald, Bill 159
Machado, Roberto 17
Macko, Joe 126
Macon, Max 52
MacPhail, Larry 13
MacPhail, Lee 134–135
Maduro (Abinun de Lima), Abigail 6
Maduro, Adela 9–10, 29, 153, 156–157
Maduro (Naar), Adela 6
Maduro, Alberto "Al" 7, 70, 153, 157, 163, 167, 173, 175, 178, 180, *182*
Maduro, Ava 154
Maduro, Carmen Cecilia 154
Maduro, Elias Levy 9
Maduro, Felipe 9, 27, 33, 42, 48–49, 70, 177
Maduro, Isabel 9, 88, 153, 156–157
Maduro (Olmo Fernández Garrido), Isolina 9, *10*, 19, 75, 151, 153, 156–157, 175
Maduro, Jennifer 152
Maduro, Jessica 152
Maduro, Joanne 152
Maduro, Jon 152, 155
Maduro, Jorge 10, 19, 22, 29, 48, 151, 153, 155, 159, 163, 173, *182*
Maduro, Jorge, Jr. 152–153, 155, 181
Maduro (Jackson), Marta 175, 180
Maduro, Mason 181
Maduro, Max 154
Maduro, Mozes Salomon Levy 6, 7
Maduro, Roberto: agent 38, 76; amateur golfer 19; with Batista 90; birth and childhood 7–8; Caribbean Series cofounding broker 17; with Castro 101, 103–104, 107, 111, *111*; Cienfuegos coowner 20–24, *24*, 25–35; Cuban Sugar Kings owner 35–39, *39*, 40–56, *56*, 57–68, *68*, 69–132, *132*, 133–145; Cuban Winter League negotiator with OB 15, 27–28; death 180; Director of Inter-American Relations, MLB 5, 170–178, *178*; Havana Cubans owner 25, 31, *31*, 32–34; Inter-American League founder 177–179; Jacksonville Suns general manager 168–170; Jacksonville Suns owner 160–164, *164*, 165–167; Los Cubanitos founder 67; Marlins Park street dedication 181–182, *182*; marriages 9, *10*, 175; Miami Stadium rededication 180–181; scout 170; stadium builder 10
Maduro, Roberto, Jr. 9, 27, 153, 157
Maduro, Salomón Mozes Levy 6–8, 151, 153, 163
Maduro, S.E.L. (Salomon Elias Levy) 6
Maduro, Suzanne 153, 163
Maestri, Amado 18
Maglie, Sal 12
Mantle, Mickey 161
Maple Leaf Stadium 43, 62, 109, 140
Marchena (Maduro), Adriana de 7, 9, 153
Marchena, Adriana Teresita de 7
Marchena, Frank de 7
Marchena, Mercedes de 7
Marianao Frailes Grises (Gray Monks) 20
Marianao Tigres (Tigers) 20–21, 24–28, 78, 89, 152
Marichal, Juan 155
Marina, Alba 67
Maris, Roger 125, 161
Marlins Park 181
Marrero, Conrado "Connie" 18, 57, 59–60, 62, 71, 74
Marsans, Armando 32
Martí, Humberto 18
Martin, Billy 180
Martin, Fred 12, 16
Martin, Johnny "Pepper" 22, 32, 105, 120
Martínez, Nancy 61
Mateosky, Ben 137
Matos, Huber 130
Mauch, Gene 122, 124–126
May, Dave 179
Mayagüez Indios 17–18
Mays, Willie 184
Mazeroski, Bill 184
McAllister Hotel 17
McDaniel (Maduro), Beatríz "Betty" 22, 153, 156
McDaniel, Betty 153
McDaniel, Ellie 153
McDaniel, Lisa 153
McDaniel, Robert 153
McDowell, Sam 166
McDuffie, Terris 16
McGaha, Mel 148, 166
McGlothin, Pat 26, 28
McGowen, Lloyd 127
Melton, Jim 41–42, 44–45, 48–52, 55
Memphis Chicks 105
Mena, Rigoberto 168
Mendoza, Mario 17
Menendez, Danny 133
Mercer (consulting firm) 2

Metropolitan Stadium 121
Mexican League 12, 77, 168, 172
Mexico City Red Devils 77, 81, 104
Miami Amigos 178–179
Miami Beach Flamingos 40
Miami Marlins (International League) 66, 69, 71, 73–76, 79, 82, 85–86, 88, 94, 100, 105, 114, 120, 145, 149, 179
Miami Marlins (National League) 181
Miami Orioles 178
Miami Stadium 30–31, 54, 66, 69, 79, 97, 115, 159, 179–181, 183
Miami Stadium Apartments 181
Miami Sun Sox 22, 70
Michener, James 97
Miller, Bob 137, 139
Miller, Paul 17, *24*, 57, **68**, 101, 103–104, 113, 132–133, 144–145, 161
Milwaukee Braves 36, 98, 140, 170
Minarcin, Rudy 69, 72, 74
Minneapolis Millers 4, 100, 121–127
Minnesota Twins 166
Miñoso, Orestes "Minnie" 27, 38, 55, 136, 158, 184
Minot Mallards 165
Miramar Yacht Club 67
Miranda, Fausto 10, *132*, 134, 147
Miranda, Willy 76, 147
Miro Cardona, José 142
Mitterwald, George 179
Mobile Bears 71
Moford, Herb 145
Molina, René 22
Monroe, Marilyn 38
Monroe, Zack 117
Monsignor Pace High School 181
Montemayor, Felipe 28
Monterey Sultans 168
Montmartre Night Club 59
Montreal Royals 13–15, 45, 47–49, 51–52, 58, 60–64, 69, 71, 74–77, 79, 82, 85–86, 91, 94–95, 99–101, 106, 109, 114, 120, 127, 129, 138–139, 148–149, 160
Moore, Jackie 171
Moorehead, Bob 115, **128**
Morehead, Seth 69
Morejón, Danny 74, 77, 79, 86, 93–96, 116, *119*, 121, 123–124, 126, **128**, 137
Morgan, Joe 168–169
Moreno, Julio 28, 41–42, 51, 57
Morton, Lew 40
Moulton, Mabel 29
Muffett, Billy 123, 126
Mulbury, Walter 17
Mulleavy, Greg 62, 64, 75, 87, 105
Muller, Monsignor Alfredo 39, *39*

Munsen, Thurman 153
Munzel, Edgar 27

Naranjo, Johnny 171
Nashville Volunteers 116
National Association of Professional Baseball Leagues 15–17, 20, 99, 172, 177
National Catholic Congress 131
National Federation League 13
National Institute of Sports, Physical Education and Recreation (INDER) 158
National League 85, 88, 105, 158, 160
National Sports Commission 15, 30
National Sports Palace 58
Navarro, Luis **128**, 144
Neal, Charlie 58
Negro League 48
Nelson, Rocky 49, 52, 62
New York Biltmore Hotel 154
New York Cosmos 175
New York Giants 20, 23, 26, 40, 70, 88, 164
New York Mets 139
New York Yankees 13–14, 42, 75, 86, 101, 120, 147–148, 151, 160–161, 166, 170, 173, 180
Newkirk, Dave 95
Newsome, Skeeter 52, 64
Nicholas, Don 67
Nin, Mario *24*
Noble, Rafael "Ray" 23, 26, 32, 40, 46, 50, 62, 85, 96
Nodarse, Dr. Lorenzo 27
Novak, Larry 109, 126, **128**, 147
Novas, Joe 75
Nunn, Howie 145–146

Oakland Oaks 23, 59
O'Doul, Francis "Lefty" 38
Offermann Stadium 95
Oh, Sadaharu 184
Olmo, Luis 12, 16
Olmo Fernández Garrido, Francisca "Fanny" 153, 155
O'Malley, Walter 104–105, 152, 161
Orange Bowl 74, 88
Orhstron, George 177
Oriental Park & Race Track 58
Oriente (club) 75
Ortiz, Roberto 11, 32, 46, 50
Osborn, Don 72, 75, 86
Osceak, Frank 86
Otero, Regino "Reggie" 38–39, *39*, 40–41, 44–45, 47–48, **49**, 50–52, 55–57, 59, 61–64, 67, 69, 75, 145
Ottawa Athletics 44, 50, 52, 54, 88

Index

Pacheco, Tony 98–101, 104
Pacific Coast League 23, 59, 120, 132, 166
Paige, Satchel 69, 71–74, 88
Palatka Redlegs 104
Panama Banqueros (Bankers) 178
Panamanian Professional League 16
Parga, Luis 20, *24*, 30, 33
Parker Field 50, 117
Parris, Clyde 74, 94
Pascual, Camilo 33–34, 158
Pascual, Carlos 32, 41
Pasquel, Jorge 12, 15–16
Paul, Gabe 28, 48, 104, 134–135, 145, 147–148, 152, 161, 168, 173
Paula, Carlos 116, *128*
Pehanick, Al 110
Pelé 175
Peña, Orlando 76–77, *80*, 82, 84–86, 94, 96, 99–100, 137–138, 146
Pendleton, Jim 137–138, 140–141, 146, 160
Pequeño, Alfredo *24*
Pequeña Copa del Mundo de Clubes (Little World Cup) 81
Pérez, Evelio 169
Pérez, Mako 67
Pérez, Tony 32
Perry Ellis International 153–154
Philadelphia Athletics 30, 41, 52, 86, 88
Philadelphia Phillies 52, 64, 69, 75, 101, 120, 148, 169, 179
Phillips, Damon 26
Phillips, John 34, 103, 108
Phillips, R. Hart 150
Piedmont League 59
Pisoni, Jim 117
Piton, Phil 172
Pittsburgh Pirates 23, 27–31, 33, 73, 101, 120, 148, 170, 175
Pope John XXIII 131
Porto, Yasel 183
Powell, Willie 48, 50, 58, 65, 75
Pozo, Justo Luis del 47
Puebla Parrots 12
Puerto Rican Winter League 16–17, 173
Pupo y Proenza, Alfredo H. 43

Quintana, Witremundo "Witty" 77, 79, 94, 95

Rabe, Charlie 99
Raffensberger, Ken 47–48, 50–51, 57, 59
Ramazotti, Bob 40
Ramírez, Antonio 172
Ramírez, Francisco "Panchillo" 77
Ramírez, Rafael "Felo" 22, 181, *182*

Ramos, Pedro 158
Rand, Dick 70
Raye, Martha 75
Red Bird Stadium 54
Red Wing Stadium 46, 59, 95, 114–115
Reese, Harold "Pee Wee" 105
Reguera, Lourdes 9
Resinger, Grover 170
Reyes, Napoleón "Nap" 32, 56, 67, *68*, 70, 73, 75, 78–79, 84–86, 89, 95–96, 98, 101, 145–146, 148
Rice, Bob 29
Richardson, Tommy 159–160
Richmond Rebels 35
Richmond Virginians 45, 49–50, 52, 59, 60, 64, 75, 85–86, 100–101, 114, 117–118, 120, 124, 148
Ricketts, Dick 109
Rickey, Branch 14, 27–30, 81, 107
Rivas, Rafael 15
Robbins, Austin "Red" 121
Roberts, Curt 73
Robinson, Frank 173
Robinson, Jackie 13–14, 127
Rochester Red Wings 37–38, 42–44, 46, 51–52, 59, 61, 63–65, 67, 70, 72, 75, 77, 83–86, 90, 94–95, 99–101, 108–109, 111–113, 120, 133, 136–137, 140, 144, 148, 152, 168
Rodríguez, Héctor 16, 40, 85, 106
Rodríguez, Oscar 15, 25
Rogovin, Saul 42, 44
Rojas, Octavio "Cookie" 106, 108, 126, *128*, 137, 146
Ronning, Al 87
Roosevelt Hotel 154
Roosevelt Stadium 144, 146, 160
Ruth, Babe 106
Rutherford, Johnny 26–28
Ryan, Joe 89

Sadeki, Ray 137
Sadowski, Ed 121
St. Louis Browns 53
St. Louis Cardinals 12, 52, 54–55, 64, 75, 86, 101, 109–110, 120, 148, 168–169
St. Margaret's Catholic School 156
St. Patrick Catholic School 9
St. Paul Saints 26
Salazar, Lázaro 81
Salazar, Maria Elvira 2
Salmón, Ruthford "Chico" 179
Salomon, Sid 65
Salon de la Fama del Béisbol Latino 5
Samson, David *182*
San Antonio Missions 97
San Diego Padres 172, 174

Index

San Francisco Giants 180
Sánchez, Máximo 76
Sánchez, Raúl 44, 60, 62–63, 73–74, 89, 98, 108, 111, 113–118, 123, 125–126, *128*, 140–141, 144
Sanguily, Dr. Julio "July" 14–17, 21
Sans Souci Night Club 59
Santiago (club) 16
Santiago, José "Pantalones" ("Pants") 82–86, 95–97
Santurce Crabbers 28, 173
Scantlebury, Patricio "Pat" 18, 50, 58–59, 61–63, 70, 72, 74, 79, 86, 96
Schaeffer, Rudy 102
Schumacher, Max 166
Scott, Barbara Ann 43
Scott, Harry 39
Scull, Angel 40, 42–44, 46, 52, 59, 67, 77
Seattle Mariners 181
Seward Park High 84
Sewell, Luke 52, 61, 64
Shaughnessy, Frank 35–36, 38, *39*, 48, 72, 77–78, 83, 85, 90–92, 95, 102, 113–114, 121–122, 127, 131, 133, 135–136, 143, 145, 159, 181
Shaw, Bob 89
Shea, William 107
Shearer, Ray 116, 118, *119*, 123, 126, 137
Shore, Ray 63
Short, Bill 117
Siebert, Sonny 166
Siebold, Harry 35
Sierra, Oscar 77–78
Simmons, Harry 82
Sisler, George 28–29, 81
Sisler, George, Jr. 134, 140, 166
Skillin, Phil 22
Slapnicka, Cy 40
Smalley, Roy 121, 125
Smith, Bob 59
Smith, Earl E.T. 88, 93, 99
Smith, Paul 41, 45, 50, 52
Smith, Reggie 68
Smith, Wendell 14
Smith, Woody 67–68, 73–74
Snead, Sam 19
Souchock, Steve 120, 148
South Atlantic League 72, 160
Southern Association 82, 105, 116, 159, 166
South Pacific 97
Spink, J. G. Taylor 11, 15, 23, 24, 99
Spokane Indians 132
The Sporting News 17, 20, 23, 25, 29, 53, 127, 144, 148, 172, 180
Spring, Jack 69
Spur Cola Colonites 17, 18

Stadium Cerveza Tropical (aka Tropical Park, La Tropical) 10–11, 13, 16–17
Stallard, Tracy 124–125
Staub, Rusty 171
Steinbrenner, George 180
Stevens, Ed 40
Stiglmeier, John C. 93, 101
Stottlemyre, Mel 169
Suárez, Miguelito 10–15, 180
Syracuse Chiefs 44, 50–52, 61, 64–65, 153, 164

Talbot, Gayle 36
Tamayo, Reynerio 182
Tampa Bay Devil Rays 181–182
Taylor, Harry 94
Taylor, Joe 44
Tebbetts, Birdie 45
Texas League 45, 50, 97, 109
Texas Rangers 180
Thomas, Frank 140
Tiefenauer, Bobby 144
Tolan, Bobby 179
Toronto Maple Leafs 38, 40, 42–43, 47–48, 51–52, 61–64, 65, 69–70, 73, 75, 77, 94, 96, 99, 100–102, 106, 109–110, 113, 147–148
Torres, Félix 137–138, 140
Tovar, César 179
Trautman, George M. 15, 17, 82, 100, 122, 127, 166
Tropical Hotel 163
Tropicana Night Club 59, 135
Trujillo, Rafael Leónidas 148

Umphlett, Tom 125
United Fruit Company 109
University of Havana 11, 103, 156
University of Miami 152, 153
University Stadium 81
Urrutia, Manuel 102

Valdés, René 85
Valentine, Harold "Corky" 59
Valentinetti, Vito 124
Varhely, Edward 42
Vedado Tennis Club 10–11
Veeck, Bill 65, 163
Venezuelan Winter League 16, 173
Verdi, Frank 112, 152
Vidal, Fernando 37
Vincent, Al 149
Virdon, Bill 52
Voice of America 162

Walker, Fred "Dixie" 64, 75, 77, 85–86, 101, 120

Walker, Harry 46, 64, 168–169
Wall, Murray 121, 126
Washington Senators 31–32, 43, 57, 77, 134, 158
Weissman, Harold 158
Wheeler, Lonnie 179
Wichita Braves 82
Wieand, Ted 106, 109–110, 113, 116–118, 121, 123, 125, *128*, 138
Wiesler, Bob 118
Williams, Don 117
Williams, Ted 33
Wills, Maury 124, 166
Wilson, Earl 122
Wise, Casey 167

Witkowski, Charles 146
Wolfson, Sam W. 160–161, 167
Wright, Taffy 52
Wrigley Field 156
Wynn, Early 84

Yankee Stadium 22
Yastrzemski, Carl 123
Yomiuri Giants 38
York White Roses 59
Young, Dick 71, 161

Zabala, Adrián 23–24
Zayas, Luis 97
Zygner, Sam 66, 181